Mudbox 2013 Cookbook

Over 60 recipes to sculpt digital masterpieces like a modern Michelangelo

Jeremy Roland

Contributions by Sagar Patel

[PACKT] PUBLISHING

BIRMINGHAM - MUMBAI

Mudbox 2013 Cookbook

First published: September 2012

Production Reference: 1120912

Published by Packt Publishing Ltd.
Livery Place
35 Livery Street
Birmingham B3 2PB, UK.

ISBN 978-1-84969-156-7

www.packtpub.com

Cover Image by Jeremy Roland (jeremycroland@hotmail.com)

Credits

Authors
Jeremy Roland
Sagar Patel

Reviewer
Sergey Danchenko

Acquisition Editor
Wilson D'souza

Lead Technical Editors
Wilson D'souza
Dayan Hyames

Technical Editors
Jalasha D'costa
Manmeet Singh Vasir

Copy Editors
Alfida Paiva
Laxmi Subramanian

Project Coordinator
Sai Gamare

Proofreaders
Maria Gould
Aaron Nash

Indexer
Rekha Nair

Production Coordinator
Melwyn D'sa

Cover Work
Melwyn D'sa

About the Authors

Jeremy Roland is a 3D Environment Artist who has worked for over 10 years in industries such as architecture, film, television, game design, and education. While studying at Virginia Commonwealth University, in both Computer Science and Communication Arts and Design with a focus in Kinetic Imagery, he began his career through an internship at the local ABC television station. Once the internship was over he moved on to the local NBC television station where he worked as a Production Assistant, a Motion Graphics Artist, and an Art Director for two years.

Once he left NBC, he moved out to the Bay Area in California where he began working in Architecture as a 3D Consultant. While continuing his consulting work as well as doing some side work creating logos for websites, he became a Lab Technician at the Academy of Art University in San Francisco. Jeremy soon began teaching modeling, texturing, and lighting classes at the academy and is currently the Lab Supervisor as well as a Teacher for the Game Design Department at the academy.

During his time at the academy he took off a few semesters to travel the world for eight months, as well as work for Golden Era Productions where he worked on films and other projects as both a 3D Artist and a Compositor. This contract job lasted about six months. On another semester off, Jeremy worked as a Visual Effects Supervisor on a music video for James Perry. While writing this book Jeremy was also juggling a full time job at the Academy of Art, a contract position as an Environment Artist at Rocket Ninja game company, and working as the Lead Technical Artist at a start up game company called Press Start. Throughout his career he has taken on many side projects, including writing this book.

My thanks go to my ever loving parents who I could never thank enough for what they've done for me. I would also like to thank Stine for putting up with my long hours of working. To all my colleagues and friends who I have learned from and enjoyed working and playing with. I would also like to thank myself for not giving up on anything I commit to.

Sagar Patel is currently a 2D and 3D Artist in the games industry. After working on multiple mobile games with Tall Chair, Inc. and CG related art with Aatma Studio, he became an Art Lead at Whitemoon Dreams, Inc. in Los Angeles, CA. Sagar is currently responsible for managing art and working with teams to maintain the vision of various properties in production.

About the Reviewer

Sergey "Treidge" Danchenko is a Digital Artist with a strong passion for 3D graphics and game development. He has worked for a number of game development studios and as a freelance 3D Artist since 2007. With a strong understanding of the technical side behind used technologies and tools, Sergey used his skills to discover non-standard solutions for using tools and his work as an artist. His other activities include partnership with NeoAxis 3D Game Engine developers and requested reviewing of relevant software products and books. More information about his work and latest news, tips, and tricks in 3D graphics, and game development is available in Sergey's blog at `http://3dg.me`.

I would like to especially thank my mother for her invaluable support in all of my endeavors.

Table of Contents

Preface

Sculpting software has changed the face of the 3D industry. Whether you are creating a character for the next Avatar movie or adding details to a post apocalyptic city in The Last of Us, 3D sculpting has become an essential tool for creating a level of realism in digital art that was much harder to achieve in the past. A couple of things that make Mudbox a better choice than other sculpting software is its ease of use, its industry-leading 3D painting tools, and its solid integration with other Autodesk products, which includes industry-standard software for 3D modeling and animation. Mudbox is also the first software to integrate vector displacement map extraction. This technology takes texture mapping one more step forward, similar to the introduction of normal maps which sparked the era of "Next-Gen" games. All in all, Mudbox is a powerful art creation tool that is only going to get better and more integrated with the industry's leading software.

What this book covers

Chapter 1, Ready? Set..., introduces you to everything you need to know to get up and running with Mudbox 2013. This chapter will cover techniques such as speeding up your workflow, downloading custom brushes and meshes from the Mudbox community, and getting a comfortable color scheme for your interface. This should be the first stop for beginners and veterans alike.

Chapter 2, Heads Up, will acquaint you with the Mudbox 2013 interface so you can easily customize and find the tools that you need. Some of the recipes will also help you set up the camera, lights, and brush properties so that you can familiarize yourself with the location of the attributes you may need to use in your future projects. This chapter is very helpful for showing you around, if you are new to Mudbox, but also has a few intermediate level techniques for those who are already familiar with Mudbox.

Chapter 3, Broad Strokes, teaches you how to work with various brushes and even create your own brushes to be saved for later use. The recipes within this chapter focus on getting familiar with the brush's properties and how to use the various brush settings to get the effects that you want. This chapter is for anyone trying to learn more about the brushes so that they can customize their tool set rather than rely solely on the default set of brushes.

Chapter 4, Fine Tooth Comb, goes deeper into the brush's customization by focusing on stamps and stencils. The techniques you will learn in this chapter will allow you to add the fine details that will bring your digital sculpts to life! This chapter will be useful for all levels but those who already use Mudbox regularly may learn a new trick or two in this chapter.

Chapter 5, Get In and Get Out, focuses on importing and exporting assets that can be used inside and outside Mudbox. You will learn things such as adding detail to your mesh with a displacement map, working with multiple objects in your Mudbox scene, and creating a terrain using an outside image.

Chapter 6, Shine On, dives into using Mudbox materials to define the look and feel of your objects. Materials include properties that define how shiny your object is and how transparent your object is, among other things. These attributes are important in defining what your object would be made of in the real world. What you learn in this chapter will enable you to make your object look as though you could touch it.

Chapter 7, Time to Paint, covers the biggest strength of Mudbox, texture painting. You will learn how to paint with projections, get rid of seams with the Clone brush, and paint various maps using Mudbox's layer system. The techniques learned here will be useful for all users from beginner to advanced.

Chapter 8, Ready for My Closeup, walks you through lighting, viewport filters, and other ways of making your work presentable. The features covered in this chapter can produce visually stunning results right within your viewport, which can then be rendered out into a turntable for your portfolio, using the final recipe of this chapter. Not only that but you will learn how to produce normal maps directly from your viewport which allows you to easily create a texture version of your sculpts that retains surface direction for lighting.

Chapter 9, One Step Forward, is all about posing your characters and models within Mudbox 2013. This chapter will enable you to bring your characters to life by giving them dynamic poses and interesting silhouettes.

Chapter 10, Get Baked, explores how you would go about extracting your sculpt's details into various types of texture maps. The maps that you get from these processes are essential for creating low polygon game assets using the information that you extract from the high polygon sculpts.

What you need for this book

For this book you will need a copy of Autodesk Mudbox and 2D image editing software such as Adobe Photoshop (`http://www.adobe.com/products/photoshop.html`) or Gimp (`http://www.gimp.org/`). I recommend using the latest version of Mudbox (2013) to follow along with this book. This is the version the book was made for, so there may be a few recipes that don't apply to the older versions of Mudbox.

The recommended system requirements for Autodesk Mudbox 2013 are listed as follows.

If you have any of the 32-bit operating systems listed below, then you will want to install the 32-bit version of Autodesk Mudbox 2013:

- Microsoft Windows 7 Professional operating system (SP1)
- Microsoft Windows XP Professional operating system (SP3)

If you have any of the following operating systems, then you can install the 64-bit version of Autodesk Mudbox 2013:

- Microsoft Windows 7 Professional operating system (SP1)
- Microsoft Windows XP Professional x64 Edition operating system (SP2)
- Apple Mac OS X 10.7.x operating system
- Red Hat Enterprise Linux 6.0 WS operating system
- Fedora 14 operating system

You will also need one of the following pieces of supplemental software for the 32-bit and 64-bit version of Mudbox 2013:

- Microsoft Internet Explorer 8 Internet browser or higher
- Apple Safari web browser
- Mozilla Firefox web browser

The following is a list of hardware requirements for the 32-bit version of Mudbox 2013:

- Windows: Intel Pentium 4 or higher and AMD Athlon 64, or AMD Opteron processors with SSE3 instructions set for support
- 2 GB RAM
- 650 MB free hard drive space
- Certified hardware-accelerated OpenGL graphics card
- Ethernet adapter or wireless Internet card
- DVD-ROM drive
- Three-button mouse or certified Wacom tablet

Here are the requirements for the 64-bit version of Mudbox 2013:

- Windows and Linux: Intel Pentium 4 or higher and AMD Athlon 64, or AMD Opteron processors with SSE3 instructions set for support
- Macintosh computer: Intel-based Macintosh computers with a 64-bit processor (Intel Core 2 Duo processor or later versions)
- 4 GB RAM

- 650 MB free hard drive space
- Certified hardware-accelerated OpenGL graphics card
- Ethernet adapter or wireless Internet card
- DVD-ROM drive
- Three-button mouse or certified Wacom tablet

Also, you must have Internet access to view or download the Mudbox documentation online. Apple Quicktime 7.0 is also recommended for viewing the Mudbox Learning Movies to get started.

For earlier versions of Mudbox as well more broken down set of requirements, you can visit this link: (`http://usa.autodesk.com/adsk/servlet/index?siteID=123112&id=14960418&linkID=11937426`). Note that if you are a student with an academic e-mail address assigned to you, then you can can get a free copy of the educational versions of all Autodesk software, including Mudbox 2013! So, if you are a student that has always wanted to learn how to sculpt, but can't afford the software or you just want to give it a try then check out Autodesk's education download section found here (`http://students.autodesk.com/?nd=download_center`).

Who this book is for

This book is for 3D artists, anywhere from beginner to advanced levels. Mudbox 2013 has advanced tools for texturing and sculpting and has a very easy to understand interface. If you have ever used any of the Autodesk 3D packages, you should be able to adapt in no time. Even if this is your first time opening a sculpting program, with this book you will learn all you need to know to put your imagination into a 3D model that you can move, rotate, and scale. The sculpts that you create can become anything from a movie character to a game asset, or even a 3D print that you can place on your desk. This book can be useful for anyone, whether it's your first time using the software or you are working professionally as a 3D artist.

Conventions

In this book, you will find a number of styles of text that distinguish between different kinds of information. Here are some examples of these styles, and an explanation of their meaning.

Code words in text are shown as follows: " This file will install the documentation into your `Autodesk\Mudbox 2013` folder by default. Next to a `.obj`, I would say, the `.fbx` is the next most widely used file type for bringing assets from one package to another."

New terms and **important words** are shown in bold. Words that you see on the screen, in menus or dialog boxes for example, appear in the text like this: " Now, click on **Import** under the **File** tab in Mudbox to import your FBX model.".

[Warnings or important notes appear in a box like this.]

[Tips and tricks appear like this.]

Reader feedback

Feedback from our readers is always welcome. Let us know what you think about this book—what you liked or may have disliked. Reader feedback is important for us to develop titles that you really get the most out of.

To send us general feedback, simply send an e-mail to `feedback@packtpub.com`, and mention the book title through the subject of your message.

If there is a topic that you have expertise in and you are interested in either writing or contributing to a book, see our author guide on `www.packtpub.com/authors`.

Customer support

Now that you are the proud owner of a Packt book, we have a number of things to help you to get the most from your purchase.

Downloading the example code

You can download the example code files for all Packt books you have purchased from your account at `http://www.packtpub.com`. If you purchased this book elsewhere, you can visit `http://www.packtpub.com/support` and register to have the files e-mailed directly to you.

Errata

Although we have taken every care to ensure the accuracy of our content, mistakes do happen. If you find a mistake in one of our books—maybe a mistake in the text or the code—we would be grateful if you would report this to us. By doing so, you can save other readers from frustration and help us improve subsequent versions of this book. If you find any errata, please report them by visiting `http://www.packtpub.com/support`, selecting your book, clicking on the **errata submission form** link, and entering the details of your errata. Once your errata are verified, your submission will be accepted and the errata will be uploaded to our website, or added to any list of existing errata, under the Errata section of that title.

Piracy

Piracy of copyright material on the Internet is an ongoing problem across all media. At Packt, we take the protection of our copyright and licenses very seriously. If you come across any illegal copies of our works, in any form, on the Internet, please provide us with the location address or website name immediately so that we can pursue a remedy.

Please contact us at `copyright@packtpub.com` with a link to the suspected pirated material.

We appreciate your help in protecting our authors, and our ability to bring you valuable content.

Questions

You can contact us at `questions@packtpub.com` if you are having a problem with any aspect of the book, and we will do our best to address it.

1
Ready? Set...

In this chapter we will cover:

- Installing Mudbox 2013 documentation
- Setting up hotkeys
- Increasing the resolution on your model
- Bookmarking the camera view
- Downloading and enabling stamps, stencils, and base meshes from the Internet
- Adding and adjusting your image planes
- Sculpting on different subdivision levels effectively
- Recording a movie while you work in Mudbox
- Setting up colors and other preferences
- Setting up your Wacom tablet
- Working in expert mode

Introduction

This chapter will help you get your preferences set up so that you can work in a way that is most intuitive and efficient for you. Whether you are a veteran or a newbie, it is always a good idea to establish a good workflow. It will speed up your production time, allowing you to get ideas out of your head before you forget them. This will also greatly aid you in meeting deadlines and producing more iterations of your work.

Installing Mudbox 2013 documentation

In addition to the recipes in this book, you may find yourself wanting to look through the Mudbox 2013 documentation for additional help. By default, when you navigate to **Help** through Mudbox 2013's interface, you will be sent to an online help page. If you have a slow Internet connection or lack a connection altogether, you may want to install a local copy of the documentation. After downloading and installing the local copy, it is a good idea to have Mudbox 2013 point you to the right location when you navigate to **Help** from the menus. This will eliminate the need to navigate through your files in order to find the documentation. The following recipe will guide you through this process:

How to do it...

1. First thing you will want to do is download the documentation from Autodesk's website. You can find the documentation for this version as well as the previous versions from the following link: `http://usa.autodesk.com/adsk/servlet/index?siteID=123112&id=17765502`.
2. Once you're on this page you can scroll down and click on **2013** for the language and operating system that you are using. The following screenshot is what you should see:

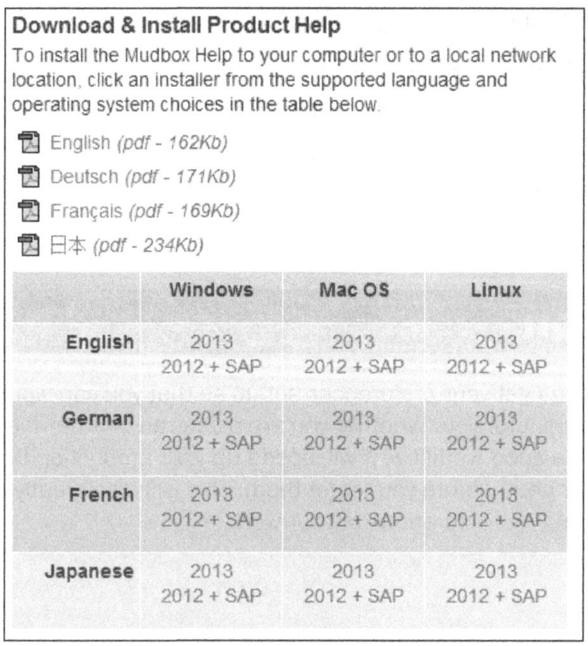

Download & Install Product Help

To install the Mudbox Help to your computer or to a local network location, click an installer from the supported language and operating system choices in the table below.

English *(pdf - 162Kb)*
Deutsch *(pdf - 171Kb)*
Français *(pdf - 169Kb)*
日本 *(pdf - 234Kb)*

	Windows	Mac OS	Linux
English	2013 2012 + SAP	2013 2012 + SAP	2013 2012 + SAP
German	2013 2012 + SAP	2013 2012 + SAP	2013 2012 + SAP
French	2013 2012 + SAP	2013 2012 + SAP	2013 2012 + SAP
Japanese	2013 2012 + SAP	2013 2012 + SAP	2013 2012 + SAP

3. Next you will navigate to the location that you downloaded the file to, and run it.

4. Now follow the prompts by clicking **Next** until the installation is complete. This file will install the documentation into your `Autodesk\Mudbox 2013` folder by default. You can change this location during the installation process if you like but I recommend leaving this as the default location.

5. After the local version of the **Help** files are installed, we need to point Mudbox 2013's **Help** menu to the local copy of the documentation. To do this, open the `Mudbox 2013` folder, click on **Windows** in the top menu bar, and click on **Preferences**. The following screenshot shows how it should look:

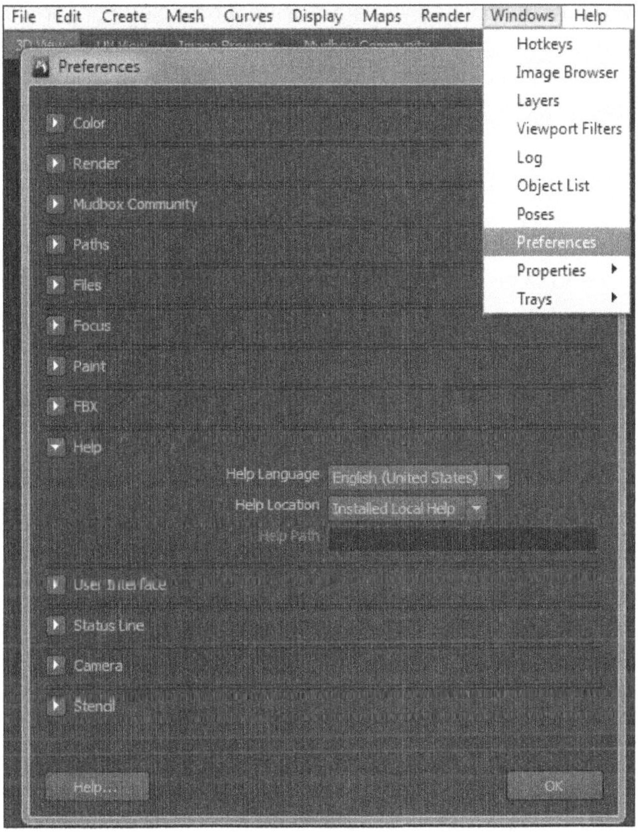

6. Next, click on the small arrow next to **Help** so that more options open up. You will notice that next to **Help Location** it says **Autodesk Web Site**. We are going to change that to **Installed Local Help** by clicking on the small arrow next to (or directly on the text) **Autodesk Web Site** and choose **Installed Local Help** from the drop-down menu. Then click on **OK**.

> Take note that if you did install your documentation to a different directory, then you will need to choose **Custom** instead of **Installed Local Help**. Then you will need to copy and paste the directory location into the **Help Path** textbox.

Setting up hotkeys

The first thing you will want to do when you start using a new piece of software is, either set up your own hotkeys or familiarize yourself with the default hotkeys. This is very important for speeding up your workflow. If you do not use hotkeys, you will have to constantly go through menus and scroll through windows to find the tools that you need, which will undoubtedly slow you down.

How to do it...

1. First you will need to go into the **Windows** menu item on the top menu bar.
2. Next, you will click on **Hotkeys** to bring up the hotkey window as shown in the next screenshot.
3. You will notice a drop-down menu that reads **Use keyboard shortcuts from** with a **Restore Mudbox Defaults** button next to it. Within this menu you can set your default hotkeys to resemble a 3D software that you are accustomed to using.

This will help you transition smoothly into using Mudbox. If you are new to all 3D software, or use a software package that is not on this list, then using Mudbox hotkeys should suffice.

The following screenshot shows the options available in Mudbox 2013:

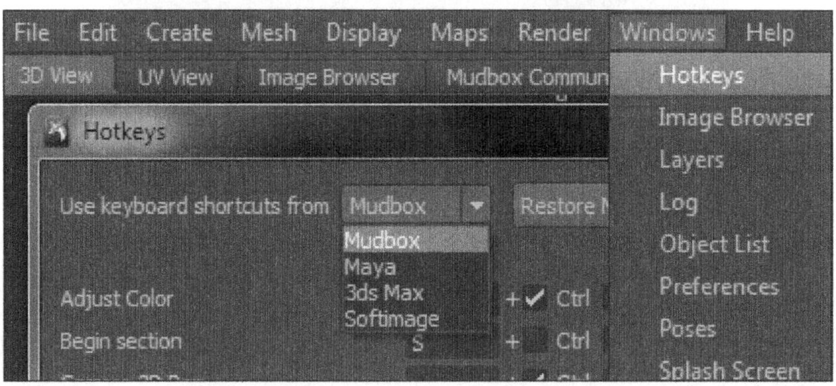

After choosing a default set of keys, you can now go in and change any hotkeys that you would like to customize. Let's say, I would like **Eyedropper** to activate when I press the *E* key and the left mouse button together. What you will do is change the current letter that is in the box next to **Eyedropper** to **E** and you will make sure there is a check in the box next to **LMB** (**Left Mouse Button**). It should look like the following screenshot:

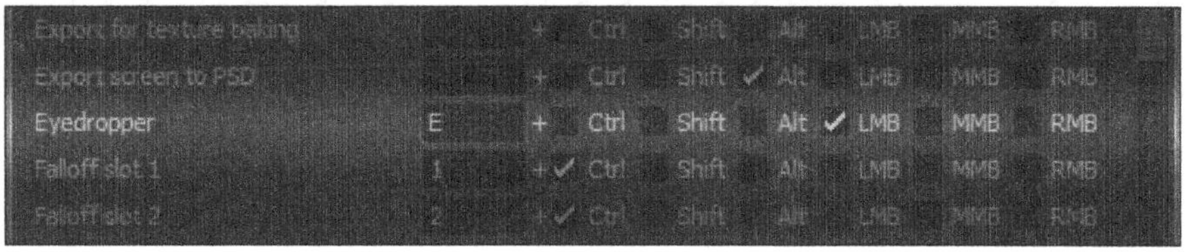

How it works...

Once all your hotkeys are set up as desired, you will be able to use quick keystrokes to access a large number of tools without ever taking your eyes off your project. The more you get comfortable with your hotkeys, the faster you will get at switching between tools.

There's more...

When you first start using a particular software, you probably won't know exactly which tools you will be using most often. With that in mind, you will want to revisit your hotkey customization after getting a feel for your workflow and which tools you use the most.

Another thing you want to think about, when setting up your hotkeys, is how easy it is to use the hotkey. For example, I tend to make hotkeys that relate to the tool in some way in order to make it easier to remember.

For example, the **Create Curve** tool has a good hotkey already set for it, *Ctrl* + *C*, for the reasons mentioned as follows:

- One reason it is a good hotkey is that the first letter of the tool is also the letter of the key being used for the hotkey. I can relate *C* to curve.
- Another reason this could be a good hotkey is because if creating curves is something that I find myself doing often, then all I have to do is use my pinky finger on the *Ctrl* key and my pointer finger on the *C* key. You may think "Yeah? So what?" but if I were to set the hotkey to *Ctrl* + *Alt* + *U* it's a bit more of a stretch on my fingers and I would not want to do that frequently.

The point is, key location and frequency of use are things you want to think about to speed up your workflow and stay comfortable while using your hotkeys.

See also

- The *Setting up colors and other preferences* recipe

Increasing the resolution on your model

Before you can get any fine details, or details that you would see while viewing from close up, into the surface of your model you will need to subdivide your mesh to increase its resolution. In the same way that a computer monitor displays more pixels when its resolution is increased, a model will have more points on its surface when the resolution is increased.

How to do it...

The hotkey for subdividing your surface is *Shift + D* or you can alternatively go into the menus as shown in the following screenshot:

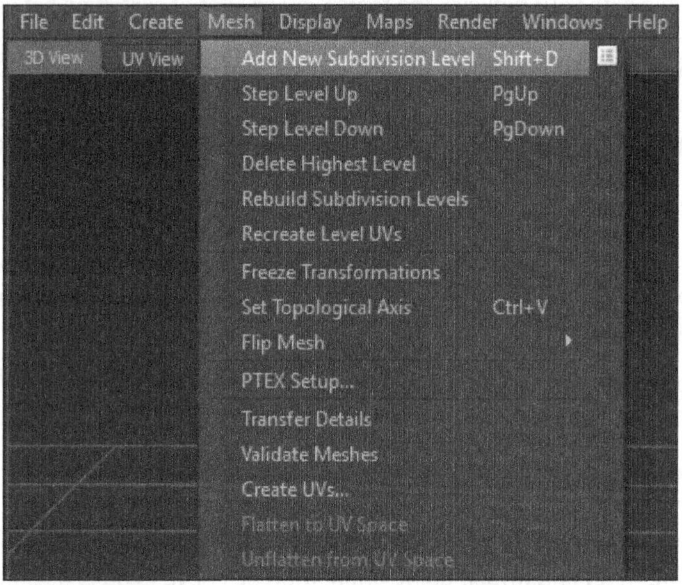

How it works...

What this does is it adds more polygons which can be manipulated to add more detail. You will not want to subdivide your model too many times, otherwise, your computer will begin to slow down. The extent to which your computer will slow down is exponential. For example, if you have a six-sided cube and you subdivide it once, it will become 24-sided. If you subdivide it one more time, it will become 96-sided and so on. The following screenshot from Maya shows you what the wireframe looks like from one level to the next:

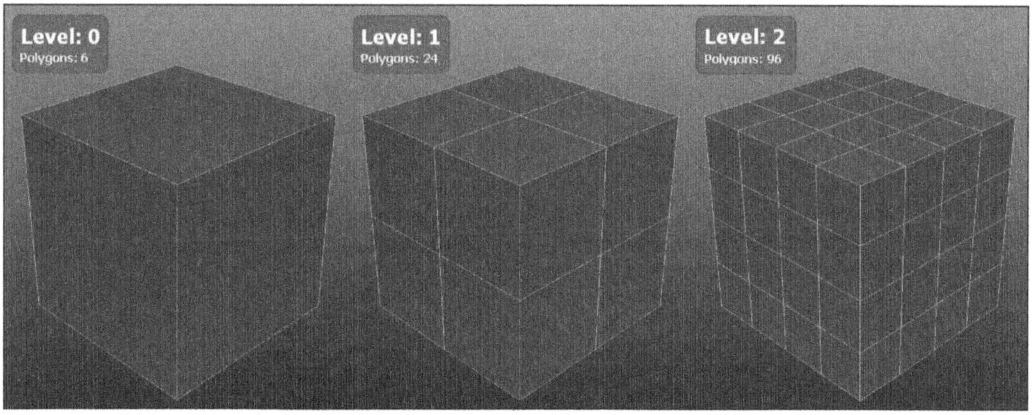

The reason this image was created in Maya is because Mudbox will only show the proper wireframe when your model reaches 1000 polygons or more.

The more powerful your computer, the more smoothly Mudbox 2013 will run. More specifically, it's the RAM and the video memory that are important. The following are some explanations on how RAM and video memory will affect your machines performance.

- RAM is the most important of all. The more RAM you have, the more polygons Mudbox will be able to handle, without taking a performance hit.
- The video memory increases the performance of your video card and allows high resolution, high speed, and color graphics. Basically, it allows the Graphical User Interface (GUI) to have better performance.

So, now that you know RAM is important, how do you decide how much will be needed to run Mudbox 2013 smoothly? Well, one thing to consider is your operating system and the version of Mudbox 2013 you are running. If you have a 32-bit operating system and you are running the 32-bit Mudbox 2013, then the maximum RAM you can get is 4 GB. But, in reality you are only getting about 3 GB of RAM as the operating system needs to use around 1 GB of that memory.

On the other hand, if you are using a 64-bit operating system and the 64-bit Mudbox 2013 version then you are capped at about 8 TB (yes, I said TB not GB). You will not need anywhere near that amount of RAM to run Mudbox 2013 smoothly. My recommendation is to have a minimum of 8 GB of RAM and 1 GB of video memory. With this amount of RAM and video memory you should be able to work with around 10 million triangles on the top level of your sculpt.

There's more...

Notice the little white box next to **Add New Subdivision Level** in the following screenshot:

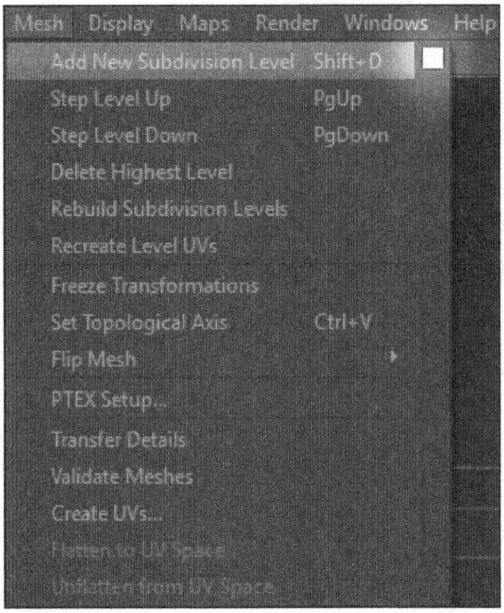

By clicking on this box, you will be given a few options for how Mudbox will handle the subdivision, as shown in the following screenshot:

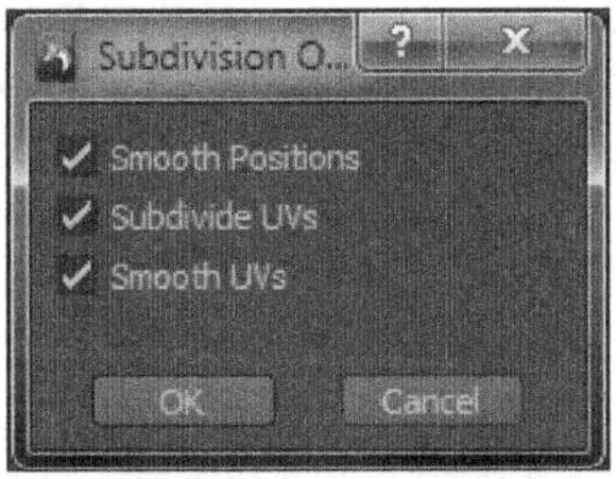

The options shown in the previous screenshot are explained as follows:

- **Smooth Positions**: This option will smooth out the edges by averaging out the vertices that are added. The following screenshot shows the progression from **Level 0** to **Level 2** on a cube:

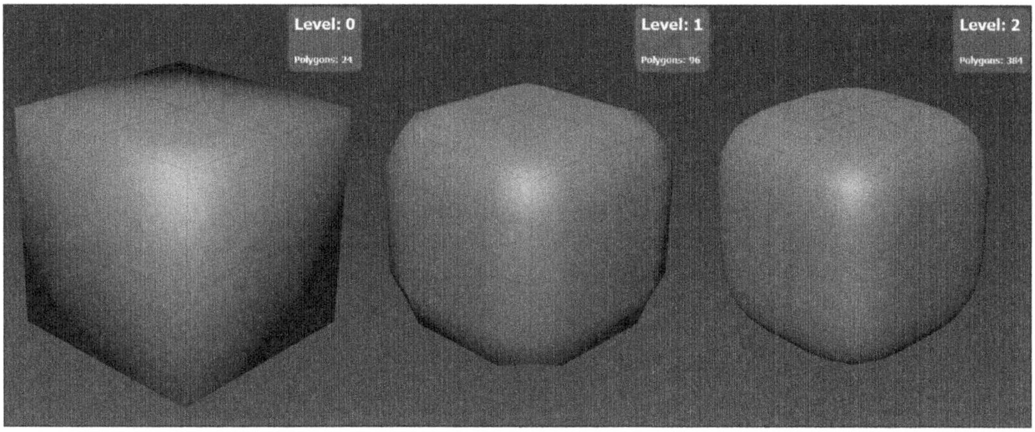

Subdivide UVs: If this option is unchecked when you create a new subdivision level, then you will lose your UVs on the object. To get your UVs back you will need to recreate the UVs for that level. This is discussed in a recipe found in *Chapter 5, Get In and Get Out*. If the **Subdivide UVs** option is turned on then it will just add subdivisions to your existing UVs.

- **Smooth UVs**: If this option is turned on, the UVs will be smoothed within the UV Borders as shown in the next screenshot:

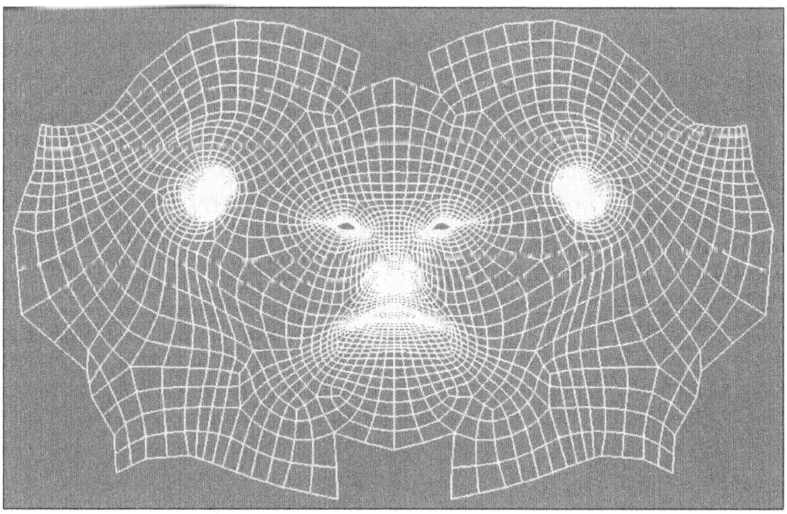

If you want your borders to smooth along with the interior parts of the shell, as shown in the next screenshot, then you will need to take a few extra steps to allow this:

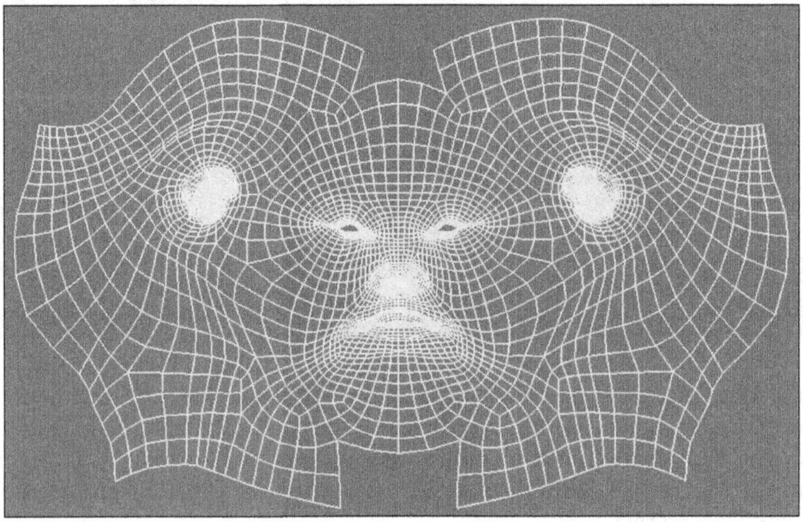

This is the method Mudbox used in the 2009 and earlier versions. In Mudbox 2010, they switched the way they handle this operation so that the borders do not smooth. Here is an excerpt from the Service Pack notes from 2010:

> *"A new environment variable now exists to alter how the Smooth UVs property works when subdividing a model: MUDBOX2009_SUBDIVIDE_SMOOTH_UV. When this environment variable is set, the Smooth UVs property works as it did in Mudbox 2009. That is, the entire UV shell, including its UV borders, are smoothed when subdividing a model whenever the Smooth UVs property is turned on. If this environment variable is not set, the default Mudbox 2010 UV smoothing behavior occurs. That is, smoothing only occurs for the interior UVs in a UV shell, leaving the UV shell border edges unsmoothed. Which UV smoothing method you choose to use is entirely dependent on your individual rendering pipeline requirements and render application used."*

This has not changed since Mudbox 2010. So, basically what you need to do on a PC is add an environment variable `MUDBOX2009_SUBDIVIDE_SMOOTH_UV` that has a value of 1. To do this you will need to right-click on **My Computer** and click on **Properties**. Then, choose **Advanced system settings** and under the **Advanced** tab click on **Environment Variables...**. Under **System Variables** click on **New...**. In the blank where it says **Variable Name** enter `MUDBOX2009_SUBDIVIDE_SMOOTH_UV` and under **Variable Value** input a `1`. Hit **OK** and it's all ready to go.

Moving up and down subdivision levels

Once you create subdivision levels using *Shift + D*, or through the menus, you can move up and down the levels you have created by using the *Page Up* key to move up in levels, or the *Page Down* key to move down in levels. But keep in mind, you will not be able to go any higher than the highest level you created using **Add New Subdivision Level** and you will never be able to go below Level 0.

Another thing to take into account is which model you are subdividing. If you have multiple objects in your scene, you need to make sure the correct mesh is active when subdividing. The following are a couple of ways to make sure you are subdividing the correct mesh:

- One way is to select the object in the **Object List** before hitting *Shift + D*.
- Another way is to hover your mouse cursor over the mesh that you want to subdivide and then hit *Shift + D*. This will subdivide the mesh that is directly underneath your cursor.

See also

- The *Sculpting on different subdivision levels effectively* recipe

Bookmarking the camera view

This recipe will teach you how to add bookmarks for your camera positions. This is great for setting up different angles that you would like to come back to.

Let's say you are working on sculpting a head and you have a photo reference of the head you are trying to portray but the pictures are from different angles. One technique you could use is to set up bookmarks of your camera in different positions around your model that match the angle of the real world cameras from the photos. This way you can switch back and forth between the different views and try to match the sculpt to the reference as best as you can.

Getting ready

Before you set the bookmark, you will want to adjust the camera position until you have the desired angle. You can do this by using whichever hotkeys you have set up for navigating through your workspace. The Mudbox default hotkeys for this are shown as follows:

- **Rotate Around**: *Alt* + left mouse button
- **Pan**: *Alt* + middle mouse button
- **Zoom**: *Alt* + left mouse button + middle mouse button or *Alt* + right mouse button

How to do it...

1. You can find the **Camera Bookmarks** tool panel on the lower right-hand side corner of your screen, as long as you haven't moved it. It is docked inside the same panel as **Stamps**, **Stencils**, **Falloff**, **Material Presets**, and **Lighting Presets**.
2. Once your angle is set, you will go into this panel and click on the little arrow at the upper left-hand side corner of the panel. This will open up a drop-down menu with the menu item **Add Camera Bookmark**. The following screenshot will help you find what you are looking for.
3. Once you have done this you will be asked to name the bookmark. One cool feature about the Mudbox **Camera Bookmarks** is that the thumbnail it produces is an exact match to your viewport to help you with remembering which angle the camera was at.
4. Now, all you have to do is click on the bookmark thumbnail and the camera will snap into place.
5. You can also hover your mouse over the thumbnail for a larger thumbnail image with the name to appear.

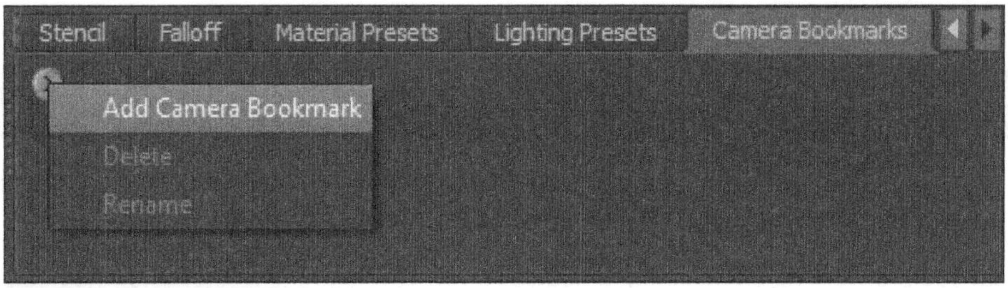

How it works...

What this does is, it takes the position and rotation of the virtual camera and stores that information into a button. It also takes a screenshot of the viewport and resizes it into a thumbnail to help you remember the angle of the bookmark.

There's more...

If you would like to rename or delete a bookmark, all you have to do is go into the same menu where **Add Camera Bookmark** is located and choose your desired menu item. Keep in mind you must select the bookmark that you would like to affect before going into the menu.

See also

- The *Setting up hotkeys* recipe

Downloading and enabling stamps, stencils, and base meshes from the Internet

This recipe will show you how to find customized stamps and stencils that you can download and use quickly, all from within the Mudbox user interface.

How to do it...

1. Once you have a stamp, stencil, or base mesh in mind, you will click on the **Mudbox Community** tab. This is located above the main viewport next to the **3D View**, **UV View**, and **Image Browser** tabs, as shown in the following screenshot. This will take you to Autodesk's **Area** website where you can view other artists' work, tutorials, or download and enable stamps, stencils, and base meshes:

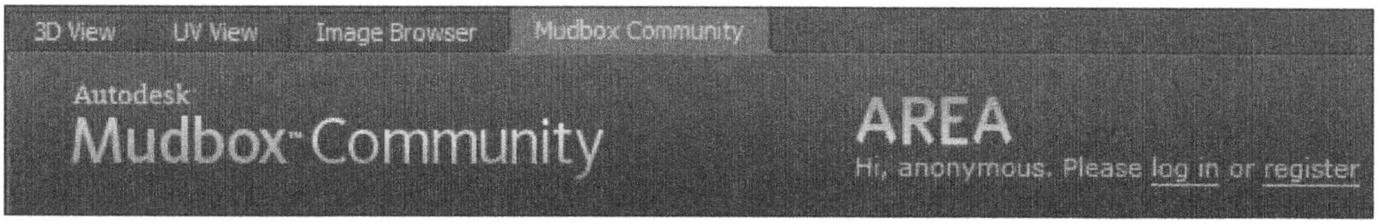

2. To get to the tools we are looking for, you will need to click on the **LIBRARY** menu item on the left-hand side of the screen, as shown in the following screenshot:

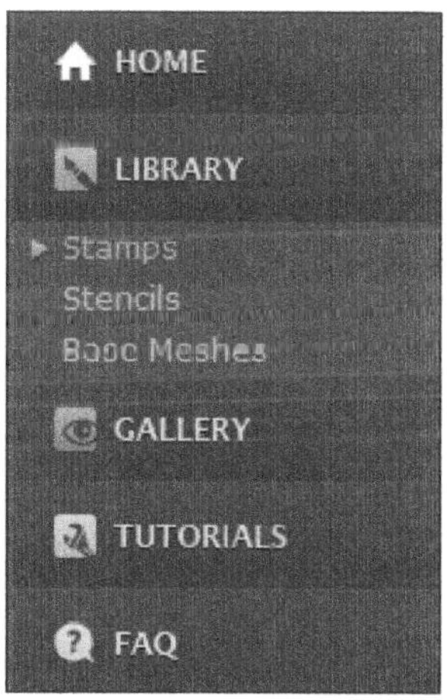

3. Once you click on **LIBRARY**, it will open up to show you the three subcategories **Stamps**, **Stencils**, and **Base Meshes**. If you click on one of these, your viewport will show thumbnail images with the name, category, artist name, size, date added, and a ranking to help you find what you are looking for.

4. On the top, right-hand side area of your viewport, you will find ways to sort the list by most recently added, most downloaded, or highest ranked.
5. There is also a search textbox that will allow you to type in what you are looking for.
6. You may also choose which category to search under, as well as how recently it has been added.
7. If you click on the button shown in the following screenshot, it will download and enable the chosen stamp, stencil, or base mesh. It will also be added to your list of stencils, stamps, or base meshes.

How it works...

The Mudbox Community window is set up so that you can easily go into a database of user-created tools to use for your own projects. You can also easily upload your own stencils, stamps, and base meshes for other artists to use.

There's more...

In order to upload a stencil, stamp, or base mesh that you have created, you will look to the bottom of the viewport where you will see the following:

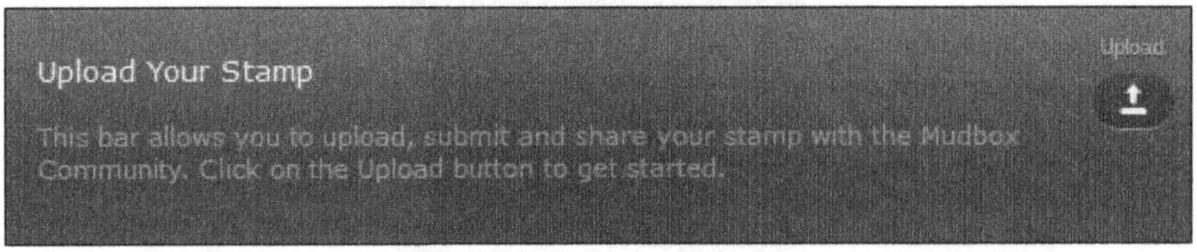

Exploring the community

You may also want to click on the image of one of the stamps, stencils, or base meshes that you find, for more information. Once you go into the more detailed view, you will be able to read the artist's description of the tool, rate the tool, report abuse, share the tool on different online networks, or quickly choose related tools.

Earn prestige in the community

Autodesk has also set up a system to give artists who contribute a lot of good tools to the community, more prestige. When you click on an artist's tool to get the detailed view, it will show their prestige level and how many points they have earned. The following screenshot shows how to earn those points and what title you will be given. This will let other artists know how helpful you are in the community, and you could impress possible employers:

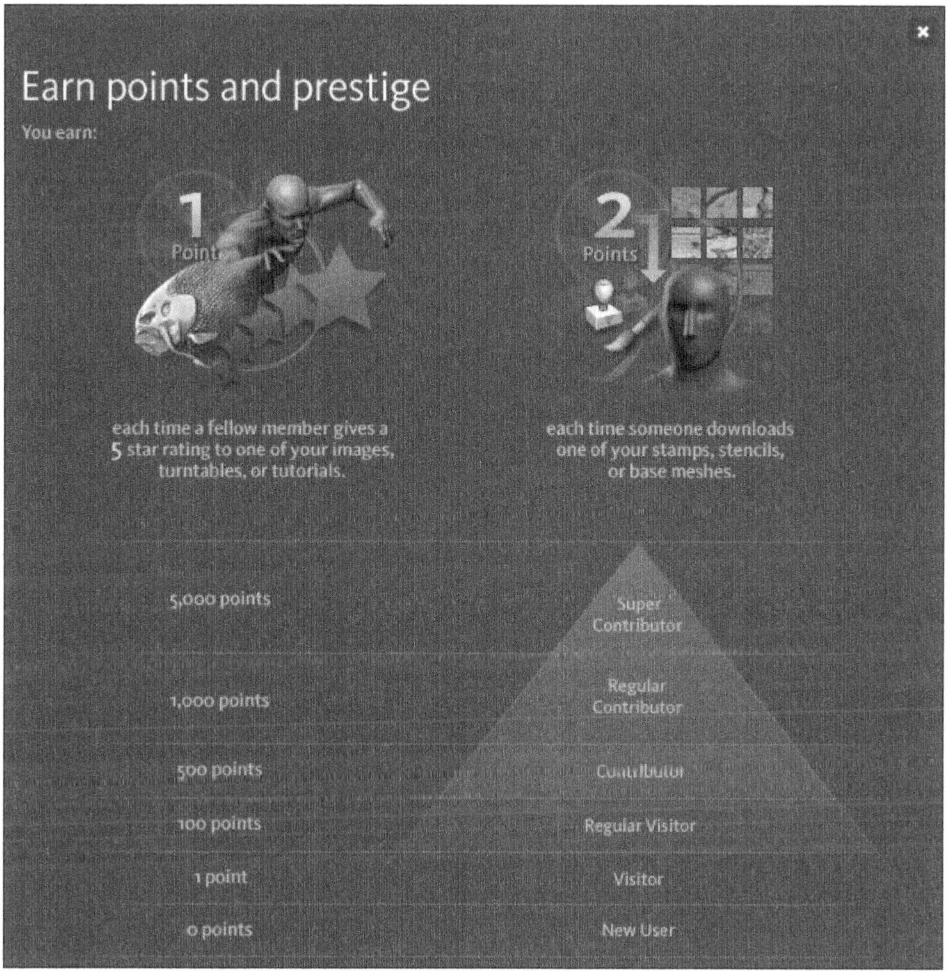

See also

- *The Setting up stamps, stencils, and image planes using image browser* recipe in *Chapter 2, Heads Up*
- *The Tricks for painting with stamps* recipe in *Chapter 4, Fine Tooth Comb*
- *The Tricks for painting with stencils* recipe in *Chapter 4, Fine Tooth Comb*
- *The Adding a stamp or a stencil to your toolbox* recipe in *Chapter 4, Fine Tooth Comb*

Adding and adjusting your image planes

This recipe will teach you how to apply an image plane to your camera/viewport so that you can look at reference photos in your workspace.

Getting ready

First you will need an image that has been saved as `.jpg`, `.bmp`, `.png`, `.tga`, `.tif`, `.gif`, or `.exr`.

How to do it...

1. To apply the image to your image plane, first go to the **Object List** tab on the right-hand side of the Mudbox workspace. It is located between the **Layers** and **Viewport Filters** tab.
2. Next, go to the list under **Name** and find which camera you would like to attach it to.
3. The default camera you are looking through is the perspective camera. If you would like to switch cameras you can right-click on the camera you would like to use and choose **Look Through**.
4. Once you have chosen which camera you would like to add the image plane to, click on the **+** next to the name of the camera. This will drop down two menu items, **Stencil** and **ImagePlane**.
5. Now, you are going to select **ImagePlane** and the properties below this window will show an option to **Import** or **Export** an image. The following screenshot is what the window looks like with the **Properties** and **Object List** tab open.

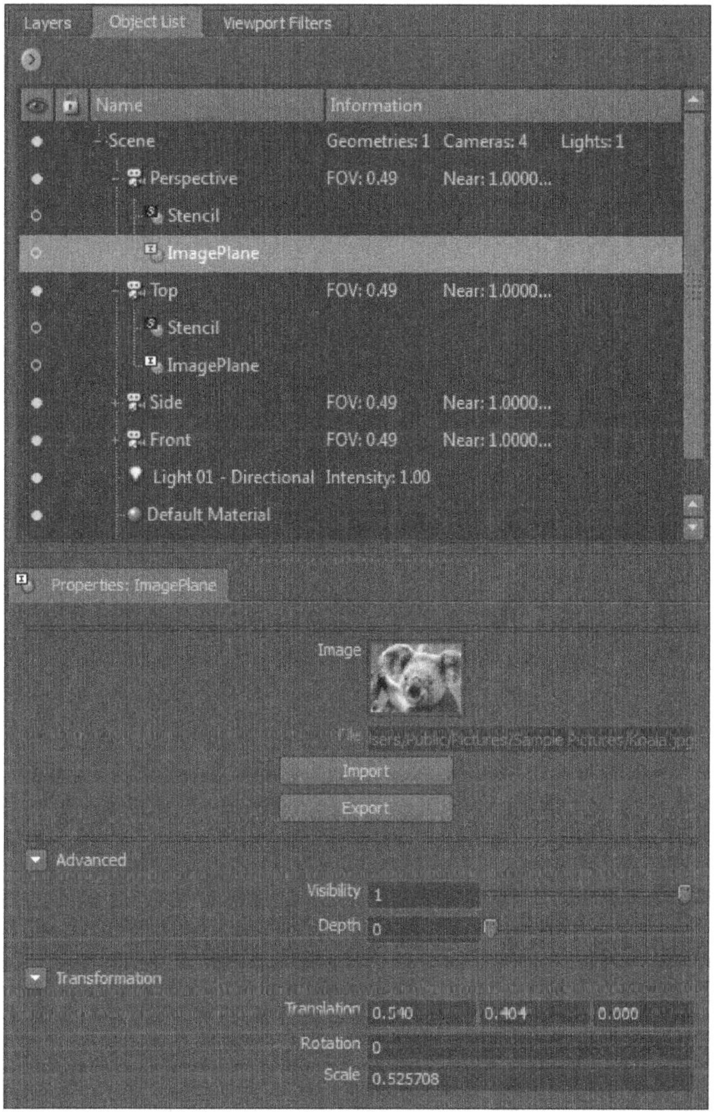

6. The next thing you're going to do is click on **Import** and choose your image file. Once it is imported you will see it appear in your viewport.

How it works...

When you apply an image to the image plane, it is basically setting up a billboard image that always faces the camera, no matter how much you rotate, zoom, or pan your camera.

The image plane will only be visible through the camera that you are looking. This can be helpful since you could apply reference images of different angles to each camera. For example, if you are working on a head, you can apply an image of the face to the front camera, and you can apply an image of the profile of the face to the side camera. This way you will be able to switch between cameras and only have the images you need from that view. Otherwise your workspace could get very cluttered with many images of all angles in one view.

There's more...

If you need to adjust the image plane, you can use the following hotkeys:

- e + left mouse button will rotate the image
- e + middle mouse button will pan the image
- e + left mouse button + middle mouse button will scale the image
- e + right mouse button will adjust the depth of the plane

Advanced properties

Under the advanced drop-down menu for the image plane, you will find settings for **Visibility** and **Depth**. You can either input a number into the textbox or you can use the slider to adjust the value.

- **Visibility**: This determines how transparent the image plane will be. The closer it is to **1**, the more visible it becomes, whereas adjusting the value closer to **0** will cause it to become more transparent.
- **Depth**: This determines how far away from the camera the image plane will sit. This will not change the size in the viewport but it will make the image appear behind the objects in your scene, or in front of them, depending on what values you use. By default, the depth slider goes from **0** to **1000**, **1000** being the farthest away and **0** being the closest. If you would like the plane to be even farther away, you can type a value into the textbox and the slider will readjust itself, making the number you input as the new maximum value. For example, if I enter `3000` into the textbox, then the slider will now slide from **0** to **3000** instead of the original **0** to **1000**.

Transformation properties

The last section in the image plane properties is called **Transformation**. This section shows and allows you to change the values associated with the image plane's **Translation** (location), **Rotation**, and **Scale**. The quickest way to alter these values is by using the hotkeys mentioned earlier, but if you would like to go in and assign values manually, this is the place to do it. Note that next to **Translation** there are three textboxes. These are for the *X*, *Y*, and *Z* coordinates of 3D space.

See also

- The *Bookmarking the camera view* recipe
- *The Setting up stamps, stencils, and image planes using image browser* recipe in *Chapter 2, Heads Up*

Sculpting on different subdivision levels effectively

This recipe will discuss how sculpting on one subdivision level will affect the other subdivision levels and how to account for this in your workflow.

Getting ready

First you will need a model that has multiple subdivision levels.

How to do it...

The basic idea is that you want to create large details on the lower levels and get finer with your details as you move up in level. This is a good idea in any medium as it allows you to get the shape, composition, and design figured out, before you start applying all the finer details only to realize that your foundation is not so great.

What is nice about Mudbox is that even if those large foundational shapes are not right at first, you can always go back down in the levels and reshape the sculpt while keeping the details you have already added.

How it works...

Mudbox stores the information from all the levels and applies any changes to all the layers. So, even if you are on a lower level and cannot see the higher level details you can still affect the shape and details of the higher levels.

See also

- The *Increasing resolution on your model* recipe
- *Chapter 3, Broad Strokes*
- *Chapter 4, Fine Tooth Comb*

Recording a movie while you work in Mudbox

This recipe will show you how to record the viewport while you work. This can be useful for creating your own tutorials or showing friends or employers your creation process.

Getting ready

First, you will need enough space on your computer to hold the movie file that you create. These files can get very large depending on what resolution you are recording at.

Then, you will also want to have your model at a point where you would like to start recording. Keep in mind this will not record audio.

How to do it...

1. To start recording, you can go to **Render** | **Record Movie** and you will see the following window after you click on it:

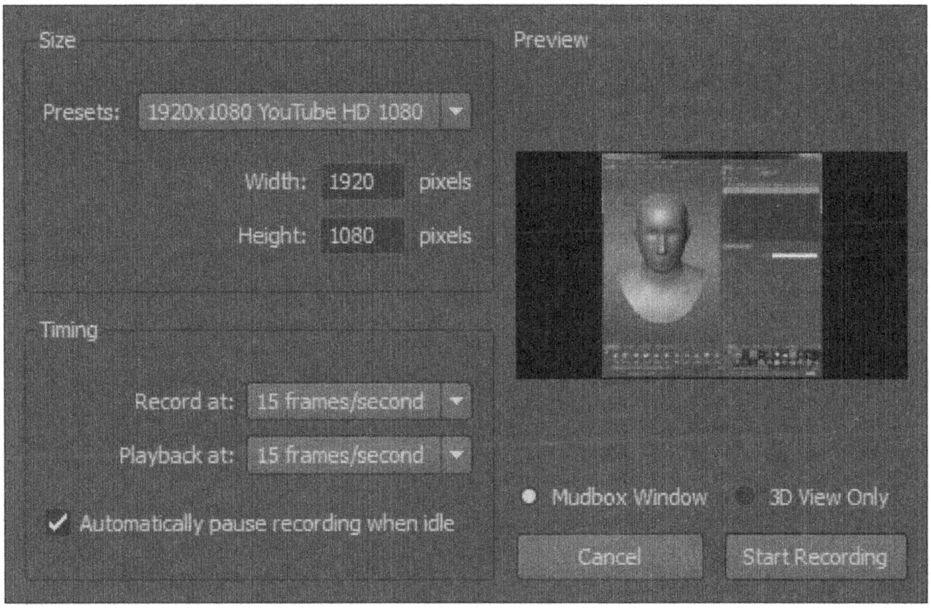

2. On this screen you will adjust the settings to what you need. The first thing you will need to adjust is **Size**. You can use the **Presets** drop-down menu or you can enter a custom resolution into the textboxes.
3. Next, you will adjust the **Timing**, giving you the ability to make the file size smaller by recording fewer frames or to speed up or slow down a sculpt. If you record with a high frames/second timing and play back at a low frames/second timing, your video will be slow and slightly choppy in its movement. If you set the record with frames per second as low and the playback with frames per second as high, you will get a fast time lapse of your work.
4. By checking the **Automatically pause recording when idle** checkbox you will save lots of time by not having to cut out all the slow parts of your video where nothing is happening. If your mouse stops moving then your video stops recording.

5. The **Preview** window shows you what the beginning of the video will look like and also what the thumbnail for the file will be. If you mark the **Mudbox Window** option you will be able to see the toolbars. By marking the **3D View Only** choice, you will only see the inside of the viewport.
6. Once you begin recording, there will be a countdown timer before the recording starts and you will have a **Pause** and **Stop** button in the lower right-hand side of the Mudbox window.
7. When you finish recording, you will see the window as shown in the next screenshot, which allows you to delete the recording or save it as one of a few different file types:

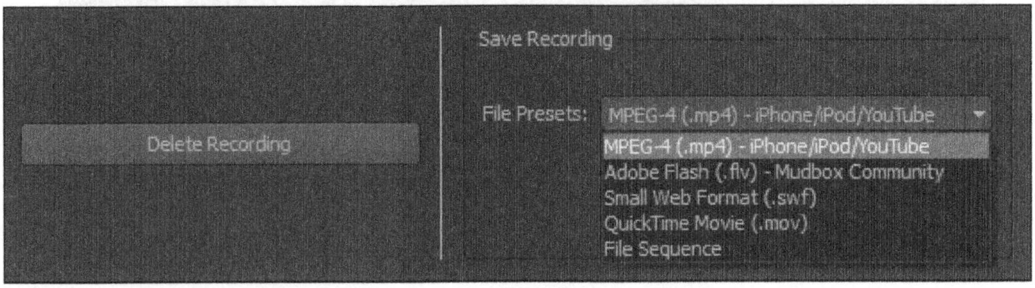

8. After hitting **Save As**, you choose where you would like to save the movie and it will create the file for you.

There's more...

You can also create a turntable by going to **Render** | **Create Turntable Movie**, which will give you this window:

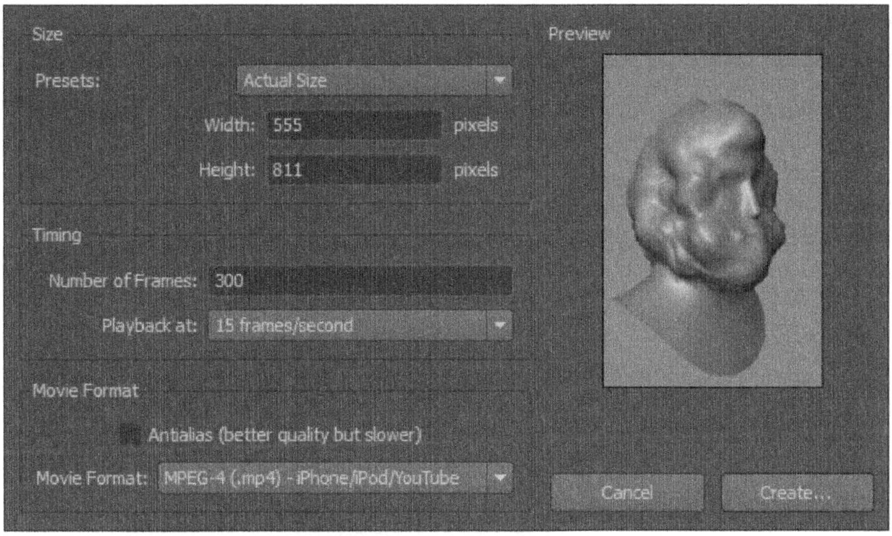

1. In the same way that you set the size of **Record Movie**, you will also need to set the size of the turntable. **Actual Size** will fit the sculpt perfectly within the window.
2. Under **Timing**, you can adjust the frames per second and the **Number of Frames** you want the turntable to be. The more frames you have, the longer it will be, and the more frames per second you have, the faster it will be.
3. The **Movie Format** section is like the **Save As** section of the **Record Movie**. Here you choose the type of movie file and you have a checkbox for **Antialias**. Antialiasing will improve the quality but it will increase your render times. This refers to the crispness of your edges.
4. Once you're ready, you can click on **Create...** and choose a place to save your file. It will start writing the file and you can see the process of the load in the bottom-left corner.

See also

- *The Creating a three-point lighting preset* recipe in *Chapter 8, Ready for My CloseUp*

Setting up colors and other preferences

This recipe will show you how to customize the colors of the Mudbox workspace. Customizing the colors will help you feel more comfortable with the user interface and allow more options for users who are color blind. In addition to this, if you are accustomed to use another software's color scheme, you can mimic those colors to allow quicker and easier adaptation to Mudbox 2013.

How to do it...

In order to adjust the colors of your workspace, you will need to go through the following steps:

1. Go into **Windows** | **Preferences** and click on the drop-down arrow next to **Color**. This will reveal the colors that you can customize as shown in the following screenshot:

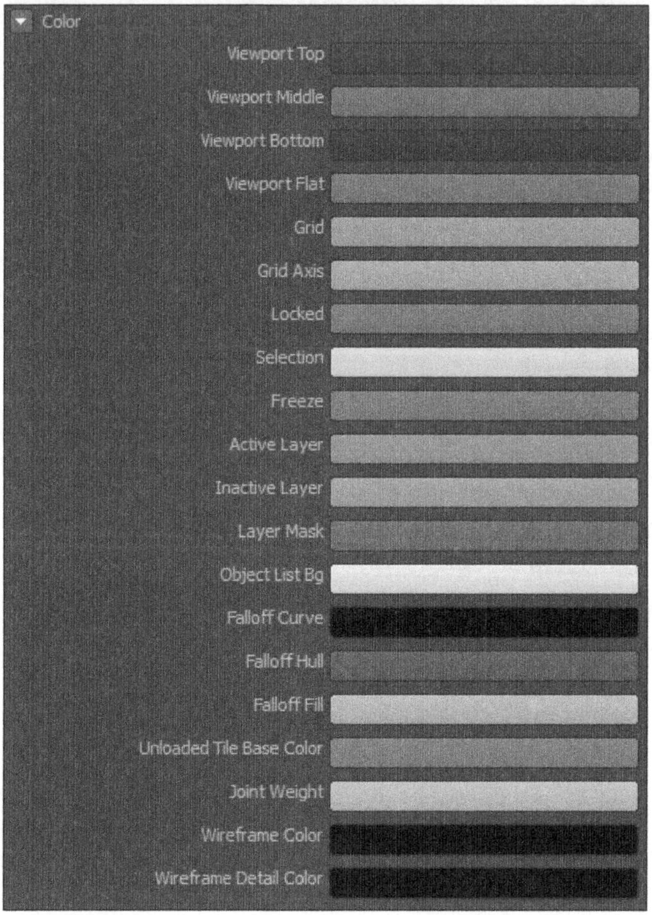

2. Now, click on one of the colors next to the element you would like to change and you will be shown the window as seen in the first screenshot of step 3.
3. There are different ways to choose your color, and once you choose the color that you want, you can store it in the swatches on the top of the window where the tiny **x**'s are. The different ways to choose a color are explained as follows:
    i. One way is to choose the dropper tool to pick a color that is on the screen. Next to the dropper tool, you have few very saturated colors along with a white to black gradient. The **Color History** thumbnail shows the previous color you had selected next to the new color you have chosen. This allows you to compare the value, saturation, and hue of your newly selected color to your previous one.
    ii. You could also use **Ring** which resembles a color wheel with a square in the middle. The square in the middle increases in saturation as you go from left to right and it increases in value as you go from top to bottom as shown in the following screenshot:

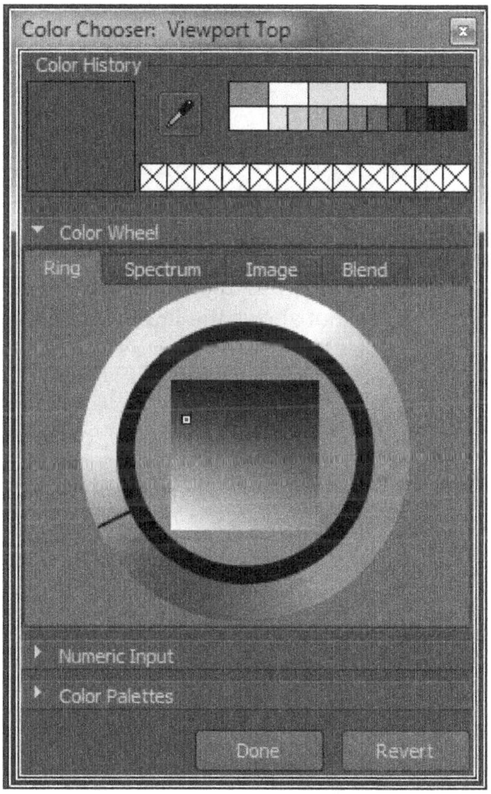

iii. Next, you have **Spectrum** which shows the different values of a color going from light to dark across, while changing hues vertically. To adjust the saturation of your color, you could use the slider below the hue and value selection window as shown in the following screenshot:

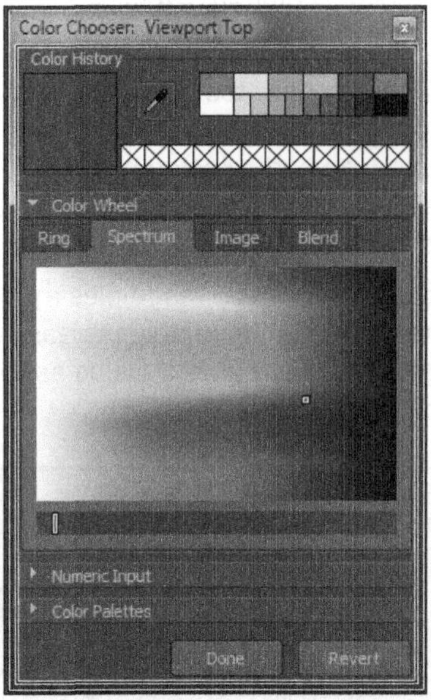

iv. Another way to select your color is from an **Image**. Once you load an image, you can aim your crosshairs at the color you would like to sample. The following screenshot shows the **Image** tab:

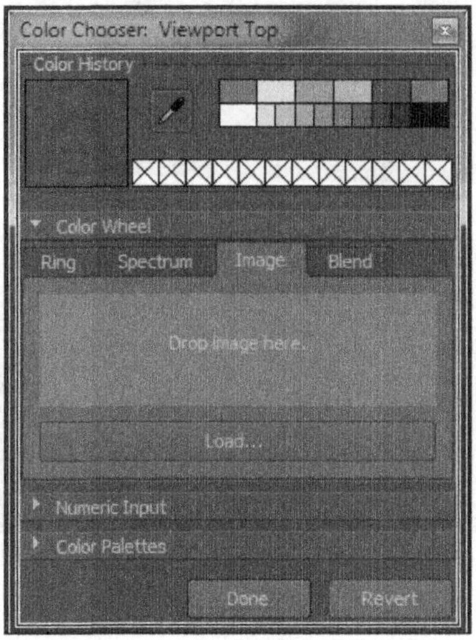

v. The **Blend** tab allows you to mix four colors and choose a color from that mixture as shown in the following screenshot:

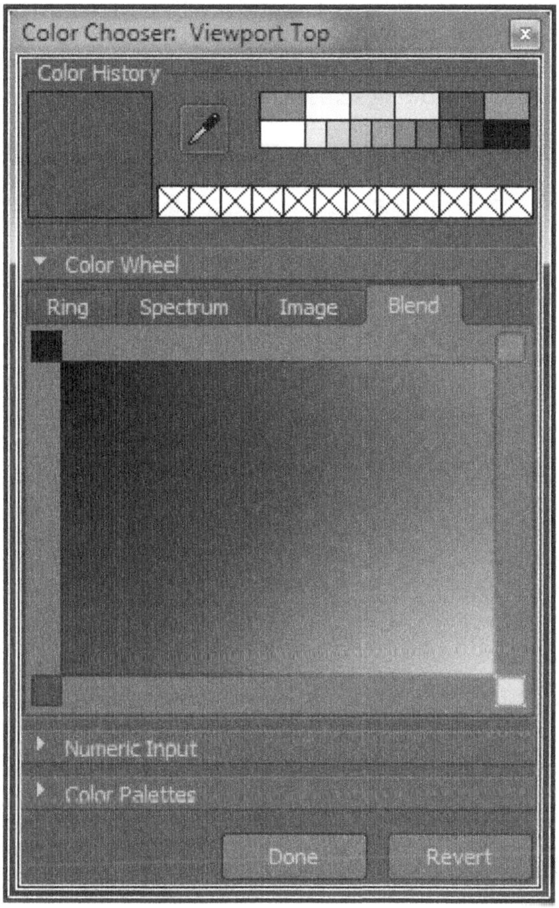

4. The next drop-down menu is labeled **Numeric Input**. This menu item consists of **RGB** and **HSV** sliders, as follows:

    i. The **RGB** sliders will let you increase the red, green, and blue channels on different sliders. You can even change the range from **0 to 1.0** or **0 to 255** depending on what units you are accustomed to working with. It is shown in the following screenshot:

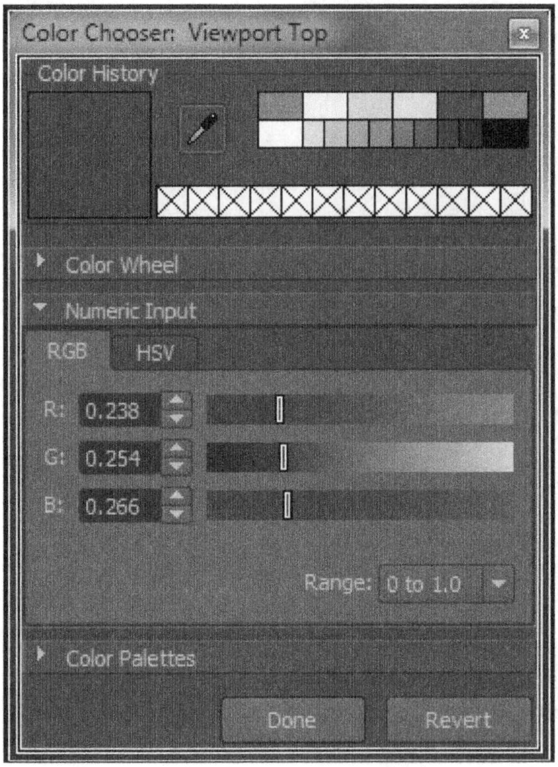

ii. The **HSV** sliders will allow you to adjust the hue, saturation, and value of a color. The hue bar will slide you through the various colors on a **0-360** scale. The saturation and value sliders are on a **0-1** range. Having a **0** in the saturation makes it gray scale while **1** is a fully saturated color. **0** in the value slider will give you black while a **1** gives you white, as shown in the following screenshot:

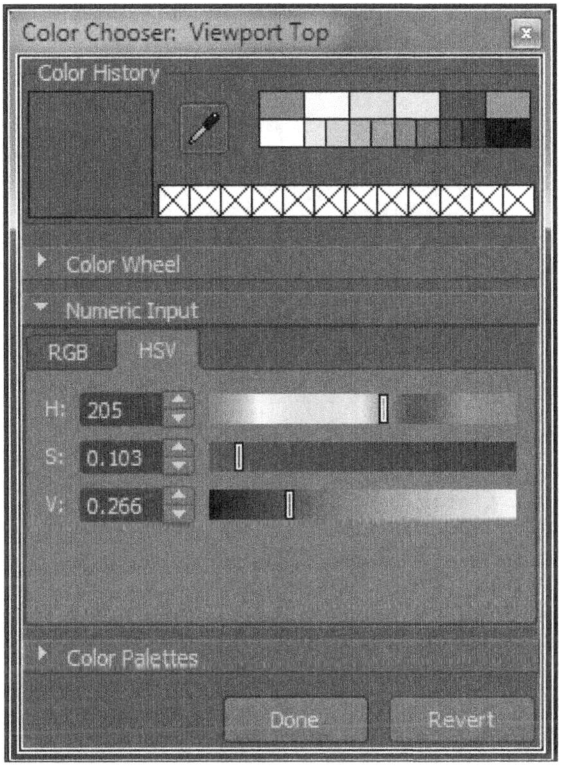

5. The final way to choose your color is by using **Color Palettes**.

   i. You can create, load, or save your own color palettes. It is usually a good idea to create a color palette that suits the need of the piece you are working on. The default palette looks like the following screenshot with a wide range of colors:

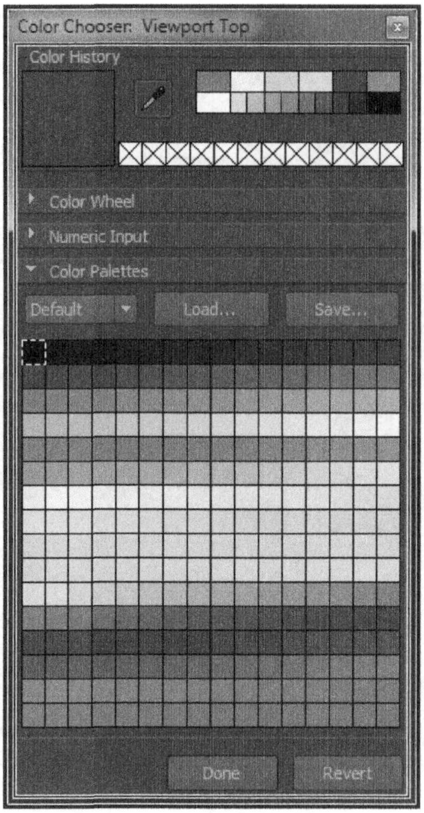

There's more...

If you adjust some of your preferences and you find that Mudbox isn't acting quite right, then you may want to go back to the default settings. As with other software of this nature, your preference settings can get corrupted at times. To fix this, you'll just need to do the following:

- Go into the **Documents** folder where you will find the **Mudbox** folder.
- Open up the `Mudbox` folder and you should see a folder labeled as the version of Mudbox that you are using. For example, if you are using Mudbox 2013 64-bit version, then the path to the **Settings** folder should be something like this: `C:\Users\yourusername\Documents\Mudbox\2013-x64`.

- Open this folder and you should see a **Settings** folder.
- Delete this folder to reset Mudbox's preferences back to its default.

Deleting this folder can fix a lot of different issues. If you notice strange things happening, you may want to try deleting this folder.

If you go into the **Settings** folder, you will notice some files inside. These files split up your settings into more specific categories. For example, sometimes you will have issues but you don't want to lose all your image-browser bookmarks or your hotkeys. What you can do in this case is save these individual files to a separate location as a backup for these settings. Once these files are backed up, go ahead and delete the **Settings** folder from your documents. The next time you run that version of Mudbox, the **Settings** folder will be replaced with the default one. Now you can try copying the backed up files back into the **Settings** folder and overwrite the default ones. This should bring your bookmarks, hotkeys, and other settings back.

As long as it is not that specific file that was corrupted in the first place, you should be back on track with no issues and the important preferences intact.

See also

- The *Setting up hotkeys* recipe

Setting up your Wacom tablet

This recipe will describe how you can set up a **Wacom tablet** for use with Mudbox. A Wacom tablet is a tablet that you can draw on with a digital pen, to allow for more organic lines and shapes in your digital paintings or sculpts.

Getting ready

First, you will need to plug in your Wacom tablet. Next, you will need to make sure you have the latest drivers for your tablet installed. You can find the latest drivers for any Wacom product at Wacom's website, `www.wacom.com/CustomerCare/Drivers`. Your tablet may have also come with a disc that has the drivers on it. You may need to restart your computer once the drivers are installed.

How to do it...

Now that you have the drivers for your tablet, you can go to **Wacom Tablet Properties** shortcut by hitting the Windows key and typing in wacom. This should reveal the Wacom Tablet Properties shortcut in your start menu list. Next, you should click on this shortcut to reveal the window that looks like in the following screenshot:

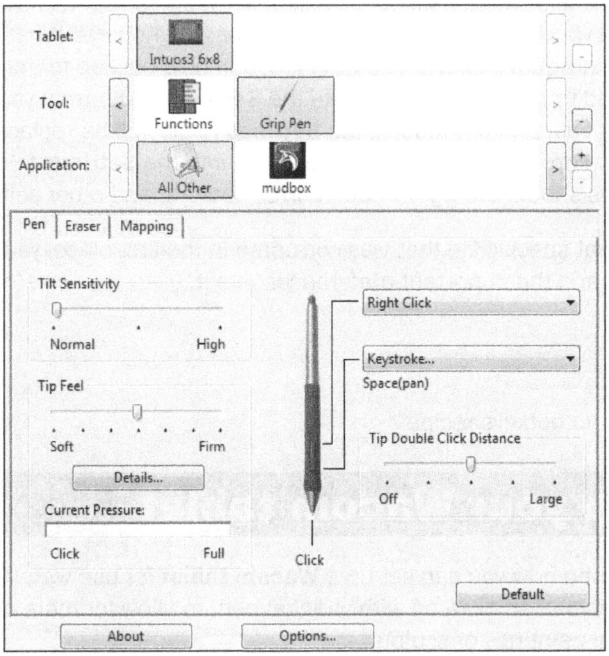

The **Tablet** section will list the tablets you have installed and connected to your machine. **Tool** is where you will choose which part of the tablet you would like to set up, the pen or the tablet itself. If you click the **+** across from **Application**, you will be able to add a customized setup for any software installed on your system. Otherwise, it will use the settings you have configured under **All Other**.

It is recommended that you set your pen buttons to **Middle Click** and **Right Click** for camera navigation. With these settings you will be able to do the following:

- **Tumble** (rotate around a center point of interest) the camera by holding *Alt* and dragging the pen tip along the surface of your tablet
- **Track** (pan up, down, left, and right) the camera by holding *Alt* and holding the button on your pen that was set to **Middle Click** while moving the pen tip just above the surface of your tablet

- **Dolly** (zoom toward and away from a center point of interest) the camera by holding *Alt* and holding the button on your pen that was set to **Right Click** while moving the pen tip just above the surface of your tablet

Alternatively, you could set up your navigation keys to use the buttons on your tablet itself. Keep in mind that you can set your tablet buttons and your pen buttons to anything you want, including a keystroke, which will allow you to enter a series of key presses. This is helpful for mapping hotkeys to your tablet buttons or your pen buttons.

You can also set the slide bar to allow you to zoom or resize your brush size or intensity. In the following screenshot, you will see an example of the tablet settings window:

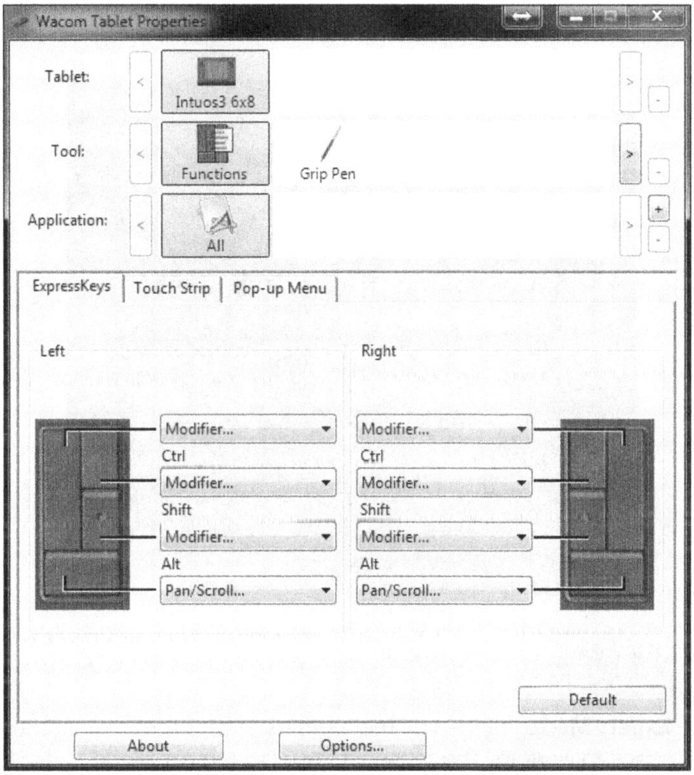

Working in expert mode

This recipe will tell you how to work in expert mode and why it is useful. Expert mode will take away all your toolbars giving you maximum workspace.

Getting ready

Before you go into expert mode, you should set up all your hotkeys the way you would like them and memorize all of the hotkeys that you will need. You can look into the recipe on *Setting up hotkeys* for more information on this.

How to do it...

The quickest and easiest way to get in and out of expert mode is to use the hotkey *T*. This will *toggle* between having toolbars or no toolbars around your workspace. If you would like to go into expert mode, through the menus you can go to **Display | Expert Mode** as shown in the following screenshot:

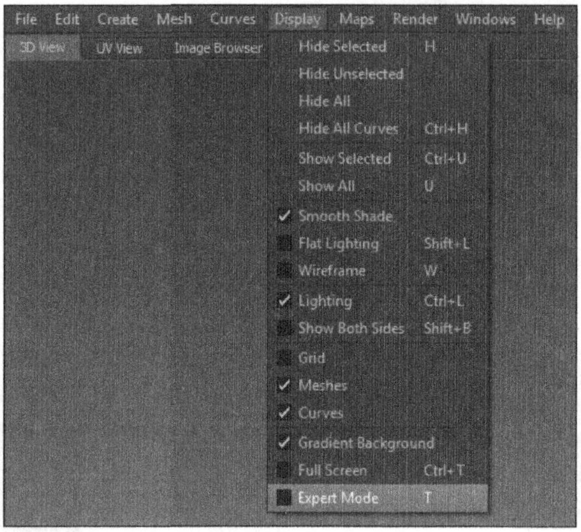

How it works...

When you enable **Expert Mode**, it hides all the toolbars except the main menu on top so that you have a larger space to work in. The reason it is called **Expert Mode** is because you will need to have memorized the hotkeys that you will use to work on your project. Also, it's a good idea to familiarize yourself with the right-click menu before using this mode.

You can also customize which toolbars disappear when you enable **Expert Mode** by going to **Windows | Preferences** and clicking on the drop-down list for **User Interface**. At the bottom of the options listed here, you will see **Expert Mode Hides:** with some checkboxes for different toolbars. The following screenshot is what the menu should look like:

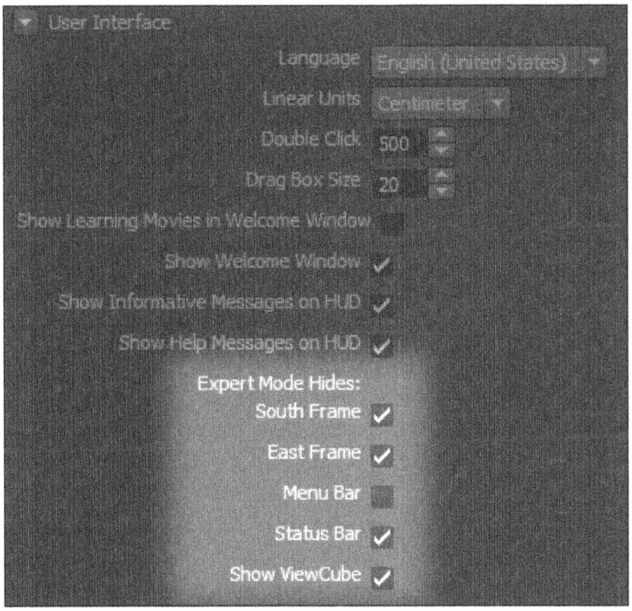

There's more...

The primary reason you would want to work in Expert mode is to maximize your viewing space on your monitor. Another thing you can do to give yourself more monitor real estate is to work in **Full Screen** mode. This mode will enlarge the Mudbox 2013 window to fit the entire screen as opposed to just your desktop area, which will leave the start menu bar in Windows.

To use **Full Screen** mode, you can go to the same menu as **Expert Mode**, under **Display**, or you can use the hotkey, *Ctrl + T*.

I recommend using these two tools together to help you focus (no distracting UI elements) so that you can see more of your models at a higher resolution on the screen

See also

- The *Setting up hotkeys* recipe

2
Heads Up

In this chapter we will cover:

- Revealing the wireframe for edge location
- Setting up a basic three-point lighting scheme
- Organizing your tabs for smoother navigation
- Locking down the camera for reference matching
- Creating a stone tile by adjusting brush properties
- Using the object list to manage multiple objects
- Setting up layers for easily adjusting sculpt details
- Setting up stamps, stencils, and image planes using image browser

Introduction

This chapter will go over some of the different aspects of the user interface. This includes the properties of your cameras, brushes, lights, and so on. The tools and techniques that you learn from this chapter will help you understand Mudbox 2013's User Interface (UI). You will also have a greater understanding on how to navigate through the UI more efficiently.

Revealing the wireframe for edge location

This recipe explains how to show the wireframe on your model. Knowing how the topology conforms to your surface will help you to accurately place the details as well as inform you of the problem areas. One thing to look out for are star shapes created by more than four edges. These can cause strange pinching issues when trying to sculpt on the surface. When you subdivide your model, these areas do not get any better. Subdividing your model will only add more edges to the star.

How to do it...

There are three ways that you can enable your wireframe in viewport.

1. First, go to **Display** and you will find a checkbox halfway down the list for wireframe. This will also show you which hotkey is assigned to this action. The following screenshot is what the menu should look like:

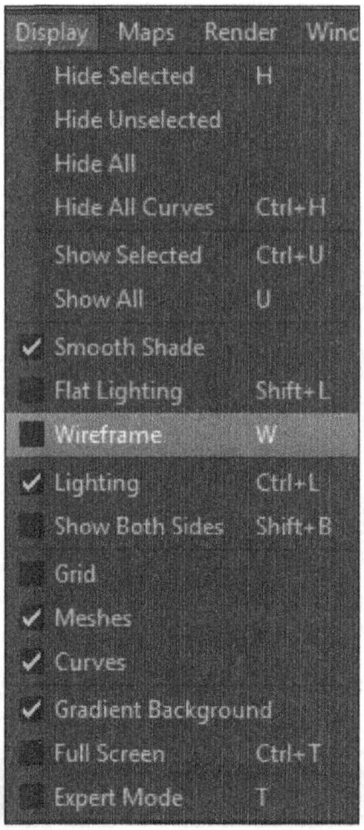

2. Another way to toggle the wireframe is to right-click inside your viewport. This menu shows some of the same options as the main menu but is condensed into fewer choices and is laid out as a marking menu. The following screenshot is what you will see when you right-click inside the viewport:

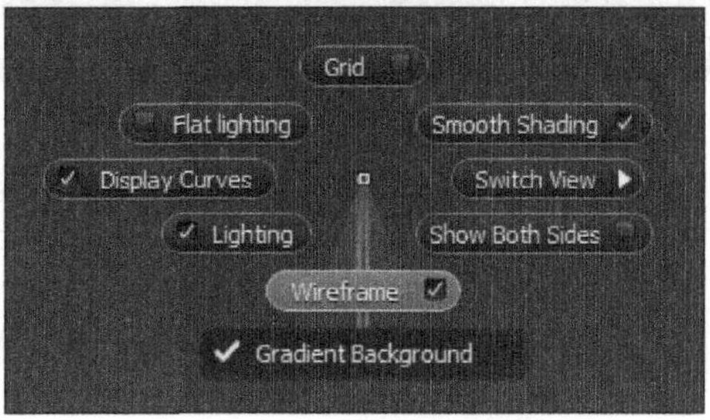

This type of menu is good for speeding up your workflow because you no longer have to scroll through menus to find the option you are looking for. If you memorize which direction your option is located in, within this menu, you can rely on gestures to use the tool that you need. For example, if you would like to toggle the wireframe quickly and you have memorized the location of this option, then you can just hold down the right mouse button (in the viewport), drag the mouse down (the location of the wireframe), and then lift your finger off the right mouse button. This will do the same thing as right clicking and choosing **Wireframe** with the left mouse button.

3. The final and easiest way is to use its hotkey, which should by default be *W* as shown next to the word "wireframe" in the main menu. Each time you hit *W* it will toggle the wireframe's visibility on and off.

How it works...

When you enable the wireframe, you are seeing a visual representation of the edges that make up your model. The more edges you have on your model the finer the detail you are able to add by adjusting the position, rotation, and size of these edges in 3D space. Essentially, all of the sculpting tools you use within Mudbox are for repositioning these edges and the vertices at the end of each edge. You should always make sure you have proper edge flow before beginning a sculpt of your model. You want to try and avoid having more than four edges meet at a vertex. This can cause issues when sculpting.

Also, take note that working in wireframe mode will increase your viewport refresh time, causing Mudbox to slow down while working with dense models or when your PC's performance cannot handle the wireframe smoothly.

Setting up a basic three point lighting scheme

This recipe will show you how to set up a basic three point lighting scheme. Three point lighting is mostly used for characters but can also be used on hero props or anything else you would like to pop out of the background.

In this recipe, I will sometimes refer to the scene that your object is in. This is for users who are bringing objects in from a larger scene. You can play around a little more with your lighting to establish a mood if you are just doing a sculpt as a standalone art piece.

Getting ready

First, you will need to know what type of lights Mudbox 2013 has. There are three light types available for use in Mudbox 2013.

- The first is the **point light** which imitates the kind of light a light bulb would emit. This type of light radiates out from a single point in all directions. An example is shown in the following screenshot:

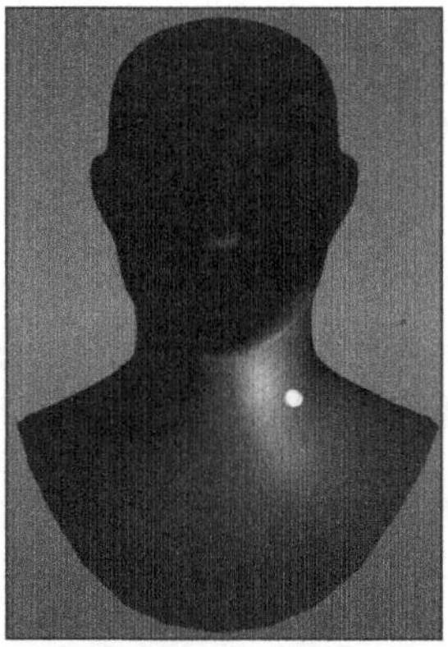

- The second light type is the **directional light** which imitates sunlight. This light will shine in one direction with an infinite distance. An example is shown in the following screenshot:

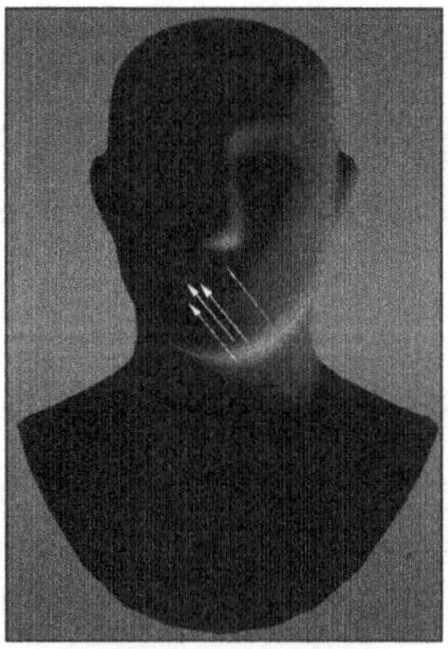

- The third light type is the **image based light**, which imitates the diffused lighting of an environment. This type of lighting uses the colors and values of an image mapped to an invisible sphere around your object as its lighting. An example is shown in the following screenshot:

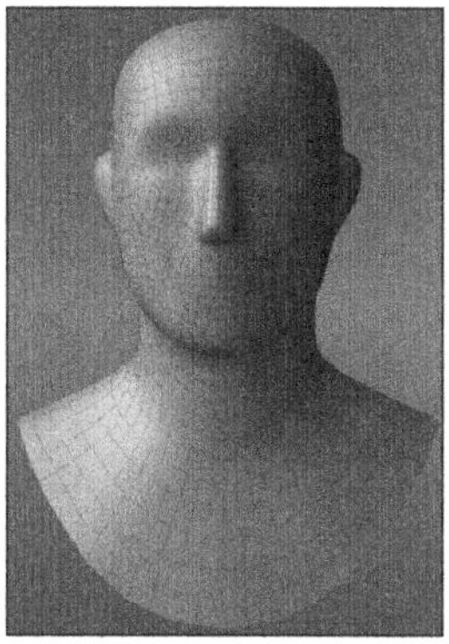

Each of the three light types have different properties. They are as follows:

1. Point light properties are as follows:
    - **Diffuse**: This is the color the light will illuminate with. If you click on the color bar next to **Diffuse**, the color chooser will pop up, which is described in *Chapter 1, Ready? Set...*.
    - **Intensity**: This determines the strength of the light. A value of zero will basically turn your light off. If you would like a value greater than one you will have to type it in as opposed to just using the slider.
    - **Light Decay**: This attribute determines how far the light will travel before it dissipates. Play around with the slider until you get the desired effect on your model.
    - **Scale**: This will change the size of the visual representation of the light itself. This will not affect the actual lighting of your object.
    - **Show Grips**: If this box is checked it will show a tool in the viewport for you to adjust the location of the point light.
    - **Show Light**: If this box is checked it will give you a visual representation of the light to help you locate the position of the light in your scene.
2. Directional light properties are as follows:
    - **Diffuse**: This is the color, the light will illuminate with. If you click on the color bar next to **Diffuse**, the color chooser will pop up, which is described in *Chapter 1, Ready? Set...*.
    - **Intensity**: This determines the strength of the light. A value of zero will basically turn your light off. If you would like a value greater than one you will have to type it in as opposed to just using the slider.
    - **Scale**: This will change the size of the visual representation of the light itself. This will not affect the actual lighting of your object.

- **Locked to Camera**: If this box is checked, it will keep the light in the same place relative to the camera. If this box is unchecked, it will keep the light in place relative to the object.
- **Show Grips**: If this box is checked, it will show a tool in the viewport for you to adjust the angle of the directional light.
- **Show Light**: If this box is checked, it will give you a visual representation of the light to help you see the angle of the light in your scene.

3. Image based light properties are as follows:
    - **Intensity**: This determines the strength of the light. A value of zero will basically turn your light off. If you would like a value greater than one, you will have to type it in as opposed to just using the slider.
    - **Locked to Camera**: If this box is checked, it will keep the light in the same place relative to the camera. If this box is unchecked, it will keep the light in place relative to the object.
    - **Show Grips**: If this box is checked, it will show a tool in the viewport for you to adjust the rotation of the invisible sphere that the image is mapped to.
    - **Image Based Light File**: This is the file that will be used to light your object. By default, Mudbox will use a file called `mudbox3PointDefault.tif`. If you click on the **...** you can choose a different file to light your scene with.

How to do it...

First you will create your key light. To create this, perform the following steps:

1. To do this you will need to go into the top menu and click on **Create** | **Lights** | **Directional**. You can come back to your light properties easily by selecting the light in your **Object List**. You can also rename the lights to help you identify each light more easily.
2. Next, you will move your light around to the location of your choice. You can do this by choosing your directional light in the **Object List** and then checking the boxes for **Show Grips** (to bring up the rotation gizmo) and **Show Light** (to see the direction the light is facing in graphic form).
3. Now rotate the light so that it is shining from somewhere close to three-quarters of an angle (or somewhere from 30-60 degrees from head on). This angle will give nice shadows to help pop out the form of the object, more specifically a face. Just remember the point of the key light is to light up the center of interest on an object while keeping true to the lighting of its surrounding environment.
4. Next, you will adjust the light's intensity. It typically sits between 0.8 and 1.5 depending on the strength of the light source. You can type this value in or use the slider until you reach a desired intensity.

5. Make sure that the color you choose matches the color of the light source. For example, you will need to add some yellow or orange to your key light if the primary light source is a candle.

It will help details pop out on your model if the key light and the fill lights, or the secondary key lights, are complimentary colors. For example, the orange candlelight, from the earlier example, may have a bluish moonlight fill, accompanied by a stronger bluish direct moonlight being used as a rim light. You could also use a lower intensity orange fill light if there are other candles around and you want orange to be the dominant color, or if you want less attention to be on the facial features.

The bust below is lit by a key light only. As you can see, one half of the face has dark shadows with hard edges. There is no fill from bounced light to show the features in the shadow areas of the face. There is also no rim light to pop the head from the background.

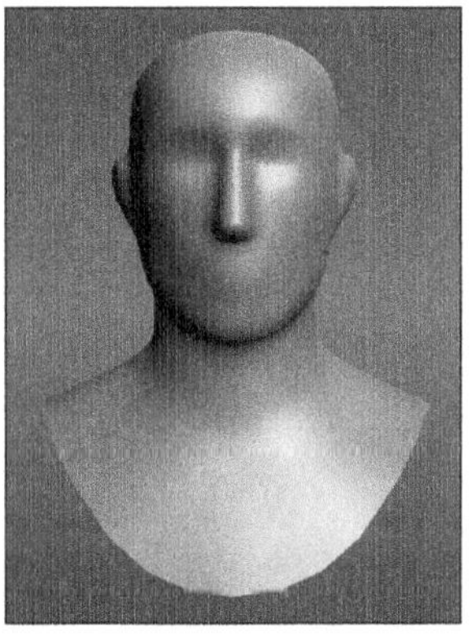

Now you will create your fill light. To create, perform the following steps:

1. This light can be created by going to **Create** | **Lights** | **Point**.
2. It might be a good time to start naming your lights since you are using more than one. Go ahead and right-click on the light in the **Object List**. Now choose **Rename Light** and give it a name such as `Fill Light` or `Orange Fill Light` if you are using multiple fill lights.

   Just remember if you are using multiple fill lights you may want to lower their intensity, as the light is additive so it may become brighter than you want it. If you want the intensity of your lights to be the same and add up to your desired intensity as a whole then you can take your desired intensity and divide it by the number of fill lights you are using.

3. To change the location of the point light, you will want to check the box for **Show Grips** and translate the light to your desired location. Since this light emits rays in all directions there is no need to rotate the light.

4. If you only have one fill light, it is usually best placed at the opposite angle from the key light. So, something like -30 to -60 degrees from the center line of your viewing angle.
5. Now you will adjust the intensity and color based on the bounced light. Also, remember that if your fill is too intense it will flatten out your model by making the shadows disappear. Too little fill and you won't see any details in the unlit areas of your model. No fill light is usually reserved for low lighting situations like candle-lit room with no windows. If there was a window you might add a bluish fill that is coming from moonlight through the window. Or you may just use a back light to represent the moonlight and leave out the fill. It all depends on the look and feel you are going for.

   A good starting point for the intensity of the fill light is to set it at half the intensity of the key light.

These things are important to think about when setting up lighting for your sculpt. It is good to have a lighting set up that is similar to the setup that your scene has or that brings out more character in your models like using dramatic lighting.

The following is an example of a head being lit only by a fill light. Notice you can only see some of the features subtly. The fill light is meant to fill in the shadow areas with a touch of illumination.

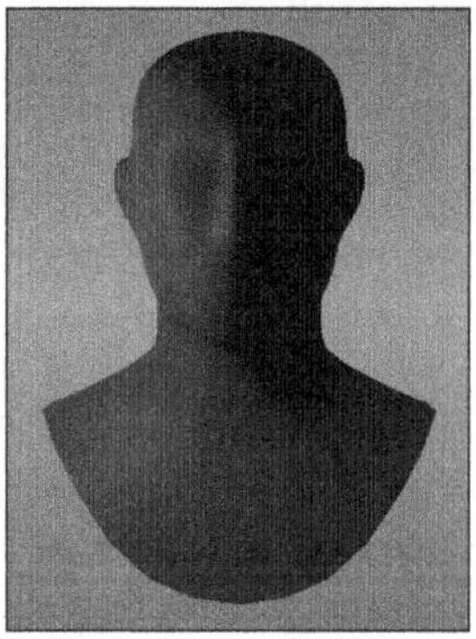

Realistically, the fill light would hit the object from all sides to different extents, due to the bounced light in the environment. In a three-point lighting scheme, you don't always need the fill to hit all areas of the model because you have a key and a rim light that will help to illuminate the model from all angles.

Last is the back light, also referred to as the rim light. To create, perform the following steps:

1. To create this light you will want to go to **Create** | **Lights** | **Directional**.
2. Now you will want to angle this light so that it highlights the silhouette of the object.
3. You may want to increase the intensity of this light for better definition.
4. The color can match a light source located behind the object in the scene and its intensity is often greater than the key light.

The bust below is lit by a rim light only. Notice how the rim light adds a thin highlighted edge to the model. This highlight can help separate a character from the background which can be very helpful when you have a character with a similar value as the background elements.

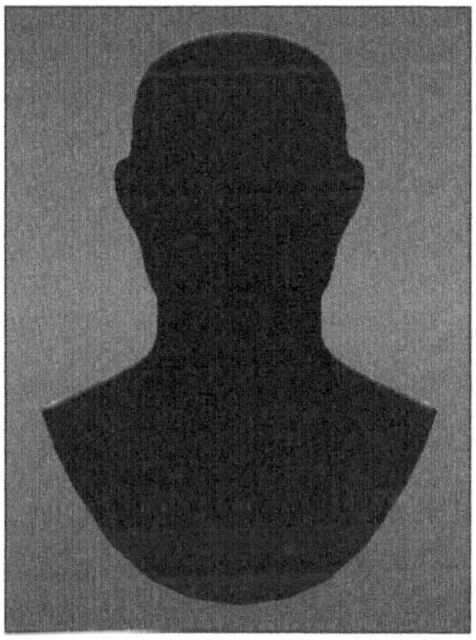

The following screenshot is an example of these three lights working together:

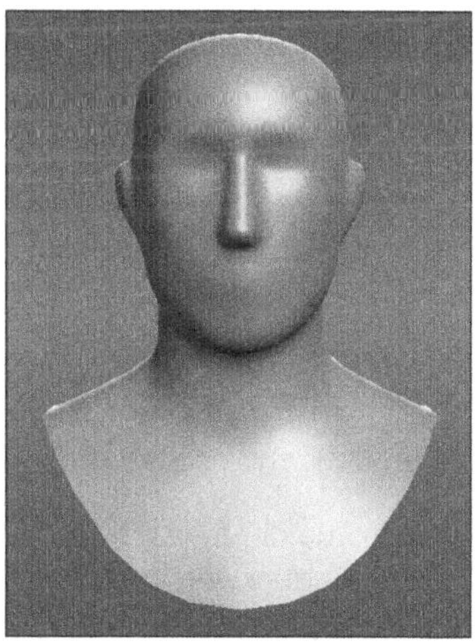

How it works...

The key light acts as your main light source. Typically this light would be either a directional light or a spot light. It will also usually be set to cast a shadow in a 3D scene since it is a direct light source. Depending on the light source, this light can be set to a variety of colors. red-orange for candlelight, bluish for moonlight, or yellow for sunlight.

The fill light brightens up the shadowy areas of the object you are lighting. This type of light simulates bounced light that you would see in the real world. You can use any type of light for this. On a blue sky, summer day, you may add a hint of blue to your fill light. If it is dusk, you may want to add a hint of purple, pink, or orange depending on the color of the clouds. You can even use image-based lighting to use the colors from an image and where they are located in 3D space. You would use an environment or reflection map to do this so that the colors are mapped in the correct location in 3D space.

The rim light or the back light is used to pop your object from the background. This light is similar to the key light in that it is usually another direct light source. The intensity of this light source is often exaggerated to give enough pop to the object.

Organizing your tabs for smoother navigation

In the 2013 version of Mudbox, they have added the ability to fully customize your interface so that you can define a layout that works best for you. This recipe will describe what you can do with your interface and how to do it.

How to do it...

Both removing and adding new toolbars to your interface is very easy. The following is a list of things you can do with the tabs located on Mudbox's main window where you can see the **3D View**, **UV View**, **Mudbox Community**, and **Image Browser**:

- First, to add a tab, you can right-click next to the existing tabs located at the top of your main window. Then go to **New Tab** and choose one of the many different kinds of tabs available in Mudbox.
- If you would like to change the order of these tabs, you can click-and-drag the tab name from its current location to the end of the list of tabs.
- To remove a tab you just right-click and choose **Close Tab**.

The rest of the tabs and windows act a little differently than the main window. This is because the main window is still using the older Mudbox version's way of customizing while everything else is using the new system for window layouts. The following is a list of ways to customize the other windows:

- First, to show or hide a tab altogether you can right-click next to the main menu, the right of **Help**, and toggle the check boxes for each window name.
- To relocate a window, you will first need to uncheck the box next to **Lock Layout** inside the **Windows** menu. Once this is done you can click and drag the top of the window into your desired location. While dragging, the windows underneath the window you are moving will shift around and there will be a preview box for where that window will land. You can move the windows between other windows, next to other windows, or even into other windows. If you drag a window into another window, then the window that you dragged will become a tab within the other window.
- You can also tear a window off into a separate floating window by double-clicking the top of the window. To re-dock the window, you can drag the window into the desired location in the interface and it will re-dock itself.
- Once you have the desired layout for your windows, you can recheck the box next to **Lock Layout** in the **Windows** menu, to keep things in place.
- If you would like to back up or share your layout, you can go into the **Windows** menu and choose **Export Current Layout....** This will allow you to save a `.mudui` file that can be imported on other computers.
- If you would like to import another user's layout, or even your layout that you are transferring from another computer, you can go into the **Windows** menu and choose **Import Layout....** Now just browse to the desired layout, must be a `.mudui` file type.
- Don't be afraid to tweak it until you get just what you need. If you can't seem to find something that works for you then you can always reset the layout to its default by going to **Windows**, in the main menu, and choose **Rest Layout**.

Locking down the camera for reference matching

This recipe will show you how you can lock down the camera so that you don't accidentally move your camera when you have it at a desired angle.

Getting ready...

First, an overview of the camera properties that you can adjust:

- **Transform**: This is the section where you can lock various movements of the camera such as rotation or zoom.
- **2D Transform**: This section allows you to scale, rotate, or reposition the view based on a 2D plane in front of the camera. You are able to disable the repositioning, rotation, and scale here as well.

- **Orthographic**: You can also change whether or not the camera is an orthographic camera or not by simply checking the box.
- Field of View (**FOV**): Next you will see the field of view which gives you a slider to adjust the lens of the camera.
- **Near Plane**: This will determine how close objects can get to the camera before they start to disappear.
- **Far Plane**: This will determine how far the objects can get from the camera before they disappear.

How to do it...

You may want to create a camera if you do not want to adjust the default camera's properties. To create a new camera you can go to **Create | Camera** in the main menu.

The fastest way to lock the camera is by going to the **Object List** and clicking in the space just before your camera name and just below the padlock icon, found at the top of the **Object List** window.

The following is the screenshot showing you where you can add the lock to your camera in the **Object List**:

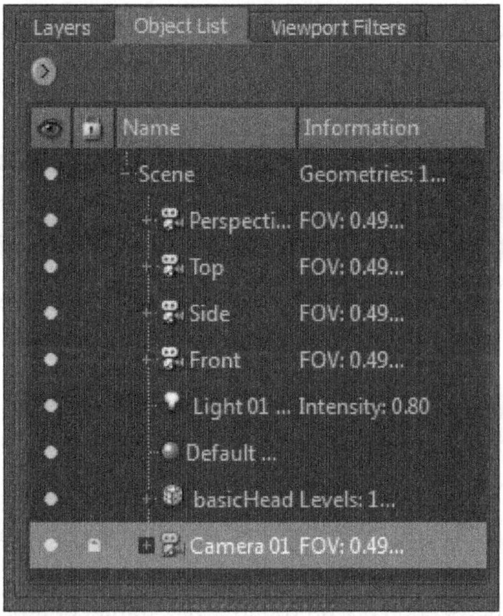

If you would like to lock the pan, rotate, and zoom, of the selected camera, you can go to the camera's properties by selecting your camera in the **Object List**. This should reveal the properties of your camera in the window below the **Object List**.

Once you're in the camera properties you can check the boxes in the **Transform** section. In the following screenshot, you can see what this section looks like in the camera's properties:

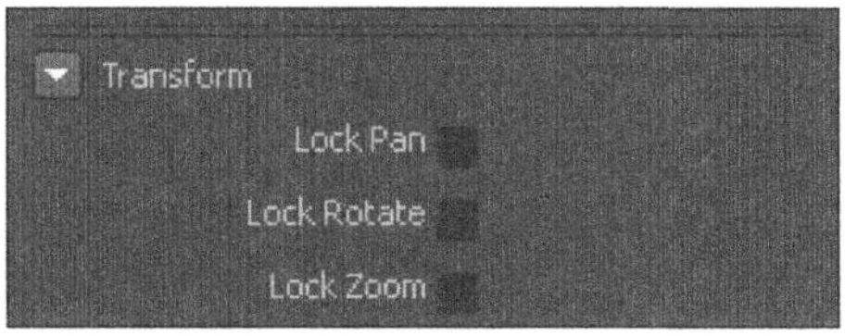

The following is a description of what each checkbox will do:

- **Lock Pan** will lock the *X* and *Y* movement of the camera
- **Lock Rotate** will lock the rotation of the camera
- **Lock Zoom** will lock the *Z* movement of the camera

See also

- *The Bookmarking the camera view* recipe in *Chapter 1, Ready? Set...*

Creating a stone tile by adjusting brush properties

This recipe will guide you through the process of creating a stone tile using a couple of different brushes with their properties adjusted. After completing this recipe, you should feel more confident in adjusting your brush settings to get the effect that you desire.

How to do it...

Perform the following steps to create a stone tile by adjusting the brush properties:

1. First thing we're going to do is hit *Ctrl* + *N* to create a new file.

2. When the **Welcome Window** pops up, select the **Cube** under **Start a new sculpture**.

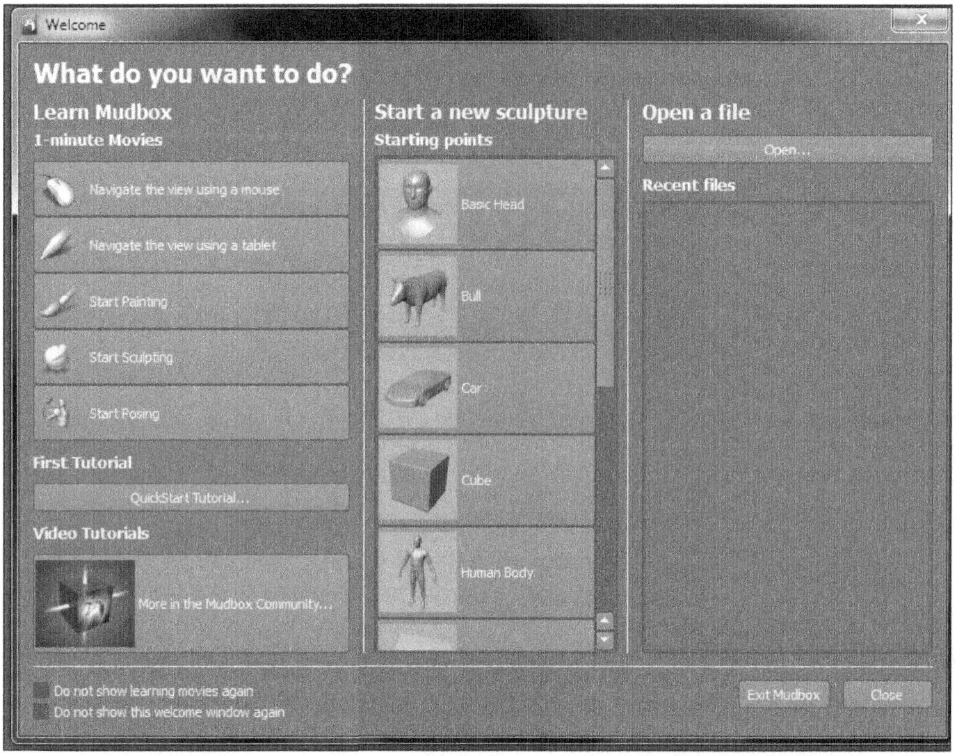

Mudbox comes with several starter meshes that you can start building upon instead of creating your own mesh from scratch. If you are starting a new project and don't see **Starting points**, found under **Start a new sculpture** in the above screenshot, that would work for your idea, then you can always go into the **Mudbox Community** tab and easily download a mesh that works for you.

3. Now click *Shift* + *D* several times until your cube reaches **Level 8**. This should give us enough resolution to get the details we need.

4. With our mesh ready to go, select the **Scrape** brush from the **Sculpt Tools** menu on the bottom-left side of the UI. The following screenshot shows what the **Sculpt Tools** menu looks like:

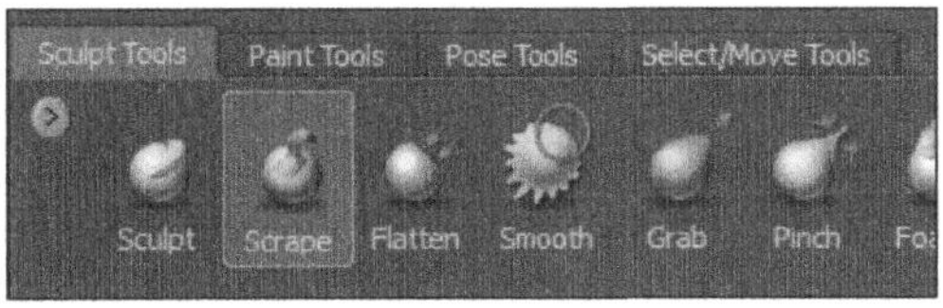

We're going to adjust the properties of this brush so that we can create believable edges to our stone tile. In order to do so, perform the following steps:

1. If we use the **Scrape** brush in its default form, it will turn out looking something similar to the following screenshot:

   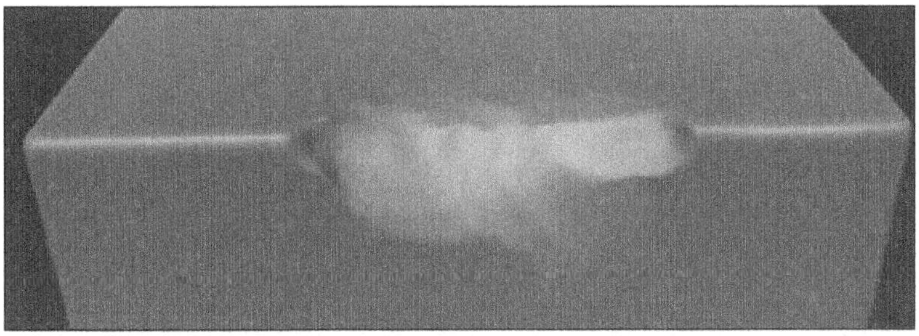

   Sure, it's a nice effect but it looks a little too waxy for our needs. To make this brush create a more faceted, heavier scrape we are going to open up the **Advanced** menu in our brush properties. This can be found on the lower right-hand side of the UI.

   Now we are going to uncheck the **Update Plane** checkbox. It should look something similar to the following screenshot:

   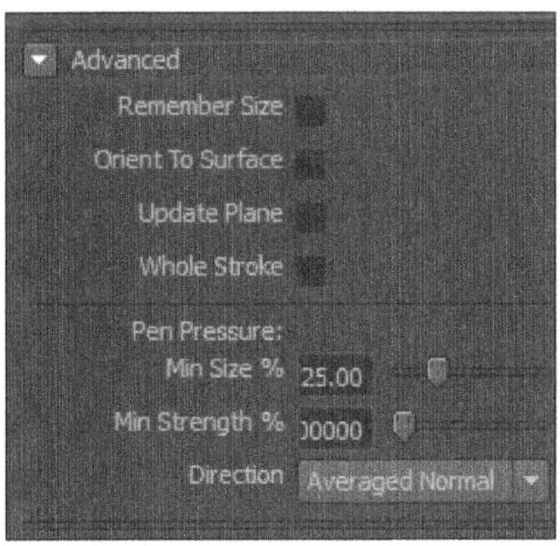

What this does is make it so the brush will scrape the surface down to the same plane that the initial stroke was made on. When this box is checked, it will scrape down to new planes as you stroke along different surfaces. As you can see in the following screenshot, the brush will now flatten the surface of your mesh using the angle of the surface you started the stroke with:

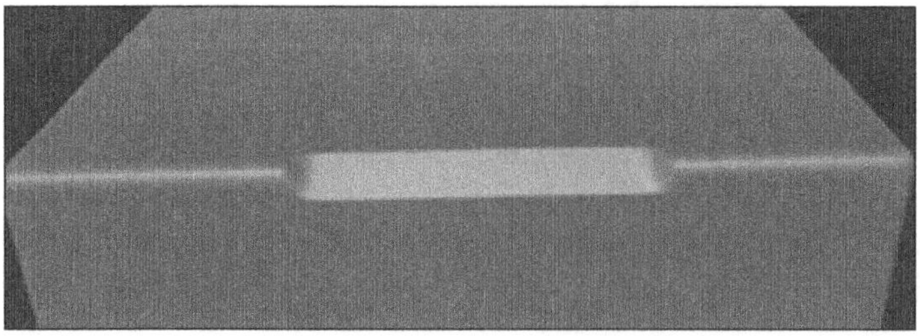

1. This still doesn't have a stone feel to it. So, what we will do now is add some texture to our **Scrape** brush. We will start by enabling one of the stamps that comes with Mudbox 2013.
2. Select the **bw_cliffFace.tif** stamp from the **Stamp** toolbar at the bottom-right side of the UI.

   You can see the names of the stamps by hovering your mouse cursor over the icon in the **Stamp** toolbar. The following screenshot will help you locate the stamp I am referring to:

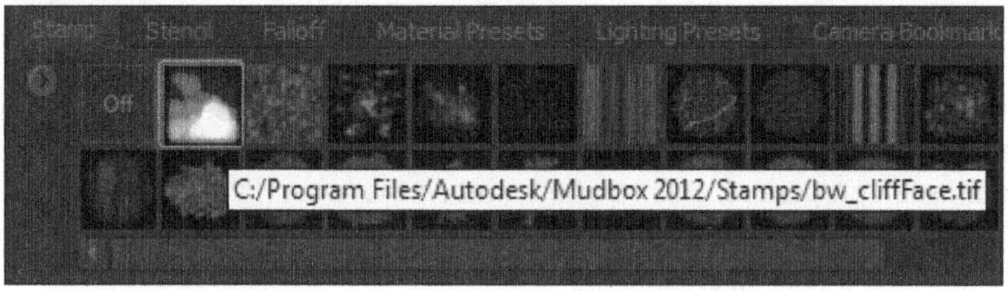

3. Now, when you test out the modified **Scrape** brush, it should look something similar to the following screenshot:

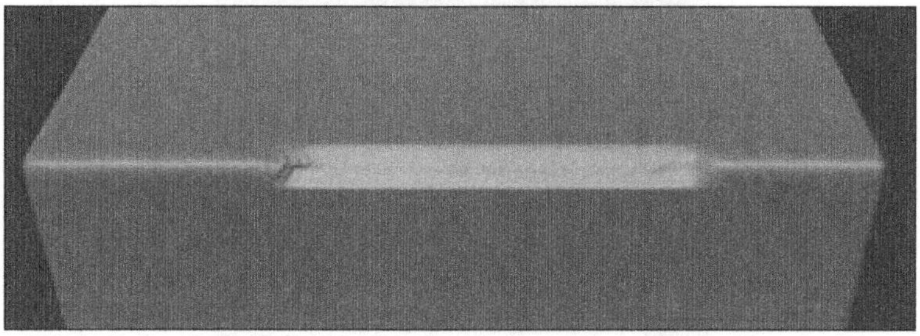

We are getting a little bit of the texture at the start and finish of our stroke but not anywhere in between. To fix this we could adjust our **Stamp Spacing**, but as you can see in the following screenshot, this would create a repetitive texture along the surface of our mesh:

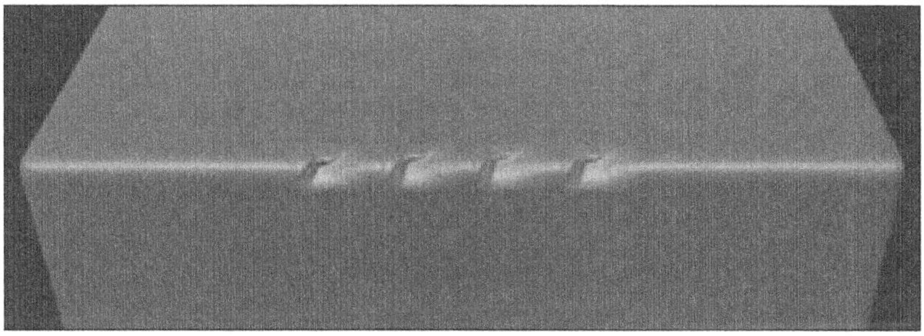

So, instead, we will set our **Stamp Spacing** to around `6.25` and check the box for **Randomize**, next to **Use Stamp Image** in the brush properties. Adjust the rotation, horizontal offset, and vertical offset sliders of the **Randomize** submenu. Your target settings should look like the following screenshot:

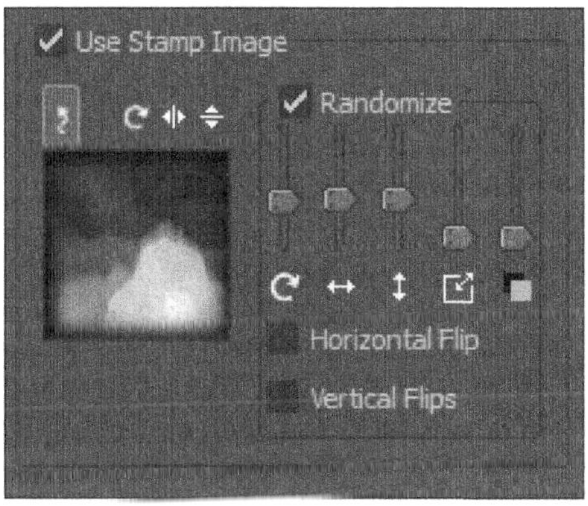

Now when you stroke the edge of your cube, it should look something similar to the following screenshot:

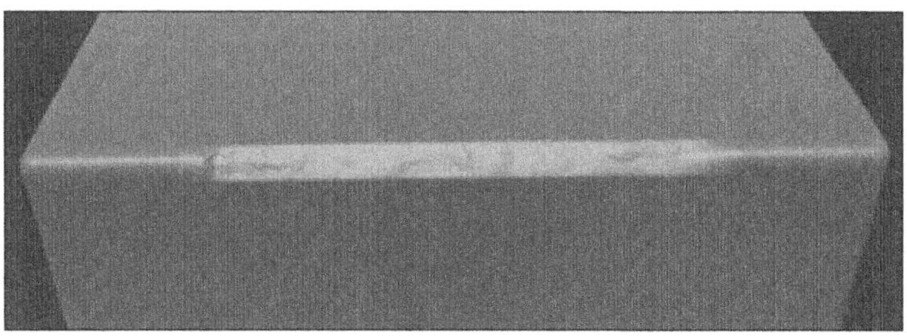

4. So, now that our brush is ready to add some edge detail, let's get sculpting! I recommend using a Wacom tablet or Cintiq for any sculpting that you do. With the pen in hand, or using the mouse, begin stroking over the edges of your cube. Continue stroking the edges of the cube and the edges that are created by your strokes until you have something that looks like the following screenshot:

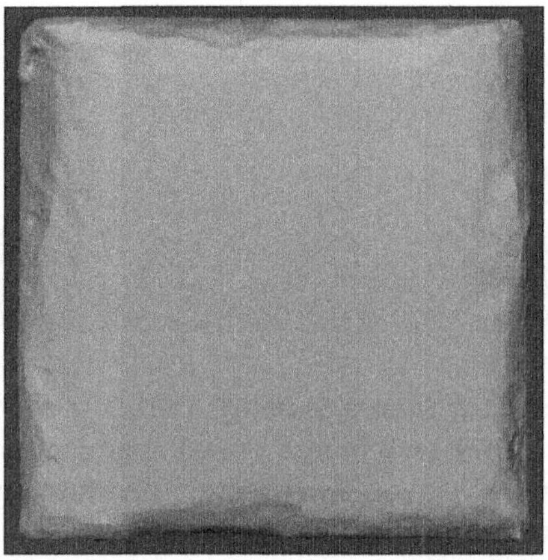

Play around with where you start your strokes. Remember, the brush will produce different results depending on where your stroke begins. You may want to undo, that is, *Ctrl* + *Z*, at times if the brush affects your model in a way that doesn't look good. This process is really just a collection of happy accidents that the randomized stamp is creating.

5. Now that the edges are taken care of we can move on to the texture on the rest of the tile. For this step, we will select the standard **Sculpt** brush from the **Sculpt Tools** menu described in the earlier steps.
6. Next, set up your brush the same way you set up the **Scrape** brush, minus the **Update Plane** checkbox. You should have the same **Stamp** enabled with the same spacing and **Randomize** checked.
7. Once you have gone through this process again, you can begin sculpting the texture onto your stone tile. Play around with the size and intensity of your brush to get some variation in the texture. When you are done, it should look something like the following screenshot:

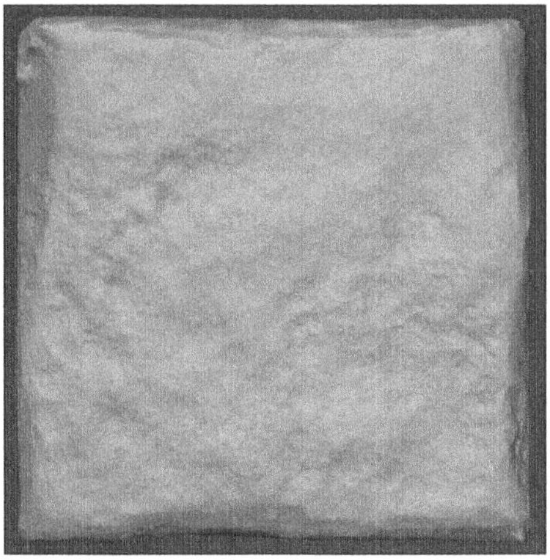

There's more...

If you want to save these brushes you are creating, you can easily do so by clicking on the small arrow just below **Sculpt Tools** in your UI and choosing **Add Tool**. Now just give it a name like `Stone Brush` or `Stone Edges`. You should see your new tool at the end of the tool list in your **Sculpt Tools** toolbar.

See also

- *The Customizing your brush and add it to your tool tab* recipe in *Chapter 3, Broad Strokes*
- *The Creating a concrete damage brush* recipe in *Chapter 3, Broad Strokes*
- *The Creating a rock wall that tiles seamlessly in all directions* recipe in *Chapter 4, Fine Tooth Comb*
- *The Setting up your Wacom tablet* recipe in *Chapter 1, Ready? Set...*

Using the object list to manage multiple objects

This recipe will help you to better understand how to use the **Object List** tab. In particular, it will help you to understand how to use the **Object List** to manipulate multiple objects in your scene.

How it works...

1. First thing we will do is bring in the stone tile that was created in the previous recipe by either importing the `.obj` or by opening the `.mud` file. If you did not go through that recipe or you did not save what you did, that's okay. You can use a **Cube** with some subdivisions on it for this recipe.
2. Once your tile has been imported you can go to your **Object List** on the right-hand side of the UI and select **cube** from the list of objects in your scene. Your object should turn yellow when you select **cube**. The menu should look like the following screenshot:

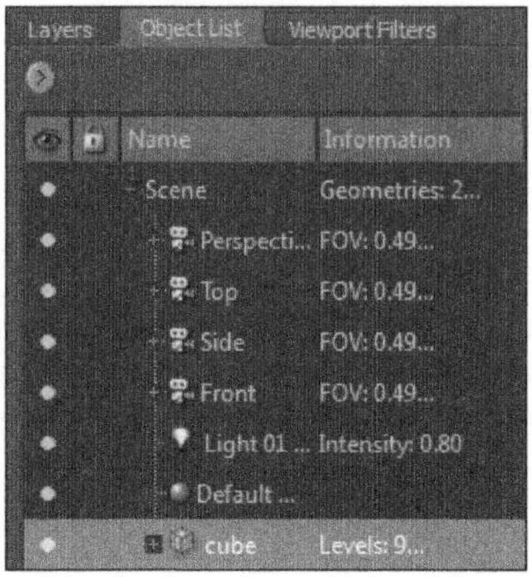

3. Now you can right-click on the word **cube** or on the object itself, and choose **Duplicate Selected**. This should make a copy of your object in your scene. The copy will be placed directly on top of the original so we will need to move one of the objects over.
4. Select one of the cubes in your **Object List** as shown in the following screenshot:

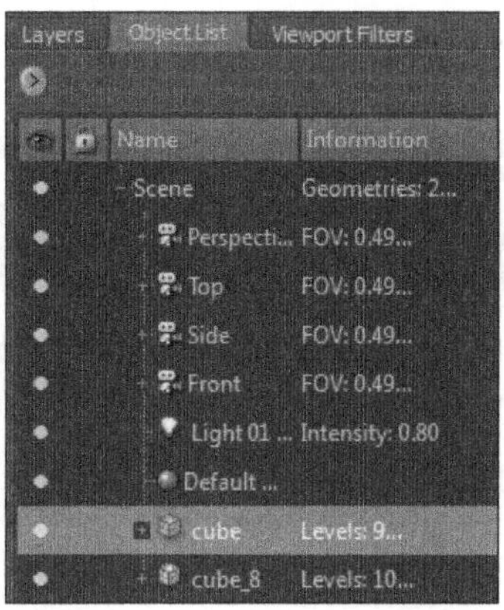

5. Using the **Translate** and **Rotate** tools under the **Select/Move Tools** tab, located in the bottom-left section of the UI, reposition one of the cubes next to the other. The following is a screenshot of the toolbar where you will find the **Translate** and **Rotate** tools.

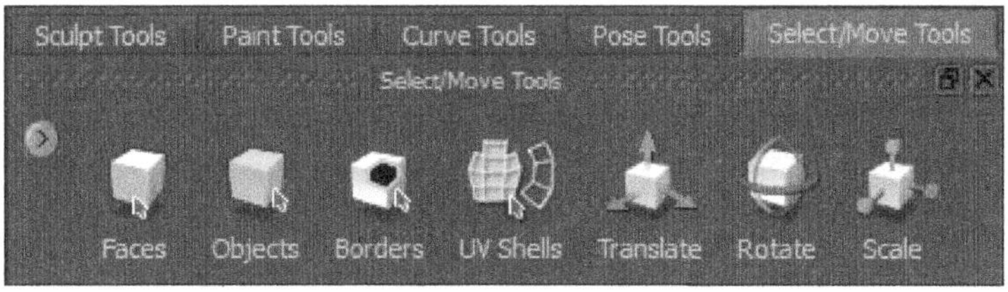

The rotation will help to hide any repetition in the texture. After repositioning your tile it should look something like the following screenshot:

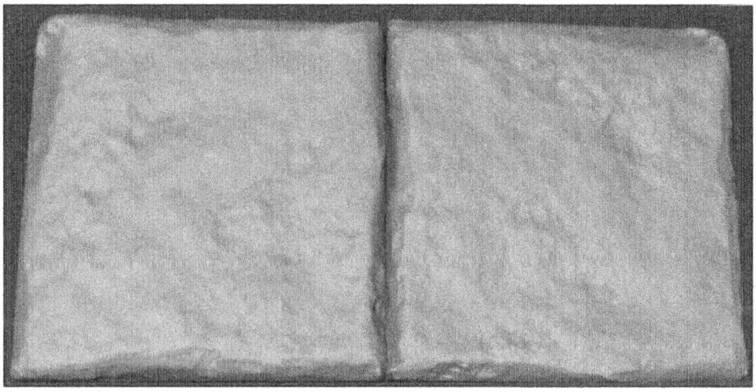

6. Now, repeat these steps a couple more times until it looks something like the following screenshot:

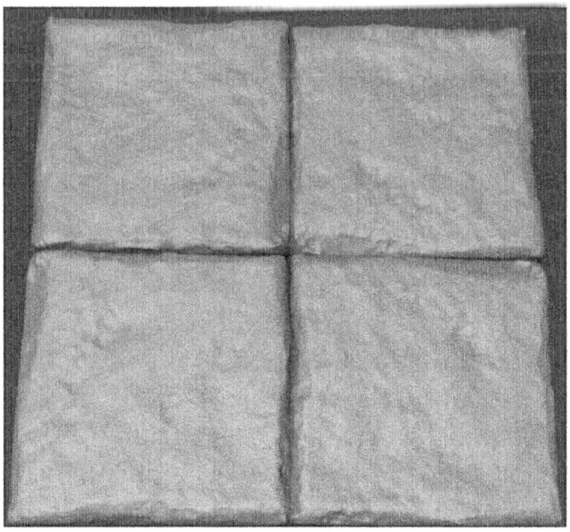

Keep in mind that if your tile has a very high resolution you may want to drop down a few levels by pressing *Page Down* on your keyboard. If your tile is 1 million polygons, then every time you duplicate a tile you are adding another million polygons to your scene. This can slow down your machine, a lot!

7. Now that you have the four tiles in your scene, you can sculpt on all four objects at the same time! Give it a try. Add some more wear and tear or add carvings to your stone. The following screenshot is an example of a stroke affecting each object without lifting the pen or mouse:

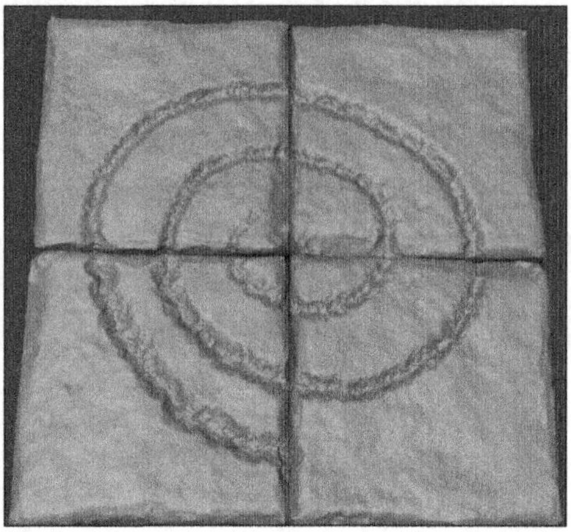

There's more...

If you would like to work with multiple objects that are not duplicates of a model already in your scene, you can choose **File | Import...** and import another object into your scene. You can follow the steps mentioned earlier to move your object into your desired position.

Keep in mind that if you need to flip your object over any axis, you can do that within Mudbox 2013. All you need to do is right-click on the object that you would like to flip and hover over **Flip Mesh** to expand the menu that lists the following flipping options:

- The first three choices (**Around X**, **Around Y**, and **Around Z**) are for flipping in world space. This means it is being mirrored across the Mudbox grid axis.
- The next three choices (**Around Local X**, **Around Local Y**, and **Around Local Z**) are for flipping in local space. This means that the object is being mirrored based on the bounding box of the object itself.
- The last two choices (**From Y-Up to Z-Up** and **From Z-Up to Y-Up**) are to correct the orientation of your object if your 3D modeling software's grid orientation is different than Mudbox's. For example, if you are importing from 3D Studio Max then *Z* axis will be up, but if you import from Maya then your *Y* axis will be up.

See also

- The *Organizing your tabs for smoother navigation* recipe
- The *Locking down the camera for reference matching* recipe
- The *Creating a stone tile by adjusting brush properties* recipe

Setting up layers for easily adjusting sculpt details

This section will discuss ways that you can organize and use your sculpt layers for more control over your model.

Getting ready

First you will need an object with multiple subdivision levels. You can do this by clicking *Shift + D* until you reach your desired poly count, or at least until it starts slowing down your computer.

How to do it...

So, what you're going to do now is:

- Hit the *Page Down* key until you reach the lowest level of your object
- Then add a layer by clicking the symbol below which it is located in the **Layers Tab**

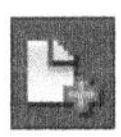

- On the lower level layers, you will sculpt your largest details, blocking in the major shapes of the object
- After you get the large shapes in, you will hit the *Page Up* key until you have enough polygons to add the next level of detail
- Then you will add another layer the same way you added the first layer
- Now you are going to sculpt the medium size details
- Now repeat those steps for all levels of detail
- When you reach the higher level layers you can begin using stamps and stencils for the finer details

How it works...

What this does is it allows you to change the large shapes later on by going to the lower levels and moving things around while preserving the finer details that are kept in the higher level layers. It will also allow you to adjust the opacity of the different levels of detail without affecting all the other details you have applied to your model.

There's more...

One more thing you can do to help keep things manageable is to keep different types of detail or detail for different areas of your model as separate layers even if it's on the same layer. This will give you more control over the intensity of those details individually and will allow you to make changes to those details without destroying the details from another layer.

Combining layers

You can also combine layers in the following two ways:

- One way is to hide all layers you would not like to combine by clicking on the circle beneath the eyeball in the **Layers Tab**. Then you right-click on one of the layers and choose **Merge Visible** from the right-click menu.
- The other way is to combine all the details from your layers and apply it directly to the model and eliminate all layers. To do this, right-click on any layer and choose **Flatten** from the right-click menu. If you do this you will lose the ability to control each set of details individually since you are eliminating those layers.

Duplicating or deleting layers

Another thing you will find in the right-click menu or your layers is the ability to delete your layer or duplicate it.

Deleting a layer will get rid of your layer and erase any details that were sculpting on that layer.

Duplicating a layer will add a new layer with the same details as the layer you duplicated. This will essentially double the intensity of the details that were sculpted in that layer.

Mirroring and flipping details of a layer

Another interesting thing you can do from the right-click menu is to mirror a detail you have already created or flip that detail over to an opposite side of the model. In order to do this, you will need to use the **Select Faces** tool and paint the faces of details you want to mirror or flip and then right-click and choose **Mirror** or **Flip** and designate which axis you would like it to mirror or flip over.

See also

- *The Increasing resolution on your model* recipe in *Chapter 1, Ready? Set...*
- *The Sculpting on different subdivision levels effectively* recipe in *Chapter 1, Ready? Set...*

Setting up stamps, stencils, and image planes using image browser

This recipe will show you how to easily start using stamps, stencils, and image planes from the Mudbox **Image Browser** tab.

How to do it...

1. First you will click on the **Image Browser** tab, which is attached to your primary viewport.
2. When you open this up you will see a section to the left, showing images that are in the current folder you are browsing. In the center of the page, you will see an enlarged version of the image you select from the section on the left. Along the top, you will see a toolbar that looks like the following screenshot (without the colored underlines):

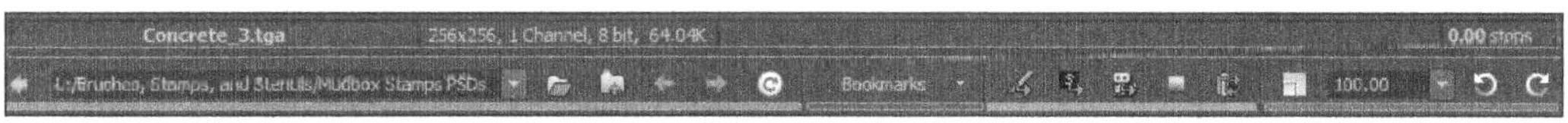

3. The blue section gives a description of the image you have selected including the name, extension, dimensions, color depth, size, and stops if it is a **High Dynamic Range Image** (**HDRI**) file.
4. The green section consists of the typical navigation tools required to locate the directory you would like to search in for images.
5. The red section allows you to add bookmarks for directories that you will be coming back to. This will make it faster to visit folders you use frequently.
6. The yellow section is where you will apply the given image as a certain tool. The following is what the icons do from left to right:
    - The first icon will set the image as a stamp.
    - The second icon will set the image as a stencil.
    - The next icon will apply the image as an image plane to your currently selected camera.

- The green square icon will let you view pixels that contain negative floating point values in green color. This is for HDRI - 32-bit floating point images.
- The last icon will refresh the image in the view.

7. The orange section will allow you to zoom in or out of your image as well as rotate it.

See also

- *The Downloading and enabling stamps, stencils, and base meshes from the Internet* recipe in *Chapter 1, Ready? Set...*

3
Broad Strokes

In this chapter, we will cover:

- Creating a concrete damage brush
- Customizing your brush and adding it to your tool tab
- Creating your own Imprint brush for adding presculpted details
- Using the Freeze brush to get hard edges and isolate your sculpting
- Using the Fill brush for detailing corners and crevices
- Matching a reference silhouette using the Grab tool

Introduction

In this chapter, we will talk about some of the different brushes you can use, how to customize them, and a few tricks for using brushes, that you may not have thought about using, for a particular problem in Mudbox 2013. With the knowledge obtained in this chapter, you will be well on your way to developing a customized toolbox that will help you get things done faster and more efficiently. If you continue to put these recipes into practice, you will build a library of brushes that can tackle any number of problems.

Creating a concrete damage brush

This recipe will show you how to create a Noise brush in Mudbox 2013. Sculpting with noise brushes is a great way to add finer details to organic objects or to add damage to hard surface models. In this recipe, we will create a brush shape in Photoshop and bring it into Mudbox 2013 to use with our sculpting tools. The brush we will be creating is targeted at sculpting concrete damage but can be used for other purposes. Having a tool like this in your library is essential for any artist who is creating photo-real assets for movies, television, print, or games.

How to do it...

To create a Noise brush, you will need a little help from an external image editing software. Go through the following steps:

1. The first thing you will want to do is use an image editing software such as Photoshop to create the shape of the brush. I will be using Photoshop because it is the most widely used industry standard for image editing.
2. One quick and easy way to get a good brush for creating concrete damage in Photoshop is to fill a layer with any color, set your foreground and background colors to black and white, and then go to **Filter** | **Render** | **Clouds** to get a nice spread of values. It should look something like the following screenshot:

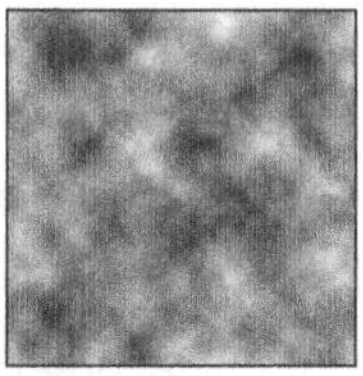

3. Next, you will need to adjust the levels to harden up the edges of the brush as shown in the following screenshot:

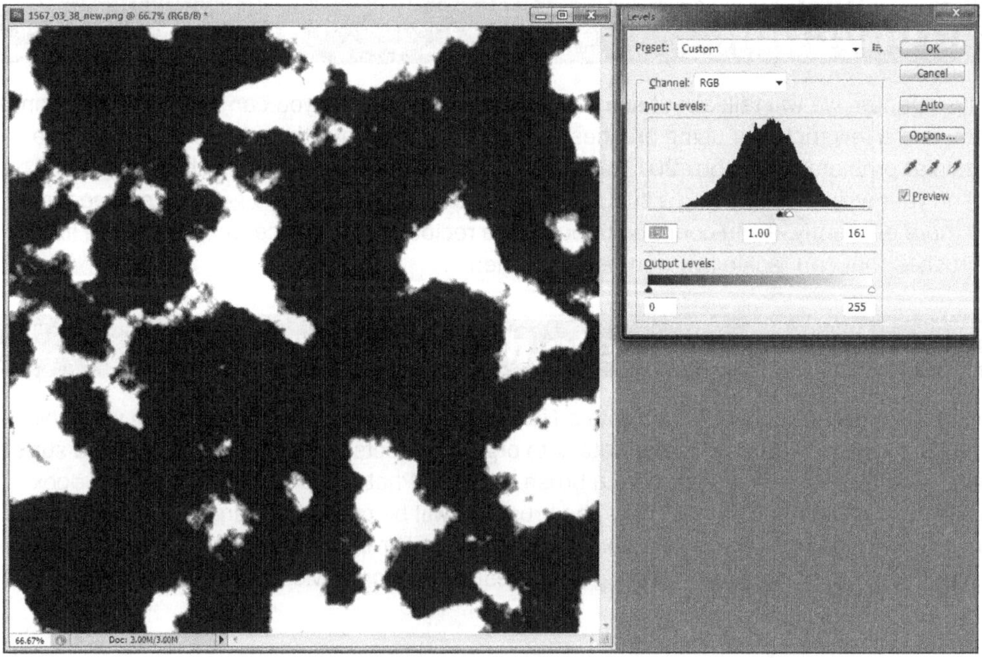

4. Now, it is important to paint out the white areas that touch the border of the image. If you leave these, you will have hard, straight lines on the edges of your brush where the white areas meet the border. Your brush should end up looking like the following screenshot:

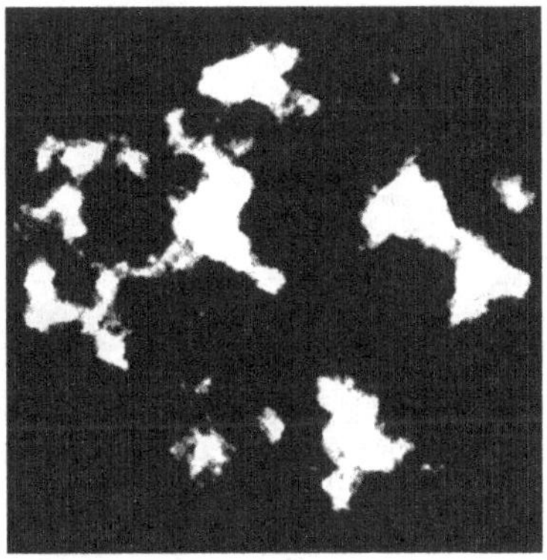

5. Now save your brush as a `.png`, `.jpg`, `.gif`, `.bmp`, `.tif`, `.tga`, or `.exr` file. I prefer using `.tga` because it works best in Maya's viewport and because it provides better quality to your images while keeping your files relatively small.
6. The next step is bringing this brush shape into Mudbox 2013. There are a couple of ways you can do this, such as the following:
   - Choose **Add Stamp** in the **Stamp** menu at the bottom right of your workspace and browse to the file you saved.

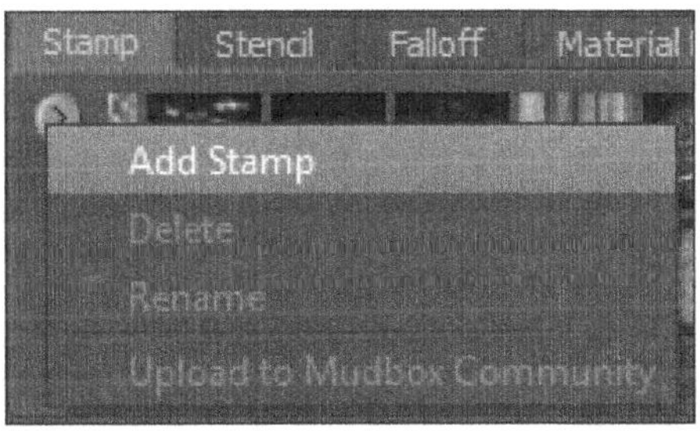

- Alternatively, you can go to the **Image Browser** tab and browse to your image. Once you find the image, you can select it and click on the **Set Stamp** button in the top menu bar as shown in the following screenshot:

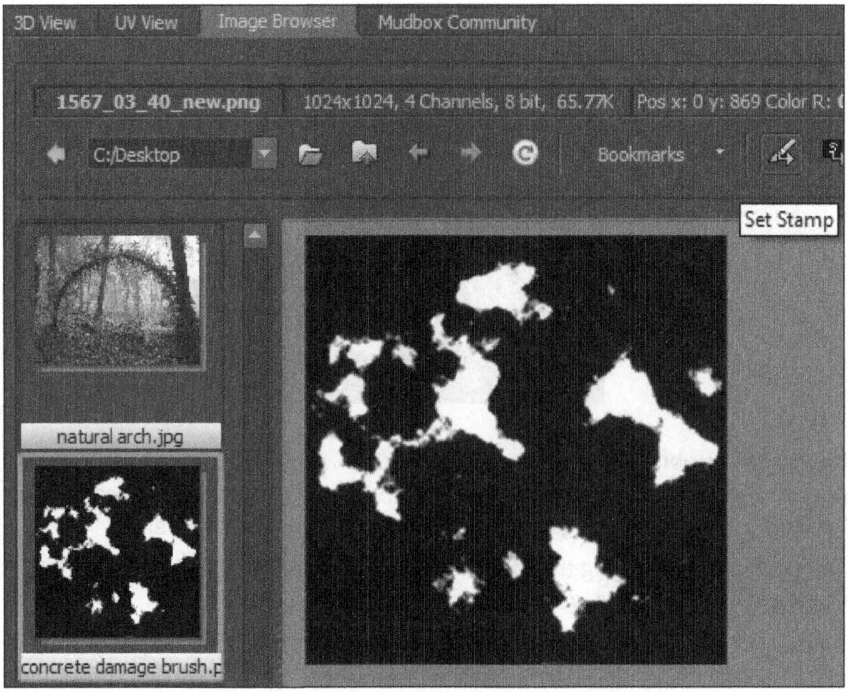

7. Once your brush shape has been imported, choose a base brush to make adjustments to. The sculpt brush will be fine. Just click on the **Sculpt** brush in the **Sculpt Tools** section in the lower-left portion of your workspace.
8. Now enable your stamp by choosing it from the thumbnails in the **Stamp** section of your workspace.
9. The first thing you will want to do is check the box for **Invert Function** under the **Sculpt Tools** properties. If you do not check this box, then your brush will raise the surface of the model instead of eating into it.

10. Next, adjust the properties of how the stamp will behave. We would like our stamp to be random in size and angle. We can accomplish this by adjusting the sliders in the **Randomize** section under the **Use Stamp Image** section of the sculpting tools properties. The following screenshot shows one possible configuration for the randomization:

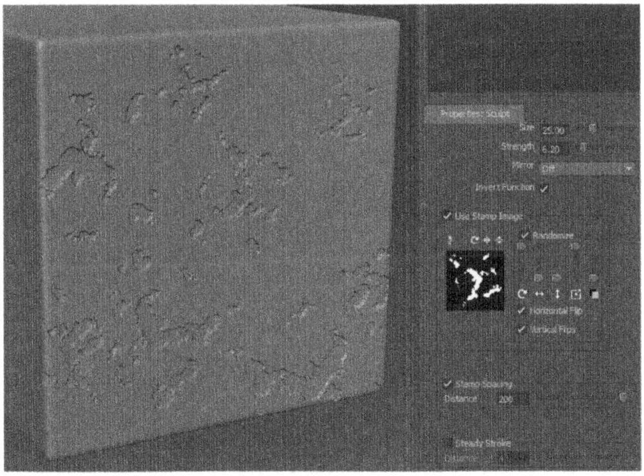

11. Now we need to make sure there is enough spacing on the stamp so that we don't stack our details. In order to adjust this, you will have to check the **Stamp Spacing** checkbox below the **Use Stamp Image** section. You may not be able to adjust the slider far enough so that your brush details won't stack. If this is the case, then you will need to type a number into the input box next to **Distance**. This will readjust the slider and make the number you type in the new maximum value.
12. The last step is to make sure your Falloff is set correctly. To adjust the Falloff you will go into the **Falloff** section present in the **Tools'** properties and adjust the image so it looks like the following screenshot. This will make sure all the details of your brush have an even intensity. You don't want this brush to fade away near the edges.

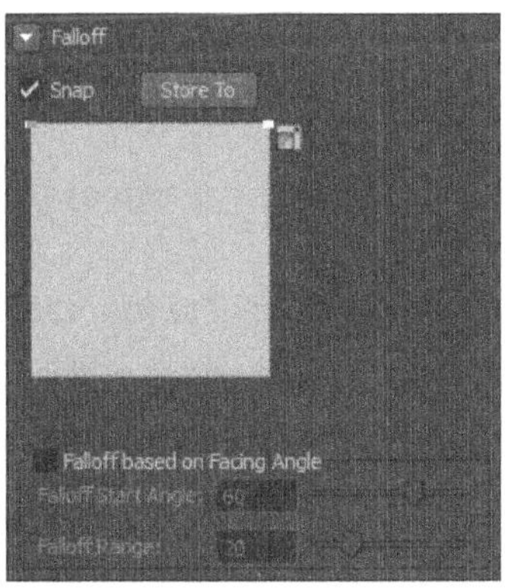

This brush can also be used to create rust and other natural corrosion. All you need to do is apply the stamp to the brush of your choice and build up the details on your model. The following screenshot shows an example of the brush:

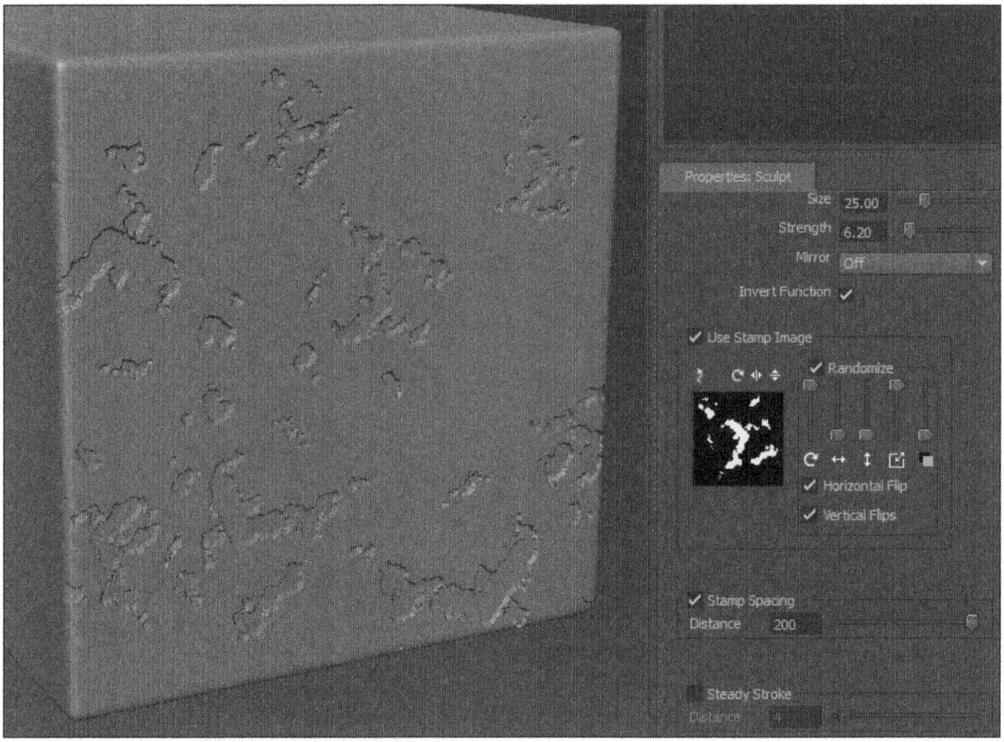

Also, try making multiple versions of the same brush to get different shapes out of the brush. This will help hide any repetition.

Keep in mind, if you want to make it look realistic you will need to build up different kinds of details, some subtle, others less so.

See also

- The *Setting up stamps, stencils, and image planes using image browser* recipe in *Chapter 2, Heads Up*
- The *Customizing your brush and adding it to your tool tab* recipe
- The *Using the Freeze brush to get hard edges and isolate sculpting* recipe
- The *Matching a reference silhouette using the Grab tool* recipe

Customizing your brush and adding it to your tool tab

This recipe will show you how to create your own brush presets. As mentioned in the *Introduction*, creating a library of brushes for different effects, such as metal scratches, dirt, weather damage, and different types of textures for representing various materials, will dramatically increase your professional value and will allow you to bring your own creations to life in a fraction of time. This recipe will guide you through the basics of creating a custom brush.

How to do it...

The following steps will help you to create your own brush's presets:

1. First you will need to choose a brush to start from. Just choose any brush from the tool tab.
2. Next, you will go into the properties of that tool and adjust the settings to what you are looking for. You can use various stamps, adjust the randomizing properties for the stamp, adjust the falloff, or anything else you can find in the **Properties** tab.
3. Once your tool settings are in place, you will want to go to the **Sculpt Tools** tab menu, as shown in the following screenshot, and choose **Add Tool**.
4. This will bring up a window for you to name the tool. Once you hit **OK** the tool will be placed in the **Sculpt Tools** tab along with all the other brushes.

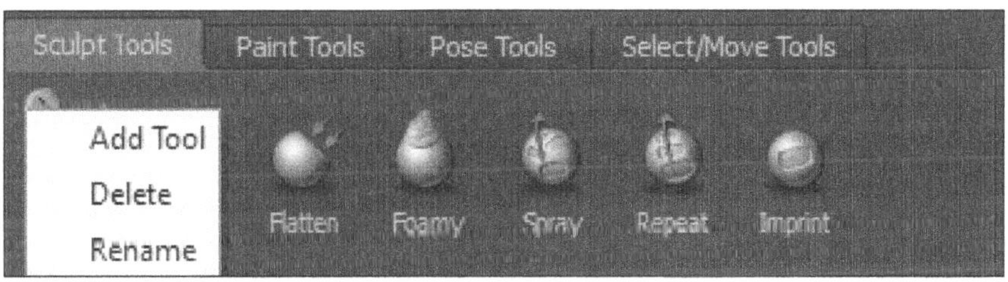

See also

- The *Creating a concrete damage brush recipe*
- The *Using the Fill brush for detailing corners and crevices recipe*
- The *Creating your own Imprint brush for adding presculpted details* recipe

Creating your own Imprint brush for adding presculpted details

This recipe will go through the process of creating a stamp from a damaged wall sculpt that will be used with the **Imprint** sculpt tool to add details in other projects. By putting this recipe into practice you will dramatically increase the speed of your workflow. As you build up a library of stamps, which you create, you will be able to create much larger assets in a shorter amount of time while still keeping things original, as opposed to using other people's stamps or the default stamps.

Try to limit the use of non original stamps because these will stand out to the trained eye, also known as job recruiters. If you do plan on using a default stamp or someone else's stamp from the Mudbox Community, then I recommend using it as a starting point for creating your own unique stamps.

How to do it...

The following steps will help you to create your own Imprint brush for adding presculpted details:

1. The first thing you will need is to create a sculpt of detail that can be re-used for many projects. For example, you might create a bolt, a wall crack, a metal dent, a small pile of trash, and so on. The sculpt I have created for this recipe is a pothole that could easily be repurposed as damage done to a concrete wall or another similar surface. The following screenshot shows the detail I will be using for this:

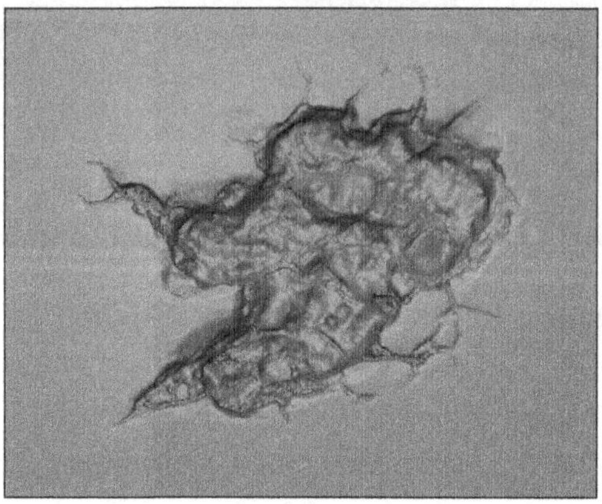

Keep in mind you may need to do a little extra sculpting depending on what real world materials you are representing. For example, if this was a hole in a brick wall, you would probably want to start from scratch since the damage would look different. The bricks would create a different silhouette around the hole and you may have little pieces of mortar and brick chunks sitting inside the hole.

2. The next thing on the list is creating an image that we can use for our stamp. To do this, you will want to switch your view to a camera that is looking at your detail head on. In my case, I created the detail facing the **Front** camera. To switch the view to the **Front** camera you can right mouse button (RMB) click on an empty space in your viewport and go to **Switch Views** | **Front View** in the following menus. The following screenshot is an example of what this menu looks like:

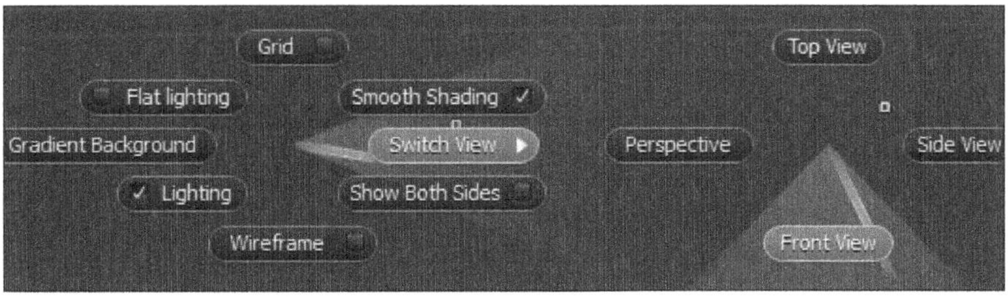

3. Now that we have the right angle, you'll need a way of capturing the detail in a black and white image that represents the depth of the sculpt. To do this, you can go to the **Viewport Filters** tab, on the top right-hand side of the Mudbox interface, and enable **Screen Distance**. Your sculpt should be showing the camera distance using white as the closest surfaces and black as the farthest away surfaces. The following screenshot is of the pothole with the **Screen Distance** filter turned on:

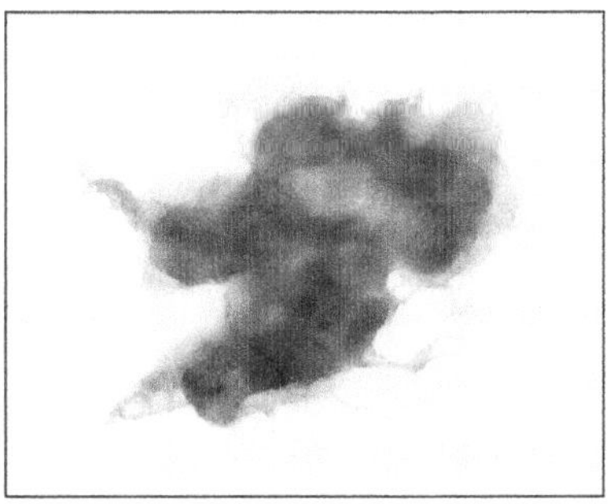

4. With this viewport enabled, you can take a screenshot by hitting the *Prt Scr* (print screen) button, on your keyboard. Now go into Photoshop, or any other 2D image editing software, and hit *Ctrl* + *N* to create a new image, and hit *Ctrl* + *V* to paste the screenshot into the image. This will paste your entire screen (including additional monitors) into the image which means you will need to crop the image down to what you want included in the stamp.
   - When you crop the image it is a good idea to keep the image at a 1 to 1 ratio, meaning the dimensions of the image will create a perfect square. The easiest way to do this is to use the **Rectangular Marquee Tool** (*M*) in Photoshop while holding down *Shift*. When you use the **Rectangular Marquee Tool** while holding *Shift*, it will make sure the selection is always at a 1 to 1 ratio.
5. Before saving the file, you need to make a couple of adjustments to the image such as the following:
   - First off, you need to invert the values of the image. You can do this by hitting *Ctrl* + *I* in Photoshop. If you do not do this then your stamp will have hard edges on its peripheries. This happens because Mudbox is interpreting the white areas of the stamp as areas that need to be pushed, or pulled if **Invert Function** is checked, while the black areas are unaffected.
   - Now, just to make sure that the blacks are fully black and the whites are fully white, known as normalization, you will want to adjust the levels of your image in your 2D image editing software. The easiest way to normalize the values of your image in Photoshop is to use the **Auto Contrast** (*Alt* + *Shift* + *Ctrl* + *L*) feature.
   - Ok, now you can save it. Hit *Ctrl* + *S*, give your file a name, and choose the TARGA format. See the following screenshot for an example of the **File name** and **Format** sections of the Save window.

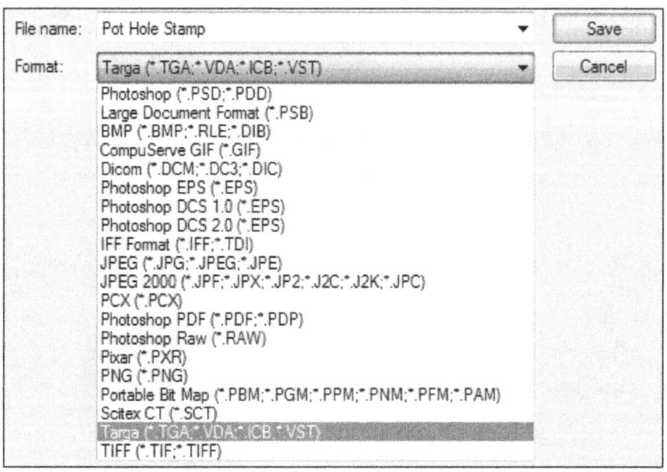

6. Your stamp image is now ready to be imported into Mudbox for use with your brushes. Just add the tool to your **Stamp** toolbar. For more information on this, you can refer to the *Adding a stamp to your toolbox* recipe in *Chapter 4, Fine Tooth Comb* of this book.
7. The next step is to select the **Imprint** sculpt tool from the **Sculpt Tools** toolbar, on the bottom left-hand side of the interface. The reason we are choosing this sculpt tool over choosing one of the others is because of the way it applies stamps to your model. Unlike the other sculpt tools, this tool works by clicking and dragging to determine the scale and orientation, of one instance, of the stamp chosen.
8. Now choose the **Stamp** you just added, in step 6, to the **Stamp** toolbar to enable it on this brush.
9. There are only two more things you need to do before the brush is ready to go, the first of which is checking the box for **Invert Function** in the tools properties.
10. The last step before you can start having fun with your new brush is to adjust the **Falloff** of the tool. Go to the **Falloff** section of your tools properties, on the right-hand side of the interface, and pull all the falloff curve handles to the top right side of the box. It should look something like the following screenshot:

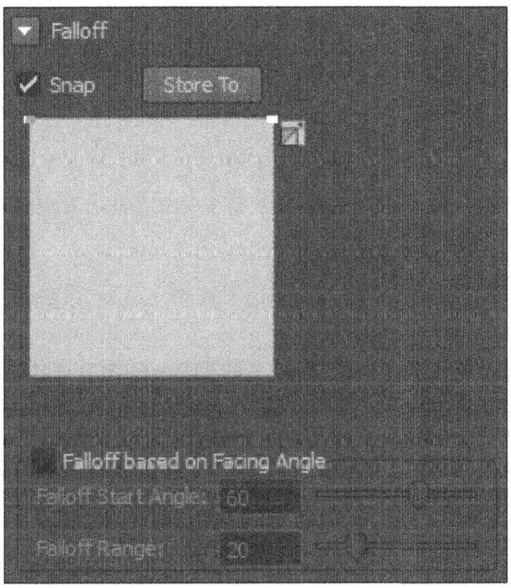

This step is needed in order to keep the details true to what you have sculpted. If you adjust the curves in any other way, you will start getting variation in the intensity of your stamp as it gets closer or farther away (depending on the curve) from the center of the stroke.

11. Now your brush is ready to go. Just click-and-drag until you have the size and orientation that you want for your detail. When you let go, it will create the detail on your model. Don't forget to adjust the intensity of your brush to get the right amount of depth. The following screenshot is an example of some details I imprinted into a cube using only this brush with various intensities:

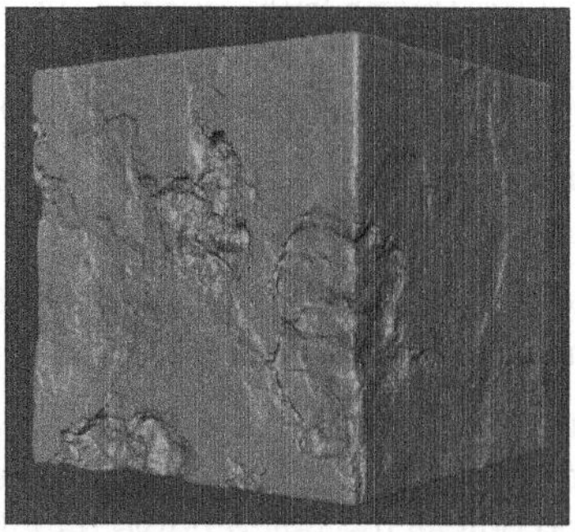

See also

- The *Creating a concrete damage brush recipe*
- The *Customizing your brush and adding it to your tool tab recipe*
- *Adding a stamp to your tool box* in *Chapter 4, Fine Tooth Comb*
- The *Creating a zipper using a custom stamp recipe in Chapter 4, Fine Tooth Comb*
- The *Tricks for painting with stamps recipe in Chapter 4, Fine Tooth Comb*
- The *Creating a custom rock stamp recipe in Chapter 4, Fine Tooth Comb*

Using the Freeze brush to get hard edges and isolate your sculpting

This recipe will show you some of the useful ways to use the **Freeze** brush. The application of this tool can be extremely helpful by blocking out interesting shapes before sculpting. It is also very useful for indicating layers of materials. For example, you might use this tool to create the inset of a window or to define the shape of a carving set in stone.

How to do it...

The following steps will help you to efficiently use the **Freeze** brush:

1. The first thing you'll need to do is choose the **Freeze** brush.

2. Next, paint the areas of the model that you would like to be unaffected by your sculpting. If you end up freezing an area that you didn't mean to, or you would just like to unfreeze certain areas with your brush to make more interesting shapes, then you can use the **Invert Function** of the tool by holding *Ctrl* while you use the Freeze brush.

   Alternatively, if you would like to unfreeze everything that you have frozen, then you can do so by using the hotkey for **Unfreeze All**, *Shift + U*. To find this without using hotkeys, you can go to **Edit | Unfreeze All** in the top menu.

3. Next, pick the basic **Sculpt** brush to pull the vertices of your model directly away from its surface. If you choose the **Bulge** brush, it will look like something is bulging out over the edge that was created with the **Freeze** brush as shown in the following sample screenshot:

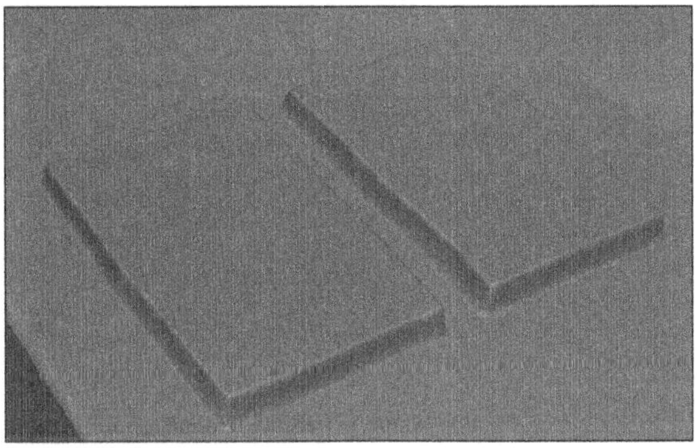

4. You can also follow up with the **Pinch** brush and the **Smooth** brush to sharpen and soften the edge. You can also use the **Knife** brush or the **Flatten** brush to add damage as shown in the following screenshot:

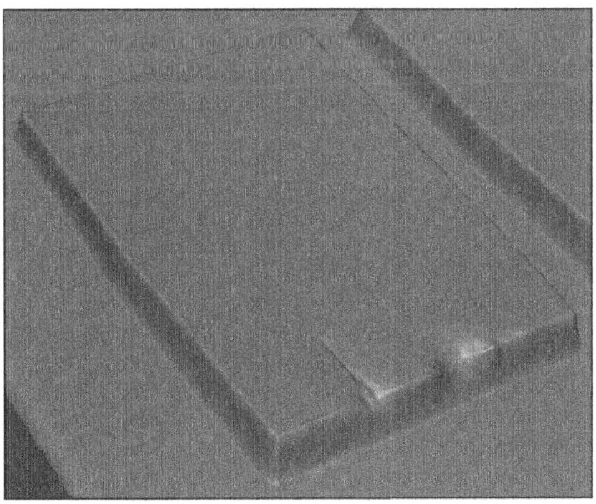

There's more...

If you enable **Steady Stroke** on your Freeze brush you will be able to control your brush stroke more accurately. **Steady Stroke** is a feature that will give you a visualization of the line you are drawing in order to help with the accuracy of the stroke. The visualization created is of a straight line starting at the beginning of your stroke and pointing outward in the direction of your mouse cursor. The stroke will not be applied until you have reached the end of this line, resulting in more control and a smoother stroke.

In order to enable **Steady Stroke** you must go into the **Properties** section for your brush and click on the empty box next to **Steady Stroke**. The properties menu should look something like the following screenshot, depending on which brush you have chosen:

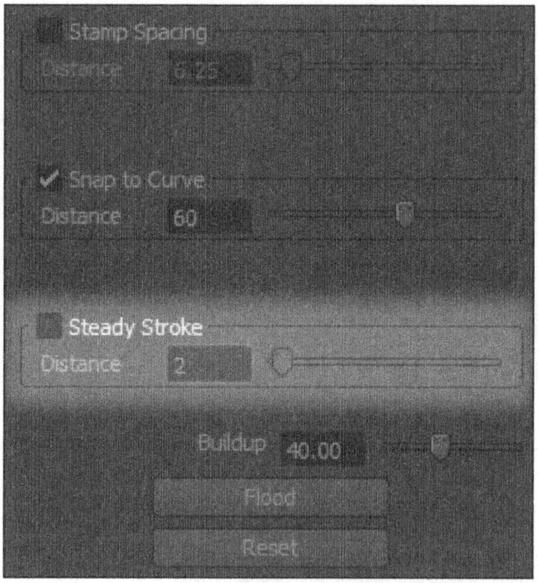

This feature works by showing you a green line (motion vector) that you can use to line up your stroke and create a more accurate line.

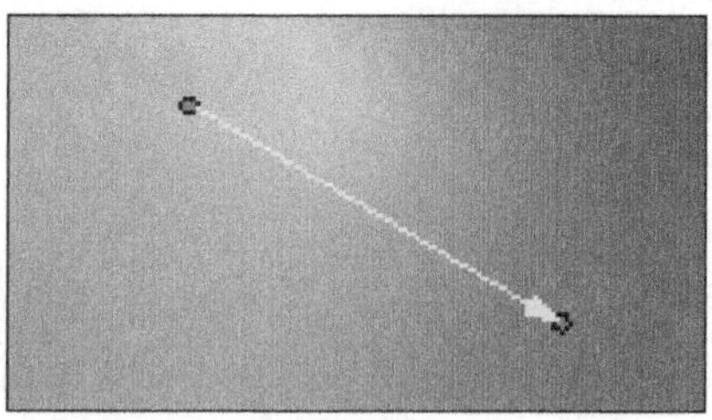

The length of the green line is determined by the value that **Distance** is set to.

See also

- The *Creating a concrete damage brush recipe*
- The *Customizing your brush and adding it to your tool tab recipe*
- The *Using the Fill brush for detailing corners and crevices recipe*

Using the Fill brush for detailing corners and crevices

This recipe will start with a simple sculpt of a brick wall that we will add detail to, using the **Fill** tool. We will also use a few of the tools learned in previous recipes to add a little extra detail. Upon completion of this recipe, you will better understand the **Fill** tool and how to use it to your advantage. The more tools you learn and customize, the more issues you will be able to solve while creating your sculpts.

Getting ready

To get ready you should create a basic sculpt of a broken brick wall. Try using the tools you have learned in the previous recipes. It is very important to practice with the tools and techniques you are learning in these recipes, in order for it to become a part of your workflow. After practicing long enough, these techniques will become second nature to you and you will be able to solve problems much quicker. You should also start customizing your own tools based on what you learn in these recipes.

The following screenshot is of the brick wall that I will be starting with. There are some issues with this sculpt that we will critique so that you can learn from these mistakes.

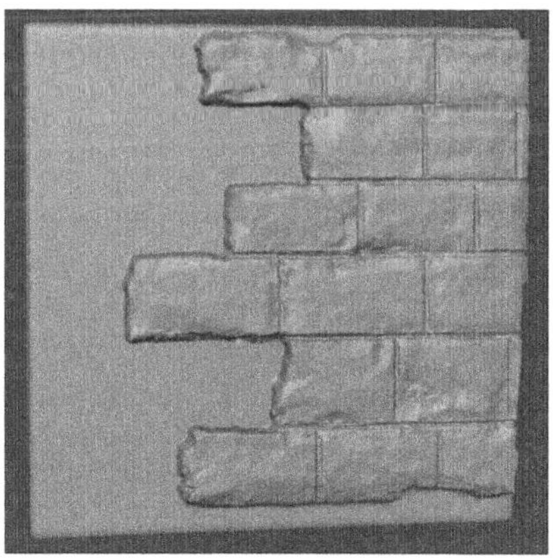

Notice that my bricks are all of different sizes. To fix this, I could go in with the **Grab** tool and pull the bricks into place, or I could use a large radius **Pinch** brush with a low intensity to close the space between the larger bricks.

You may also notice that my bricks defy the law of gravity in some areas. To fix this, I could go back and use the **Erase** tool where bricks are floating or just sculpt in some more bricks to support the ones above. Believability is something you should look out for when creating sculpts. Think about each element in your asset and ask yourself, would this make sense in the real world.

If you were to ask yourself this question again, you might find that the bricks are too shallow to make sense. To fix this, I could go in and either duplicate the sculpt layer a couple of times to get the extra depth or I could go in with the **Amplify** brush and boost the depth and details across the entire sculpt. There would probably be some cleanup needed after doing this, but that is to be expected.

I find a lot of beginners who tend to leave out the finishing touches after completing a technique. If you are making adjustments to a large area of your model, it is very likely you will need to go in and make small fixes where it is needed. This step should not be skipped if you are creating a finalized asset. If you are creating a concept sculpt, that is a different story. For concept sculpts, you can be as loose as you want, and leave out the fine details as long as you are getting your idea across.

Of course, the best thing to do is collect and use reference when you are creating any real world object. This will help you get the scale, silhouette, shapes, and details correct, right from the start.

How to do it...

Using the unrefined sculpt shown in the previous screenshot, we will now add some details to the grout and along the outside edge of our sculpted detail. The **Fill** brush will find the average location of all the vertices within the brush's radius and pull the deepest vertices toward that average. This allows you to fill in any crevices in your sculpt without affecting any of the details that are protruding from the surface of the model.

This tool can also be useful if you want details on the outside edge of a protruding surface but you do not want to affect anything beyond a certain distance. The distance of the brush's effects are determined by the size of the brush. Remember it is taking the average of the vertices within the brush's radius, therefore a larger brush size will extend the distance of the detail that is applied while a smaller brush will be limited to a smaller distance.

Now let's put this tool into practice by performing the following steps:

1. Select the **Fill** brush from the **Sculpt Tools** toolbar.

2. Choose a stamp that will add some noise to the grout (the space between the bricks).

   The following screenshot will show you a close-up of the bricks without the added detail:

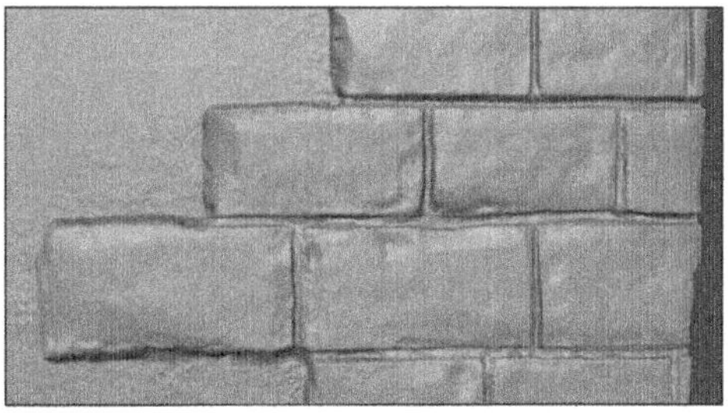

3. Now begin to paint over the grout areas of your brick wall sculpt. Once you go over all the grout areas of your model it should look something like the following screenshot:

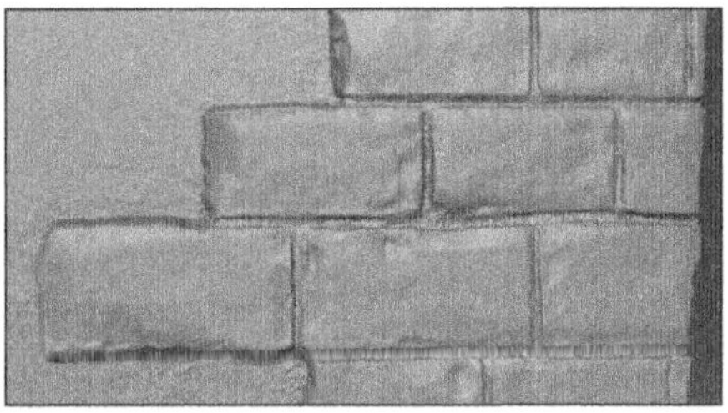

4. Now you can try out the outer edge trick. You can test it out with the same stamp you chose for the grout. Try different size brushes and paint along the outer edge of your outermost bricks. It might look something like the following screenshot when you are done:

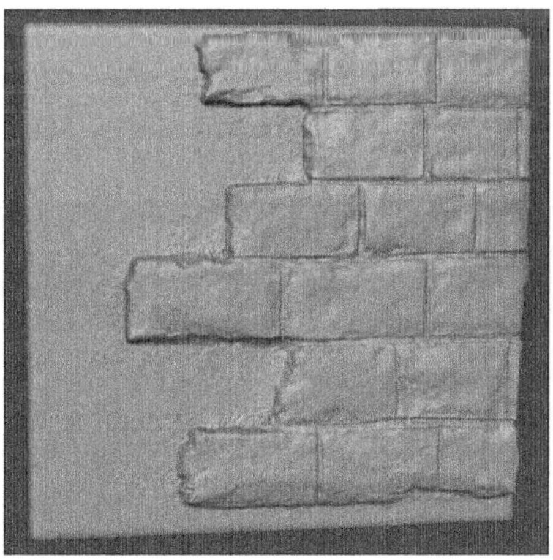

There's more...

Now we can play around with some of the tools you learned earlier in this chapter:

- Select the **Imprint** brush you created in the recipe *Creating your own Imprint brush for adding presculpted details*.
- Now start applying this brush, with the stamp you created, to your brick wall at varying intensities and sizes. When you're done it should look something like the following screenshot:

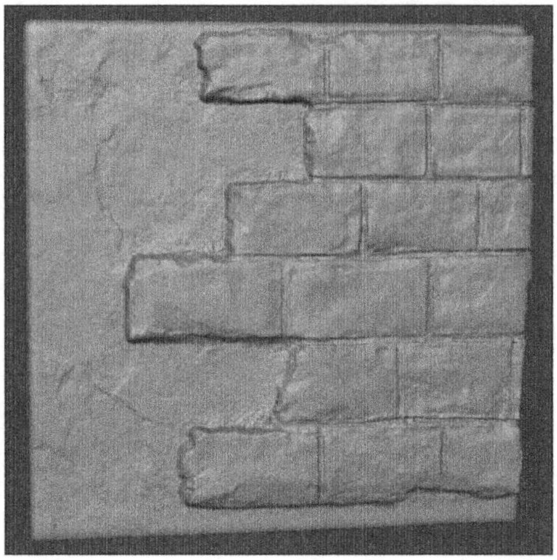

See also

- The *Creating a concrete damage brush recipe*
- The *Customizing your brush and adding it to your tool tab* recipe
- The *Creating your own Imprint brush for adding pre sculpted details* recipe
- The *Using the Freeze brush to get hard edges and isolate sculpting* recipe

Matching a reference silhouette using the Grab tool

This recipe will show you how to use the **Grab** tool to line up your model's shape with a reference image. Keep in mind you can do this before and after you have added details to your model.

Getting ready

The following steps will help you to ready yourself in order to use the **Grab** tool:

1. First you will need the model that you will be sculpting.
2. Next go to **Object List** and right-click on the **Front**, **Side** or **Top** camera and choose **Look Through**. This all depends on which profile you are trying to line up.
3. Once you have brought in a model and chosen the camera angle that you plan on matching, you will want to go to the **Image Browser** tab and search for the image you would like your sculpt to match.
4. Then you will click either the **Set Stencil** or the **Set Image Plane** button on the top menu bar. If you are only using the image as a reference to line up your model, then using **Set Image Plane** will be fine. If you would like to paint features from the image onto your model using the **Projection** brush, then you will want to use the **Set Stencil** button.
5. When your image plane or stencil is set, you will go back to the **3D View** and adjust the image plane or stencil's properties until you have the desired **Translation**, **Rotation**, **Scale**, and **Visibility** level.

How to do it...

Once you have readied yourself, perform the following steps to match a reference silhouette with the help of the **Grab** tool:

1. Once you have everything set up, you will select the **Grab** brush either by selecting it in the **Sculpt Tools** tab or by hitting the *3* hotkey (unless you have reassigned it).
2. Next you will go into the brush's properties and choose **X** in the drop-down menu for **Mirror**. This is if you are doing a symmetrical profile such as the front view of a face.
3. You will proceed in adjusting your brush's size depending on how large the forms, which you are shifting, are.
4. Then all you have to do is push and pull areas of the vertices around until you have matched the image.

The following screenshot is a simple example of a base head mesh that has been manipulated using the **Grab** brush so that it matches its reference:

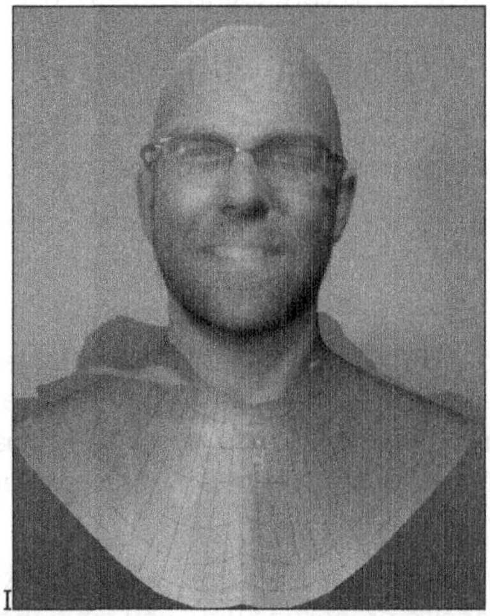

In the following screenshot, you can see what the head mesh looked like before adjusting the silhouette with the **Grab** brush:

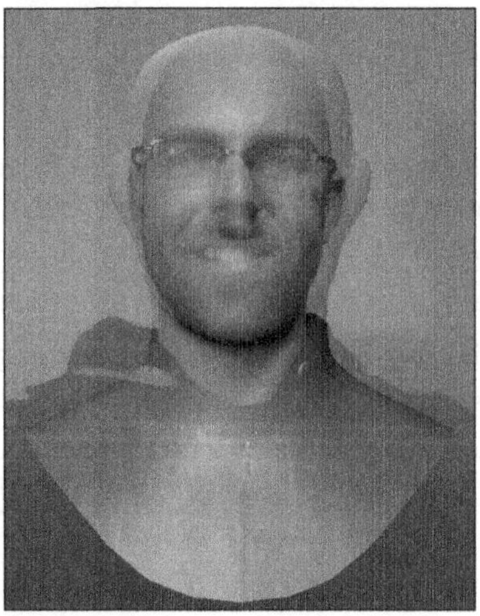

See also

- The *Customizing your brush and adding it to your tool tab recipe*
- The *Using the Freeze brush to get hard edges and isolate your sculpting recipe*

4
Fine Tooth Comb

In this chapter, we will cover:

- Creating a zipper using a custom stamp
- Creating a custom stencil from a stone wall carving
- Creating a rock wall that tiles seamlessly in all directions
- Tricks for painting with stencils
- Tricks for painting with stamps
- Adding a stencil or stamp to your toolbox
- Creating a custom rock stamp

Introduction

This chapter will show you different tools and tricks you can use to add finer details to your models. These finer details are mostly achieved by using stamps and stencils to help you sculpt.

While working your way through these recipes, keep in mind that the details you sculpt are limited to the resolution of the mesh you are sculpting on. If you plan on extracting texture maps from your sculpt, then the detail is also limited by the resolution of the texture maps that you extract.

The fine-detailing stage of a project is the stage that most beginner and intermediate artists tend to be in a hurry to get to. It is important to step back and look at your sculpt with a critical eye, to determine if your foundations are strong. Are your silhouettes creating interesting shapes? Do the shapes convey the feeling that you want the viewer to experience? Does your model have a focal point? Do other details in your model support the focal point? Are your proportions correct? It's easy to jump into detailing too soon which can end up being a big waste of time.

No matter how much detail you put into a piece of art, it will never make up for having strong foundations. Once you have the strong foundations in place, you can move on to the detailing phase, which is the fun part! This is where you make things believable.

To get better at detailing, you will want to pay close attention to everything you see in the real world. Learn how things work and how they are built. Study architecture, macro photography, Do It Yourself instruction manuals, or anything really!

Another mistake beginners make is that they do not pay close enough attention to how one material or object connects to another. For example, a beginner may model a door, but forget the hinges, or they might leave out the skirting board on a wall.

Another important thing to think about when adding details is the environment that the asset lives in and what kind of wear and tear it would endure. Is your asset located in an area that gets flooded? If so, you may want to add water damage or discoloration at the base of your model. Is your rock sitting in the middle of a river or a stream? If yes, then you probably should round out those corners and edges. The rocks you find in rivers or streams are usually rounded due to tumbling and erosion. Tumbling is when a rock gets carried by water and hits other rocks in the water causing any rough edges to break off and smooth out.

The detailing phase gives you the chance to tell a story with your model. Try adding elements to your models that hint at certain events that may have taken place around your object. This will add more depth, make your model more believable, and can help support the story you are trying to tell with your art. The story should also drive your creativity, acting as a guide for what your asset is going to look like.

Whether it's for a movie, a game, or a scene you have created for yourself, the recipes in this chapter will give you some of the tools that you need to make convincing sculpts for your future projects.

Creating a zipper using a custom stamp

This recipe will show you how to create a stamp which you can use to create a zipper. This technique can be applied to many other uses such as stitching and other repeated elements.

Getting ready

First thing you will need to do is create an image that will be used as your stamp. To do this, I will be using Adobe Photoshop, but any image editing software will do.

The following image is what I created for the zipper stamp using simple tools in Photoshop.

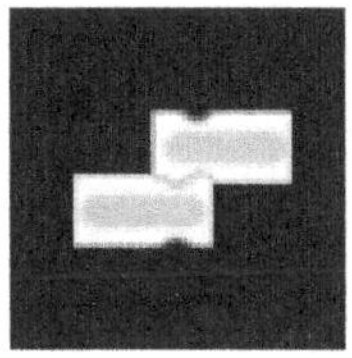

Keep in mind, the higher the value, the stronger the intensity of your stamp. The black areas will not affect the model while the white areas will affect the model the most.

How to do it...

The following steps will help you create a stamp, in order to create a zipper:

1. First you must choose a brush that can use a stamp. All of the sculpt brushes except for the **Freeze**, **Grab**, and **Eyedropper** brushes can use stamps. Each brush will have its properties set differently, so you will have to choose a brush that gives you the desired effect. For this brush we will choose **Sculpt Brush**.
2. Once you have chosen **Sculpt Brush**, you will need to add the stamp we just created. To do this, you can either use **Image Browser** or you can go to the menu for the stamp toolbar located in the bottom, right-hand side of the workspace.
3. Now your stamp should show up at the end of the list of thumbnails. Select it to activate it on your current brush. Choosing **Off** will disable it. The following screenshot shows the **Stamp** tab displaying all the available and custom stamps:

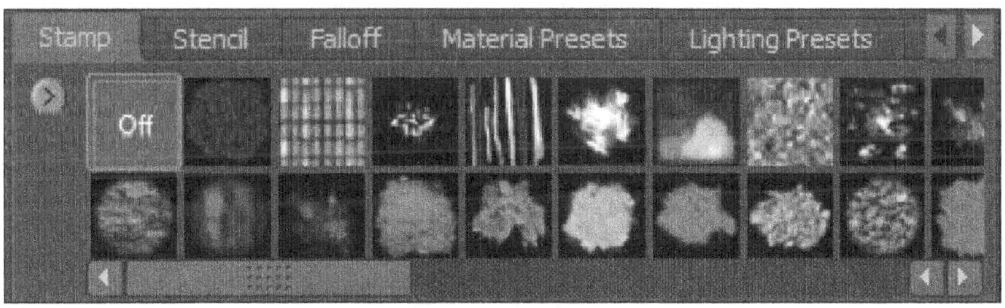

4. Next thing you will need to do is adjust the brush's properties. It should look something like the following screenshot. The important settings are oriented to Stroke, getting the **Stamp Spacing** correct depending on the size of your stamp, and the **Falloff** set so that there is no falloff. **Steady Stroke** is optional.

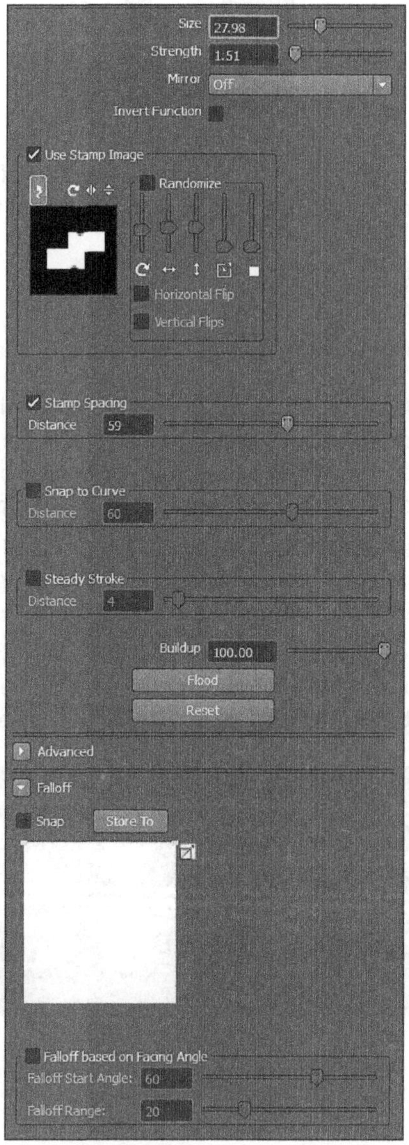

5. All that is left is to draw a zipper onto your model.

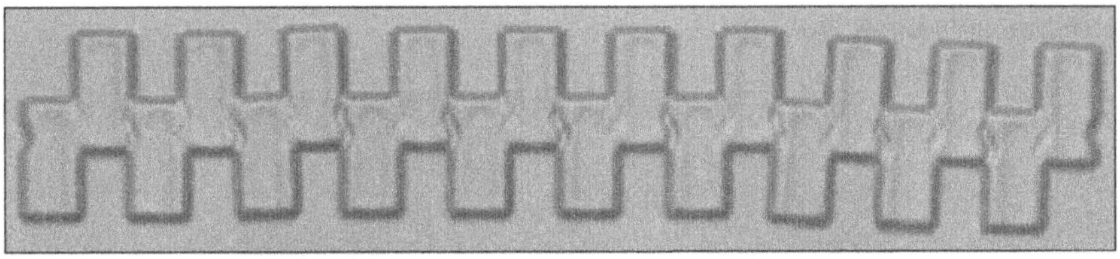

Creating a custom stencil from a stone wall carving

This recipe will show you how you can take one of your sculpts and create a stencil from it that can be used on other models. Using this technique will help you build a library of details that you can come back and reuse. Even if you do not want to use the exact same details in another project you can use the stencils, created using this method, as a starting point for a new sculpt or stencil.

How to do it...

1. The following steps will help you create a stencil from one of your sculpts: The first thing you will do is create a sculpt of the details you would like to use as a stencil. For this example, I used curves (as seen in the following screenshot) to help with the spirals and straight lines.

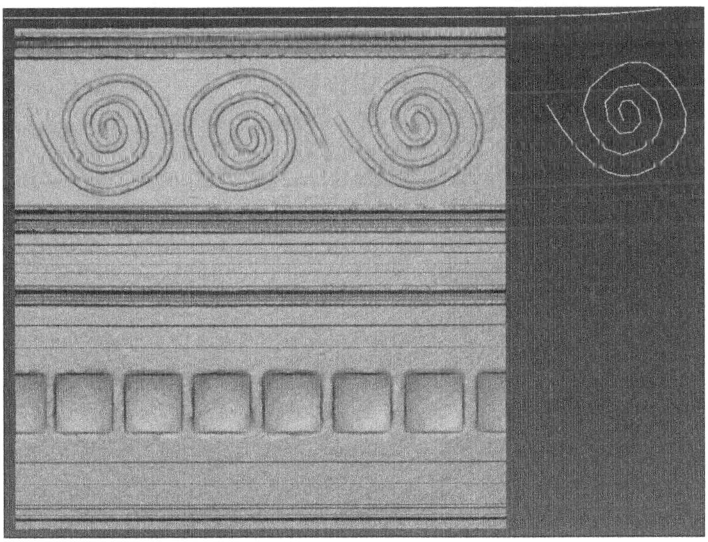

2. Now you will go into **Top** view so that you are looking at the sculpt straight on. One way to do this is by going to the **Object List** window, right-clicking on the **Top** camera, and choosing **Look Through**.

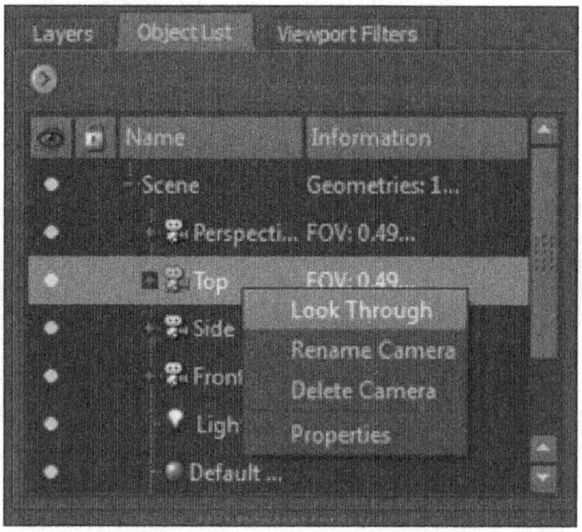

3. Another way you can do it is by using the right-click menu. After clicking into an empty area in the Mudbox viewport, you can hover over **Switch View** and choose **Top View** from the next menu that pops up. The following screenshot shows what the menus should look like:

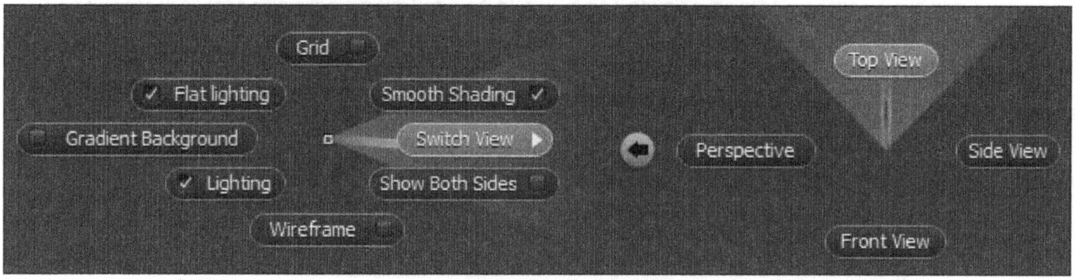

4. The next step is to go to your **Viewport Filters** tab, turn and choose **Screen Distance**, then click on **Save 16 bit Image**.

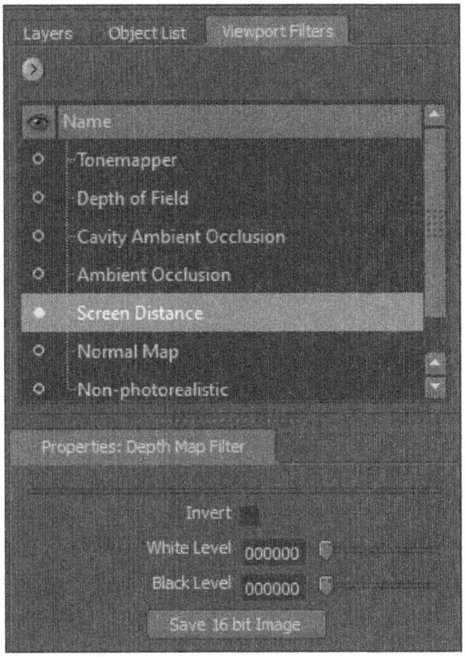

5. The image that is saved can now be set as a stencil. You can do this by either going to **Image Browser**, choosing the image, and using **Set Stencil** or you can go to the **Stencil** toolbar menu, choose **Add Stencil**, then choose your stencil's thumbnail from the toolbar. The following screenshot will show you what the example stencil looks like. The dark areas will affect the surface less than the white areas.

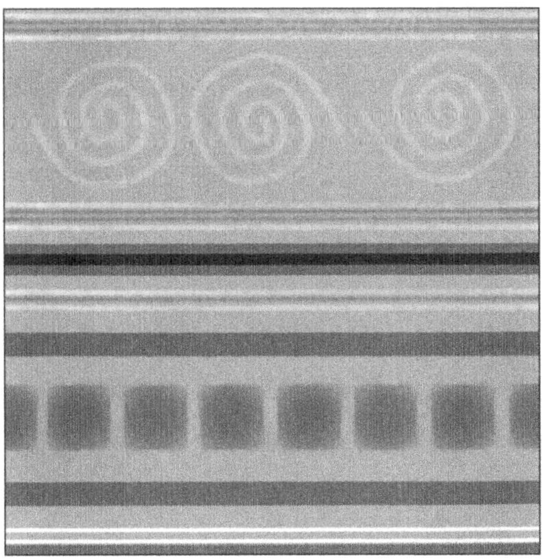

6. Notice the image is created using existing height values. Any concave detailing will be lost in the orthographic representation.

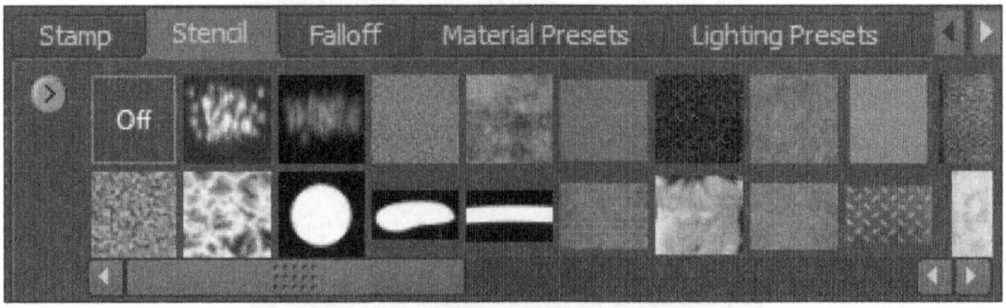

7. Now you can use this stencil on another sculpt. The following screenshot shows what the example stencil looks like in action. This is a good way to lay down some initial details on your model, then you can go back and add wear and tear or any other details that will hide the repetition.

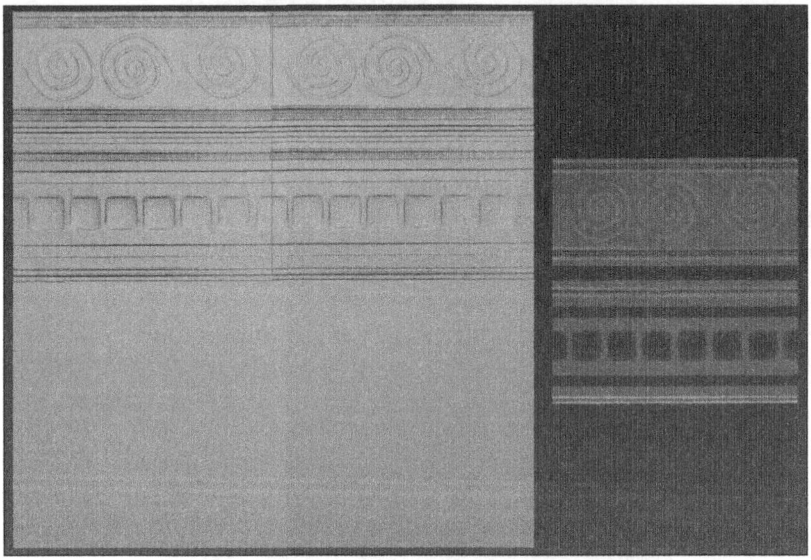

Here is a list of controls to change the visibility, size, rotation, and position of your stencil:

- *Q* will hide the stencil
- *S* + MMB will move the stencil
- *S* + LMB will rotate the stencil
- *S*+ RMB will scale the stencil

8. You'll notice that there is a seam between the two instances of this stencil. To correct this, we can bring our stencil image into Photoshop and paint out the seams. First, open up the stencil in Photoshop.
9. The next thing we need to be able to do is see our seams so that we can paint them away more easily. In order to do this you should go to **Filter** | **Other** | **Offset...** in the Photoshop menu.
10. When the options box pops up, you will set the **Undefined Areas** to **Wrap Around** and the **Horizontal** setting to half of your image's resolution. This will relocate your seam to the center of the image. The following screenshot shows what the options box should look like:

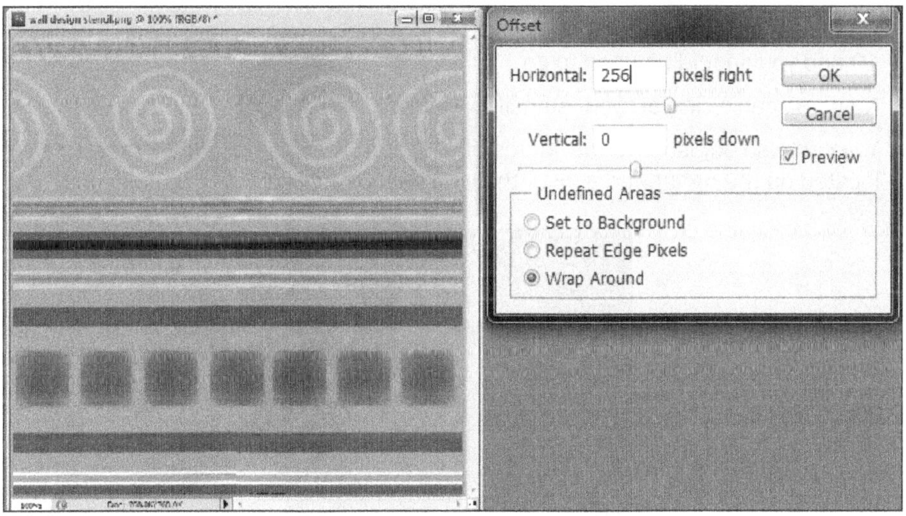

If you are not sure what your image's resolution is, you can go to **Image** | **Images Size...** and it will bring up a window with your image resolution displayed.

11. Now, by using a combination of Photoshop's **Brush Tool** and **Clone Stamp Tool** you will paint out the seam. As long as you don't make any changes to the outside edges of the image, you should be seam-free (only horizontally in this case). The following screenshot shows the wall design with no seams:

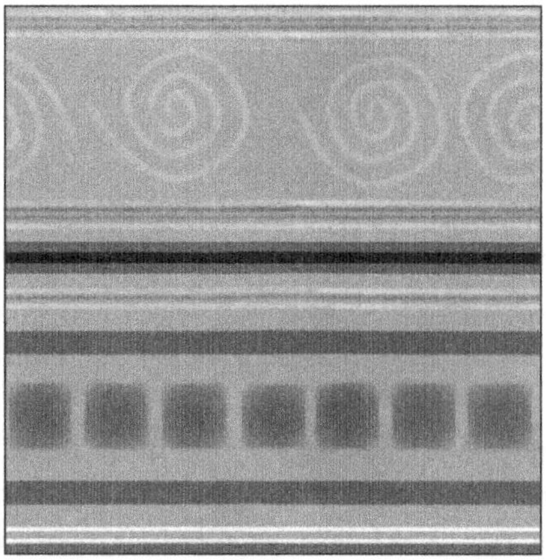

12. You may notice that the spirals are cut off on the sides. This is because we need to **Offset** the image again to get the details into their original placement. Repeat step 10 and you should be good to go.
13. Now, you can re-import your stencil to Mudbox.
14. You can also adjust other attributes of your stencil by going to the **Properties** toolbar located on the right-hand side of the workspace after selecting your stencil.

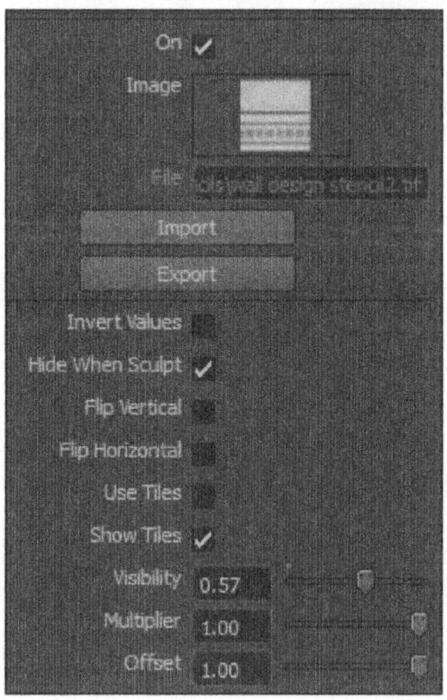

15. If you are working with a seamless stencil you can check the box for **Show Tiles** and for **Use Tiles**. This will tile your stencil allowing you to paint seamlessly across your model. The following screenshot shows these attributes in use:

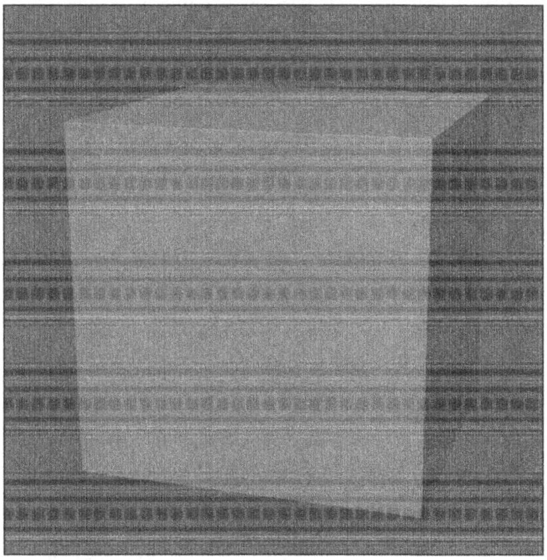

There's more...

If you are creating a tiling sculpt like the one shown in the previous screenshot, you can also use Mudbox's new tiling plane feature. If you would like to know more about this feature you can read through the next recipe.

See also

- The *Tricks for painting with stencils* recipe
- The *Creating a rock wall that tiles seamlessly in all directions* recipe

Creating a rock wall that tiles seamlessly in all directions

This recipe will teach you how to create a seamless tiling rock wall sculpt using the new tiling plane feature in Mudbox 2013. We will use some of the basic stamps that come along with Mudbox to create a rock texture that can be tiled in any direction without having any seams. This technique is very useful for games because it allows you to cover a lot of space with texture and not have to create unique details over a large area. You can save a lot of time by using this technique when creating an environment.

Getting ready

First, we need to set up our tiling plane. To do this you'll need to go to **Create | Tiling Plane**. This option will bring to a window an output that looks like the following screenshot:

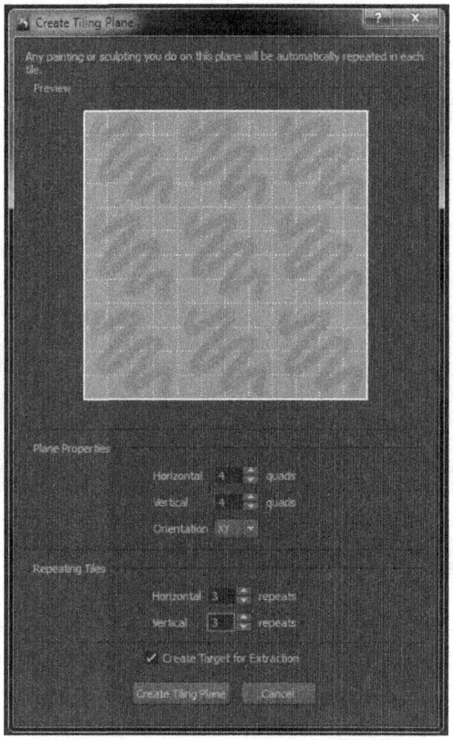

The settings in the previous screenshot are the ones we will use for this recipe. The following is an explanation of the options for your tiling plane:

- The **Plane Properties** section tells Mudbox the number of polygons you would like each plane to consist of. It also tells Mudbox what orientation to take within the scene, meaning which direction it is facing.
- The **Repeating Tiles** section defines how many tiles will be placed that have the details repeated. For example, with the **Horizontal** width and **Vertical** height set to **3**, it means that the details you sculpt will be shown nine times in a 3 x 3 square.
- The checkbox labeled **Create Target for Extraction** is so that you can export the results to a texture map that you can use for game assets.

How to do it...

Once you have created your tiling plane, you can begin to sculpt your rock wall. Choose the **Sculpt** tool from your **Sculpt Tools** tray and then choose a stamp from the **Stamp** toolbar in the bottom right-hand corner of the Mudbox interface. The following screenshot is an image of the stamp that I will be using for this recipe:

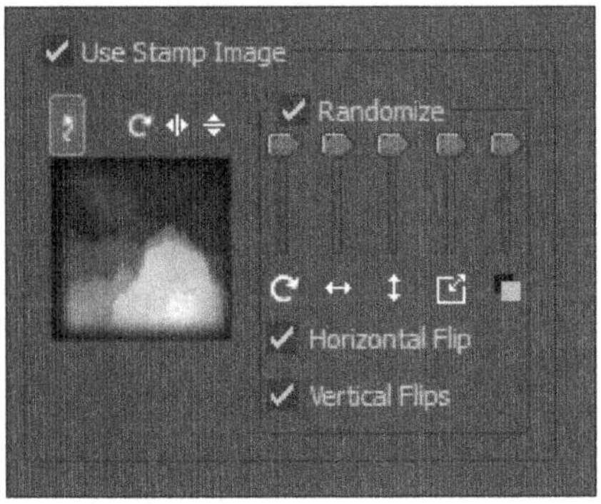

You will notice that I have the **Randomize** checkbox turned on with each of the sliders maxed out. This will vary the stamp on every stroke. This makes the stamp more effective at hiding repetition. If you'd like, you can use one of the other default stamps that come with Mudbox or even a customized one that you have made yourself. After just a few strokes, you will have a very basic rock wall texture. You will notice that whenever you complete a stroke, the plane will update all the tiles with the details you have added. Since the details are repeated on a 3 x 3 grid, you may want to target your sculpting toward the center tile for more accurate detailing. The following screenshot is an example of what you may come up with using the stamp shown previously:

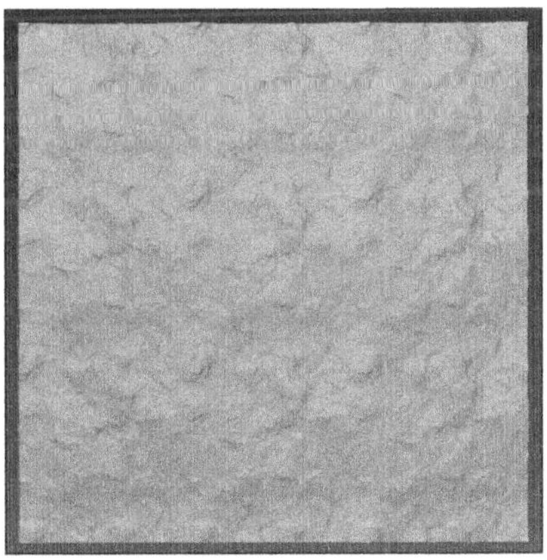

If you are just making pretty pictures in Mudbox then you can stop here. But, if you would like to extract texture maps from this sculpt to be used in a game engine, then you will need a normal map.

To extract a normal map, perform the following steps:

1. Go to **Maps** | **Extract Texture Maps** | **New Operation** in the main menu.
2. Next, input a name for the extraction. This is so that you can easily come back to this window with the settings you choose. This is helpful when you need to go back and extract a map from another object with the same settings or if you need to tweak the settings of an extraction you have already made.
3. To set up the extraction settings for a normal map you will need to check the box next to **Normal Map**. The following screenshot will show you the settings you will use for this extraction:

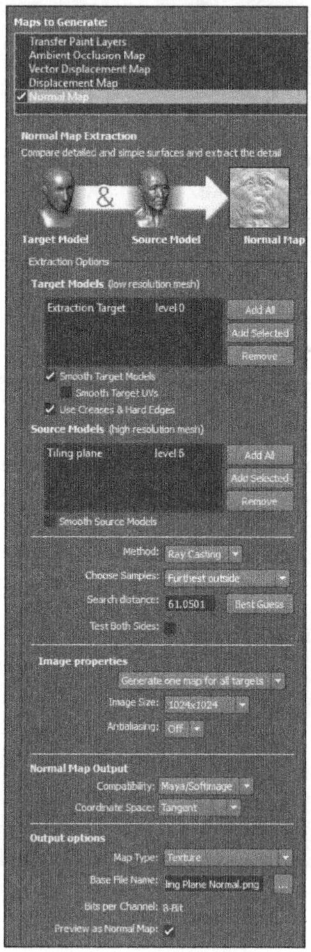

4. An important thing to note is that, for tiling planes, your target model is going to be the **Extraction Target** that was created when you first made the tiling plane. Normally, you would just choose a lower level of your model that you would like to use as your game resolution model.
5. The **source model** will be the highest level of your sculpt so that you are capturing all the details that you put in.
6. You can adjust **Image Size** to whatever you would like your final normal map to be.
7. Make sure to choose **3D Studio Max** from the **Compatibility** drop-down if you are using 3D Studio Max to view your normal maps.
8. Next give your image a **Base File Name** by clicking on the **...** next to the designated textbox. This is how you will choose the file type and location that the normal map will be extracted to.
9. Now, hit the **Extract** button at the bottom and wait a moment for the extraction to occur. The following screenshot is an image of what the normal map looks like for the wall shown previously:

See also

- The *Creating a custom stencil from a stone wall carving* recipe
- The *Adding a stencil or stamp to your toolbox* recipe

Tricks for painting with stencils

This recipe will show you a few tricks you can use while painting with stencils.

Getting ready

To get ready, you will just need to select a stencil that you would like to use and make sure it is enabled.

How to do it...

The following steps will help you perform an unobstructed tiling texture painting:

1. One trick you can use to paint with a tiling texture without the stencil obstructing your view is to resize your stencil to the desired size and move it off to the side.
2. Then select the **Use Tiles** checkbox.
3. Next, deselect the **Show Tiles** checkbox. This will allow you to paint a texture onto your model without anything obstructing your view.

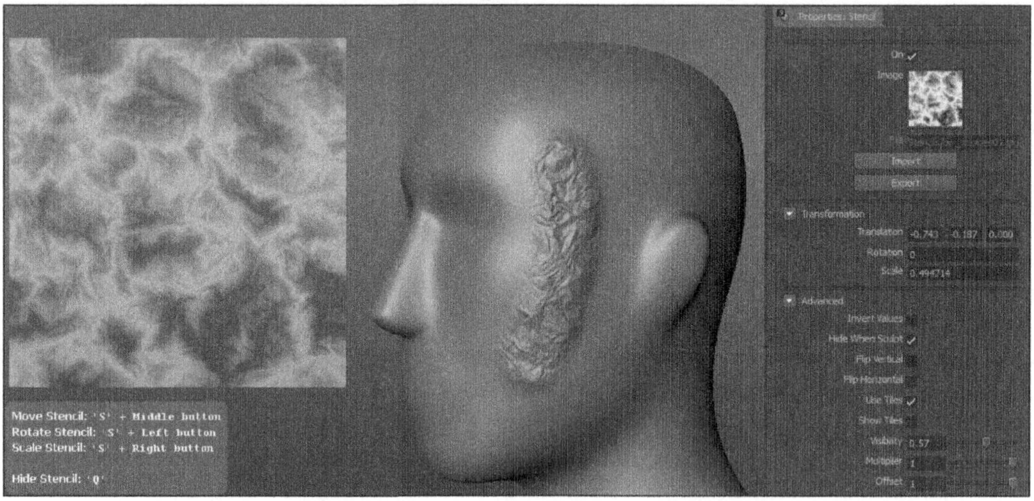

Using a stencil to define proportions

For this trick, we will use a stencil to define the proportions on a relief sculpt. Other techniques that will be used in this project, but are not thoroughly examined, are the **Freeze** brush, **Sculpt** brush, importing multiple meshes, duplicating objects within Mudbox 2013, capturing a screen image, among others. If you would like more help with these techniques, you can read more in the recipes that cover these techniques.

First off, I would like to give credit to **Chidi Okoye**. He is the artist whose work, Lolo Mask, I am using as a direct reference for my sculpt, shown in the following image:

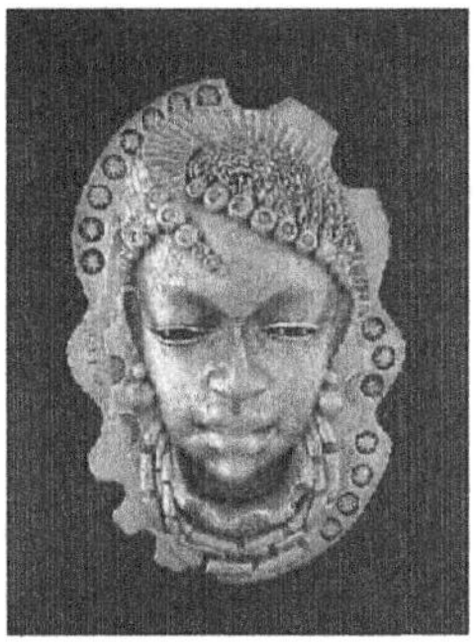

4. To implement this technique, you will first bring your reference or concept into Photoshop and draw lines for the main shapes in the image using white on black. Save this image as a `.png`. This line drawing will be used as a guide for keeping your proportions on target. The following is an example from this project:

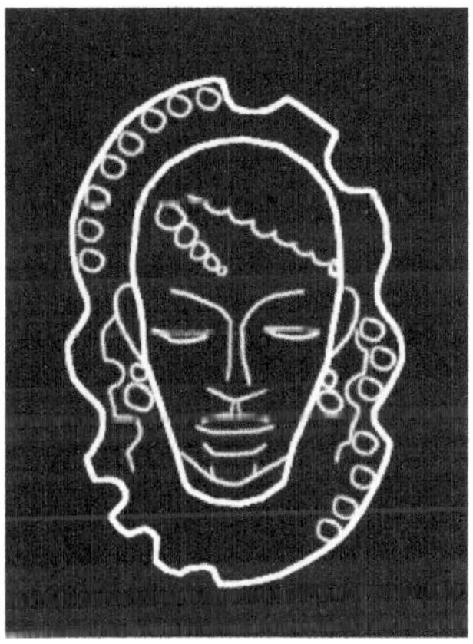

5. Next, you will need a plane to sculpt onto. Go ahead and create a plane in Mudbox by clicking *Ctrl* + *N* (**New Scene**) and choose the **Plane** from the **Starting points** section of the Welcome window.
6. Now hit *Shift* + *D* until you get to level 6. This should give you enough detail to sculpt in the details we will be adding.
7. The next step is to get a good angle to sculpt from. Click on **Top** on the view cube inside the Mudbox **3D View**. This will aim the camera directly down onto your plane.

8. Now you'll add the stencil we created in step 1. Go to the **Stencil** toolbar in the bottom right-hand side of the Mudbox 2013 interface, click on the arrow, and choose **Add Stencil**. Now, navigate to the `.png` that you just saved to enable this stencil.

9. To save the position of the camera and the position of the stencil you can go to the **Camera Bookmarks** toolbar at the bottom-right of the interface, click on the arrow, and choose **Add Camera Bookmark**. This will add a bookmark to this shelf that will bring you back to the same camera angle and will activate, plus reposition, your stencil to its current state.

10. Now you can use the stencil in two ways. One way is to turn it on and off, from the bookmarked camera angle, to make sure that your details are lining up. The second way is to sculpt onto a new layer of the plane and use this layer as a guide. To do this you will need to add a new sculpt layer and use the **Sculpt** tool to scribble over your stencil while this new layer is active. Your plane should look like the following screenshot:

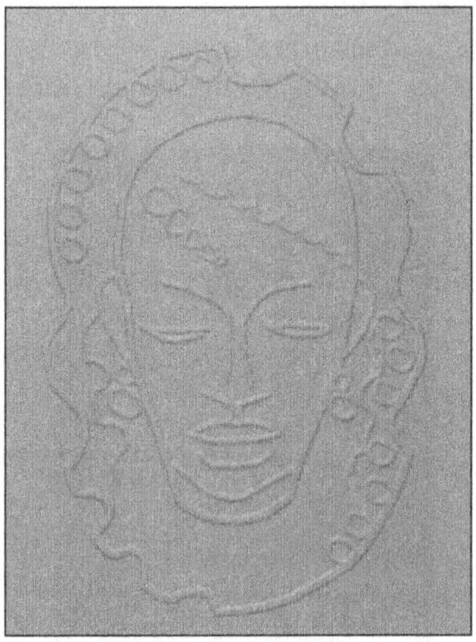

11. Now you can turn this layer on and off as you need it. Go ahead and rename this layer as `Guide`. For the real sculpting, you will be using new layers, not the guide layer.

12. With your guide in place, you can now use the **Freeze** brush to start blocking out the main shapes of your sculpt. The following screenshot is what you should see after the first shape is blocked out:

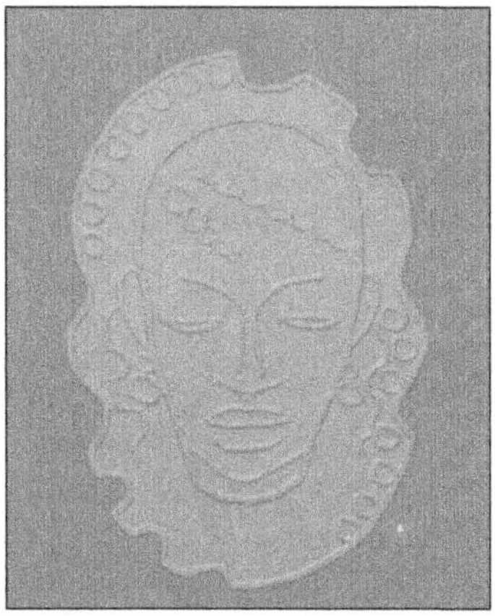

13. Now fill in the smaller areas, with the **Freeze** brush, where the sculpt will not be pulled forward. The following screenshot is an example of the first frozen blocked out shape:

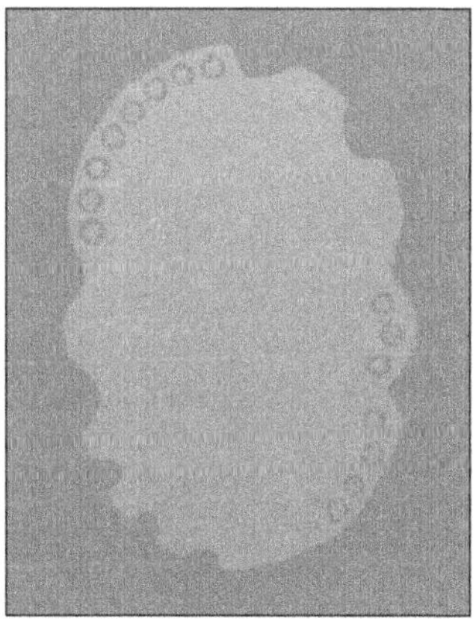

14. Now select the **Sculpt** brush and set up the properties as seen in the following screenshot:

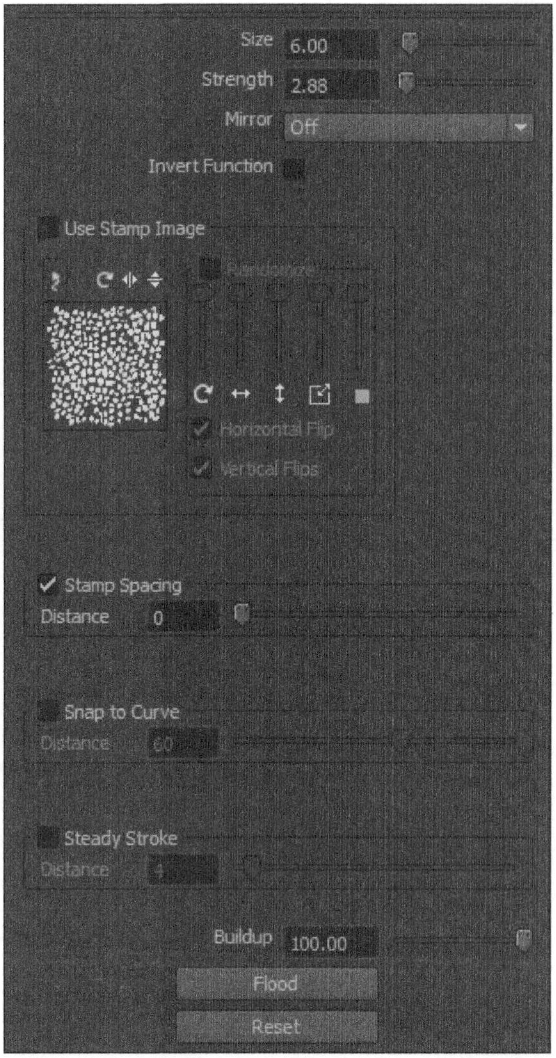

15. Next, sculpt over the blocked out areas without lifting your finger or pen. This will make sure that the sculpt height will plateau at the strength you have given your brush and will remain consistent across the entire shape. Your sculpt should look like the following screenshot:

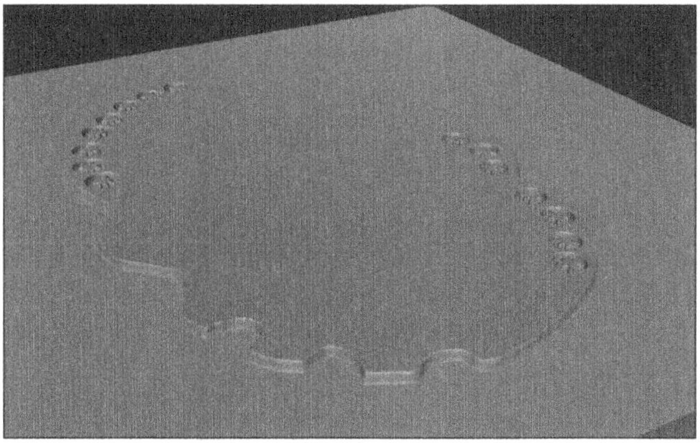

16. Your next step is to create the raised gear shapes on the surface you just sculpted. Using the stencil as a guide, or the guide layer, begin blocking out the gear shapes. When you are done, you should have a frozen sculpt that looks like the following screenshot. Keep in mind that it is not necessary to block out the earrings. The area that the head will cover can be sculpted on and it will not hurt anything.

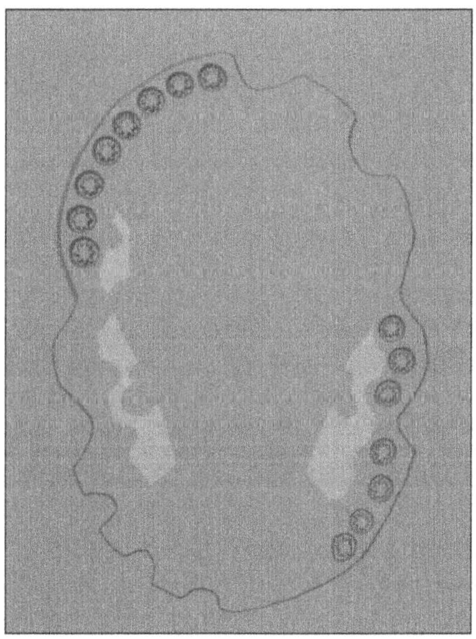

17. Now, using the **Sculpt** brush with a falloff set to something similar depicted in the following screenshot, you will use the size of the brush to define the rise and fall of this detail on the model:

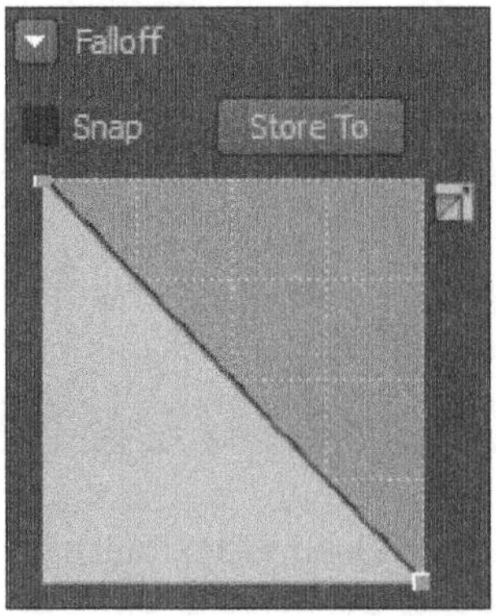

18. When you complete this you should have a sculpt that looks like the following screenshot. Keep in mind you may need to use the **Smooth** or **Flatten** brushes to help smooth out this detail.

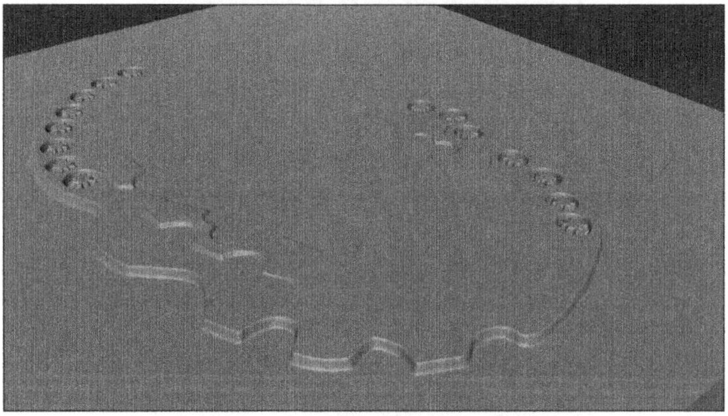

19. For the head, import the Mudbox default `Basic Head.mud` file. This mesh can be located (for 64-bit Windows) at `C:\Autodesk\Mudbox_2013_EFGJ_Win_64-bit\x64\Mudbox\Program Files\Autodesk\Mudbox2013\Meshes`. Just go to **File** | **Import**, browse to this location, and click on **Import**.
20. Now, using the **Translate**, **Rotate**, and **Scale** tools, get the head in place using your stencil as a guide. Once it is in place, you may need to use the **Grab** brush to line up some of the features better. Also, don't forget to add subdivision levels to your head before sculpting. The lined up head mesh should look something like the following screenshot:

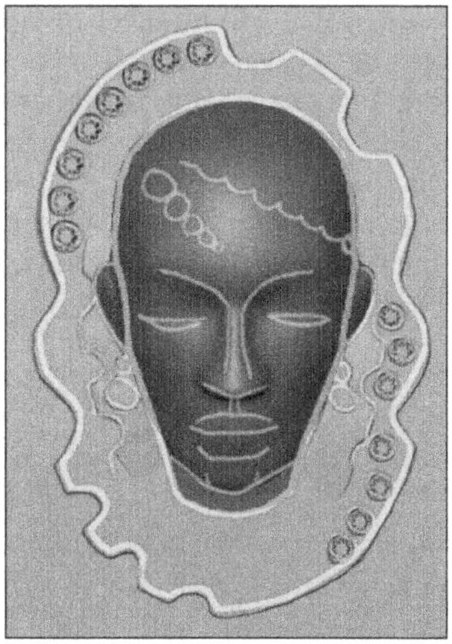

21. For the head sculpting, I am not going to go through all the steps but what I will tell you is that I used Mudbox primitives, duplication options, the **Sculpt** brush, the **Grab** brush, the **Smooth** and **Flatten** brushes, a little bit of Maya **Import/Export** (for the necklace) and a few of the basic Mudbox stamps (for the hair). The following is an image with progress shots, till the completion of the first pass on this sculpt:

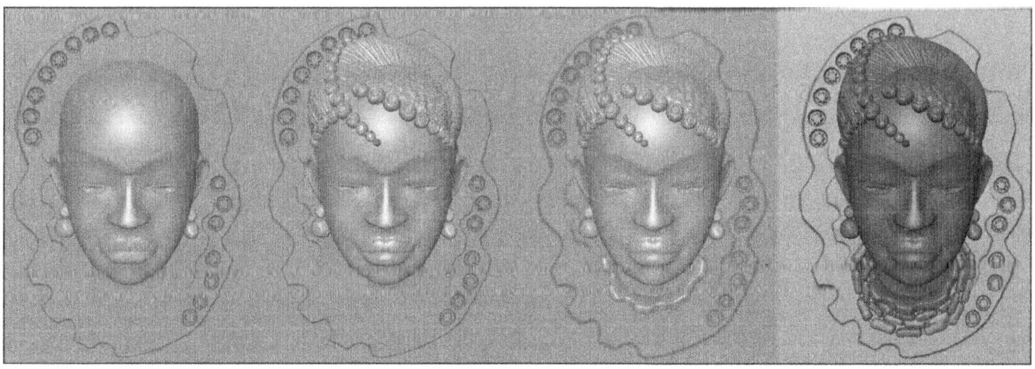

22. Next we can turn this sculpt into a normal map that can be used in games. First, you need to turn on the normal map viewport filter by going to the **Viewport Filters** tab on the far right and clicking on the dot next to **Normal Map**.
23. Make sure that you are in your top view and then go up to **Render** | **Save Screen Image** and save an image that is 4x the screen size.
24. Open up your new large normal map image in Photoshop, select the **Crop** tool, hold *Shift* and then click on **+** , drag over your sculpt details and press *Enter* when it is centered. This will make sure that the aspect ratio of your image is squared.

25. Now reduce your image size by going to **Image** | **Image Size...** and set it to 2048 pixels wide by 2048 pixels high. Now save the file. For games, your textures need to be powers of two. By saving this image with the dimension 2048 pixels wide by 2048 pixels high, it means you can always reduce the size to 1024 pixels wide by 1024 pixels high, 512 pixels wide by 512 pixels high, 256 pixels wide by 256 pixels high, and so on, if you would like to at a later date. It is usually better to keep as much resolution as possible for flexibility in the future. The following screenshot is what your normal map should look like:

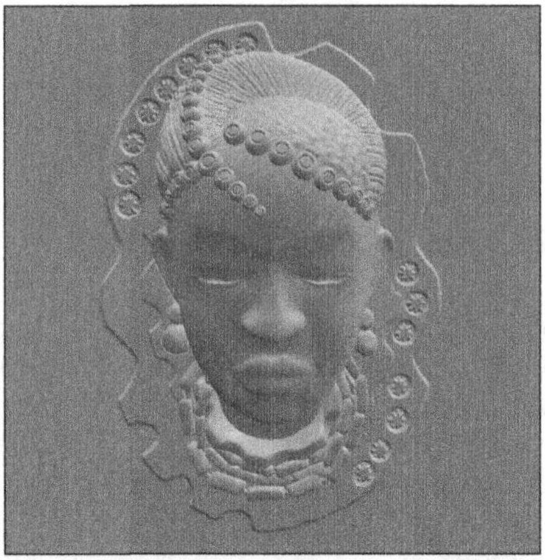

Tricks for painting with stamps

This recipe will show you a few tricks you can use while painting with stamps.

Getting ready

To get ready you will just need to select a stamp that you would like to use and make sure it is enabled.

How to do it...

The following steps will help you obtain straight lines on curved surfaces (paint mode):

1. One trick you can do to get straight lines on a curved surface, such as the stitching or lettering on cloth, is to select **Flatten to UV Space** in the **Mesh** menu. Keep in mind this will only work when using paint tools. Any sculpting you do while the mesh is **Flattened to UV Space** will go away when you **Unflatten from UV Space**.

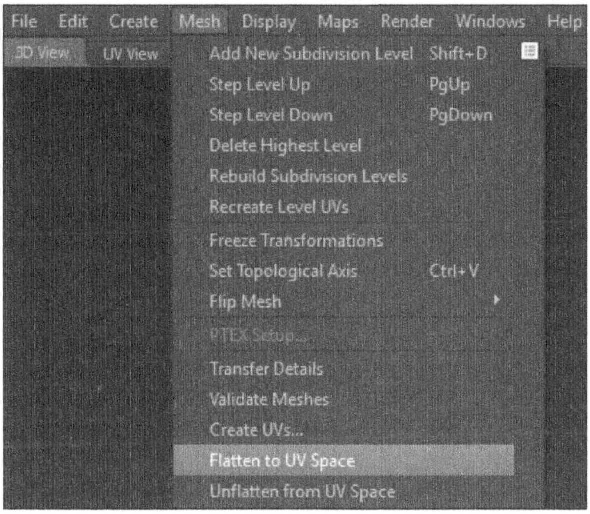

2. Next you will select your desired stamp and set the spacing to what suits your purpose.

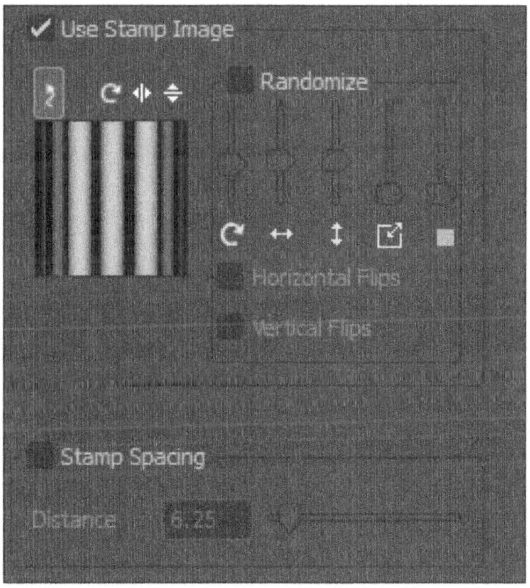

3. Also, you will want to make sure your UVs are laid out in such a way that any line work is not on a diagonal. This will cause aliasing issues meaning your straight line will look jagged as shown in the following screenshot:

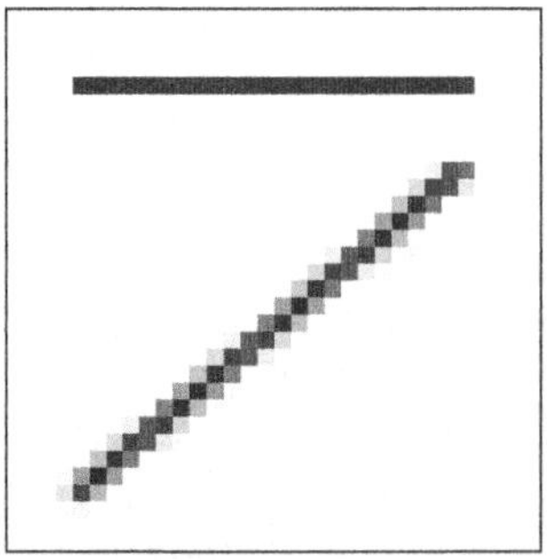

4. Then you can enable **Steady Stroke**, found in your brush's properties. The following screenshot is what you should see in the brush's properties:

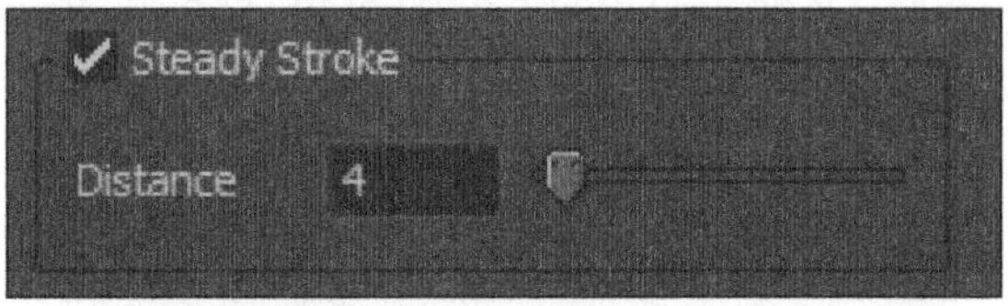

5. Alternatively, you can use **Curves** to make sure that your line is straight. You can read about **Curves** in *Creating a zipper using a custom stamp* recipe. The green line in the following screenshot is a curve and can be used in the same way as a *straight edge* would be used outside the digital medium:

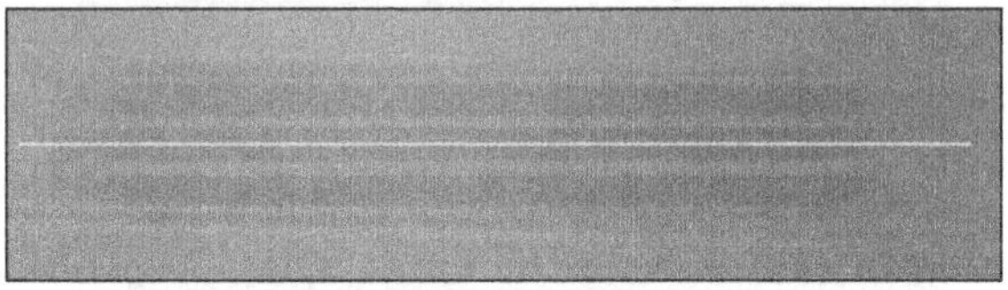

6. Now switch to the front camera view by going into the **Object List** and right-clicking on the **Front** camera and choose **Look Through**.

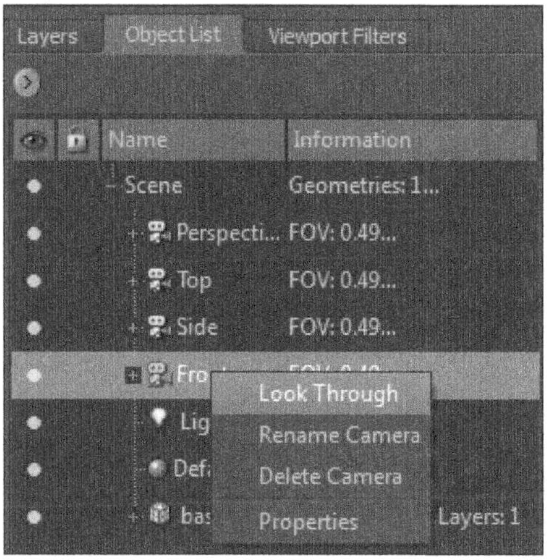

7. With everything set up you can now paint straight lines onto your object, no matter what the 3D form looks like. The following screenshot illustrates the same:

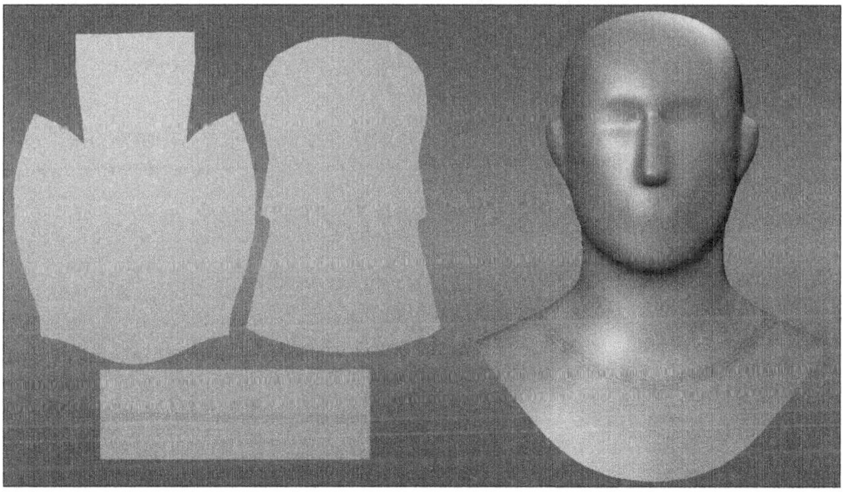

Adding a stencil or stamp to your toolbox

This recipe will show you how to add a stencil or stamp to your toolbox. Knowing how to add stamps and stencils to your toolbox is an essential skill that you will use time and again.

Once you go through this recipe, I recommend creating a few brushes that you can add to your toolbox so that you can start experiencing what makes a good stamp or stencil.

The default stamps and stencils can be very handy as well. Try them out and see what kind of effects you can produce.

How to do it...

Adding a stencil to your toolbox is very simple. The following steps will help you to add a stencil to your toolbox:

1. First you will need to go into the **Stencil** tool tab in the lower right-hand corner of your workspace.
2. Now, click on the menu for this tab and choose **Add Stencil**.

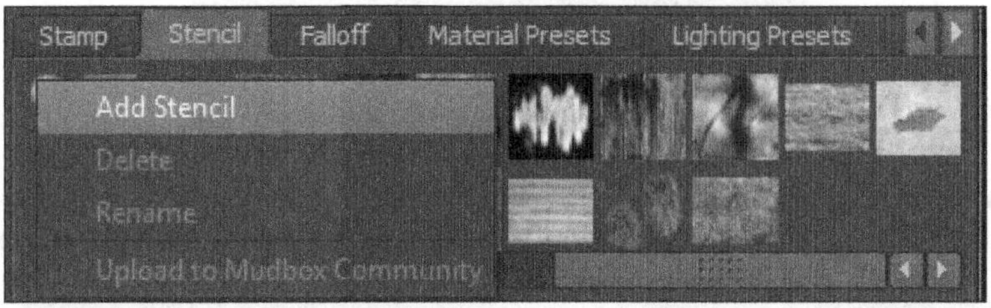

3. Browse to the image that you plan on using as a stencil and select it. You should now see the image in your tool tray.
4. Adding a stamp can be done in the very same fashion. First, what you will need to do is go into the **Stamp** tool tab in the lower right-hand corner of your workspace.
5. Now, click on the menu for this tab and choose **Add Stamp**.

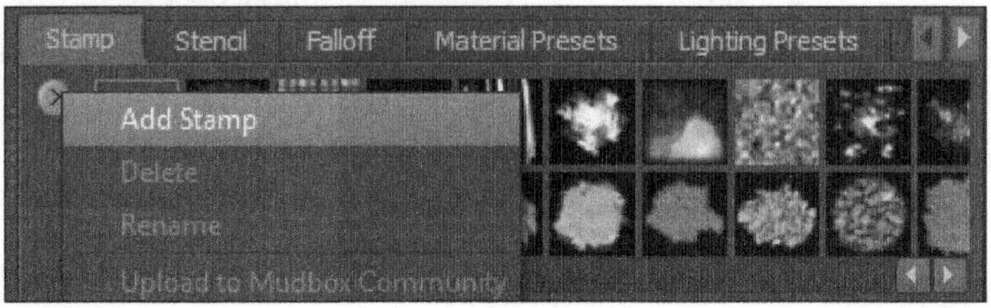

6. Now browse to the image that you plan on using as a stamp and select it. You should now see the image in your tool tray.

See also

- The *Tricks for painting with stencils* recipe
- The *Creating a custom stencil from a stone wall carving* recipe
- The *Creating a custom rock stamp* recipe

Creating a custom rock stamp

This recipe will show you how to create your own stamp using an image editing software.

Getting ready

In order to create your own custom stamp, you will need to find or create an image that suits the type of stamp you would like to create. For example, if you would like to sculpt claw scratch marks, you might use four or five lines to drag along the surface. On the other hand, if you would like to sculpt in the texture of a rock you would need a good image of a rock with the details you would like to come through.

How to do it...

The following steps show how to make a stamp meant for sculpting a rock texture:

1. First, find a good starting image like the one in the following image farthest to the left:

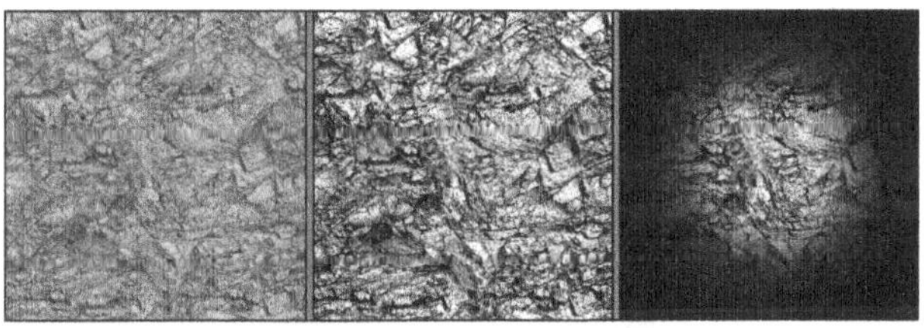

2. Next you will want to desaturate the image, (*Ctrl* + *Shift* + *U* in Photoshop).
3. Now you are going to adjust the levels (*Ctrl* + *L* in Photoshop) to something like you see in the following screenshot. Your image should now look like the image in the center from the previous image.

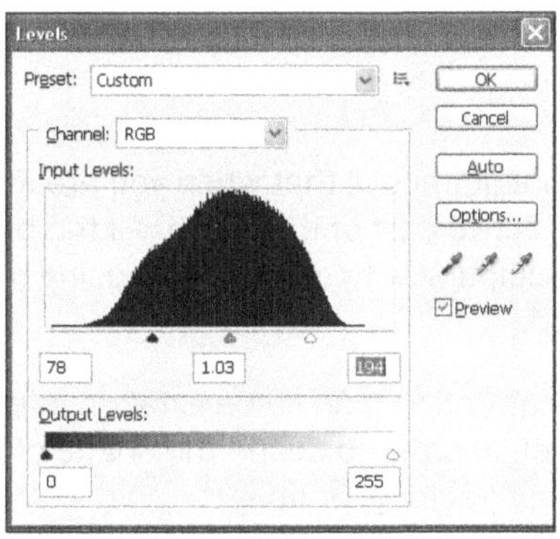

4. Next you will create an alpha channel to define the shape of the brush. To create an alpha channel in Photoshop, you can go to the channel's window and create a new layer. This should give you a layer that can be called **Alpha 1** and should be all black.

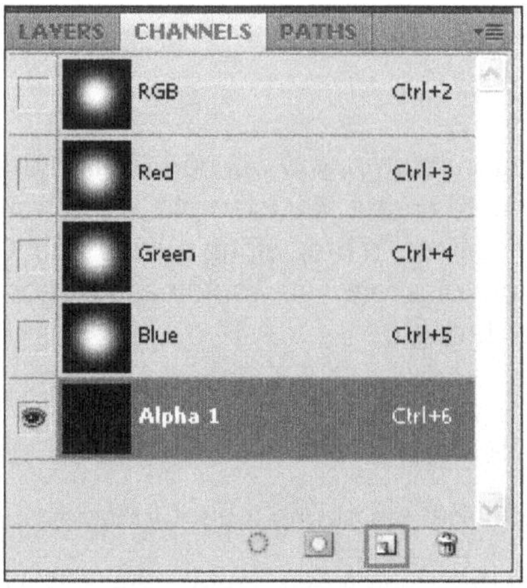

5. Next you will draw a white dot on the alpha layer with soft edges to designate what parts of the image will be active.

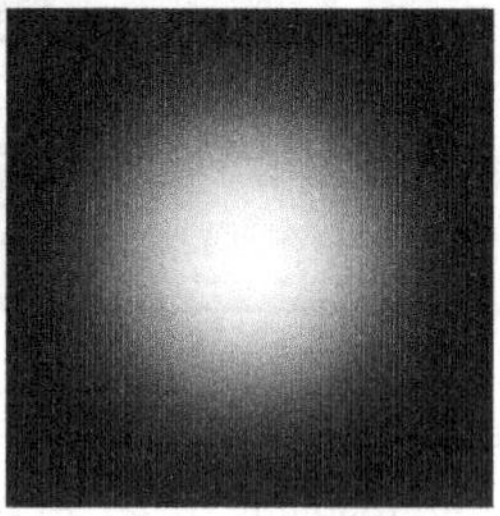

6. Now just save it out as a 32-bit TGA file and you can go into Mudbox and choose **Add Stamp** in the **Stamp** toolbar.

How it works...

One thing you should know about stamps is that when you are in the **Sculpt** mode, any part of the image that is white is an active part of the brush. All the black areas will not affect your model. Essentially, when sculpting with stamps, it is using the values of your stamp to determine what detail is applied.

While in the **Paint** mode, hue, saturation, and value is taken into account. Also, black areas will still be applied to your model. In order to define the shape of your stamp while in the **Paint** mode you will need an alpha channel for your image.

See also

- The *Using a stamp* recipe
- The *Adding a stamp to your toolbox* recipe

5

Get In and Get Out

In this chapter, we will cover:

- Flattening to UV space
- Deleting the highest level of resolution on your model
- Blocking out a rough Mayan pyramid using a displacement map
- Importing, exporting, and working with multiple objects within Mudbox 2013
- Creating a terrain

Introduction

This chapter will be covering the various ways to import and export your models as well as handling the UVs within Mudbox 2013. Understanding model pipeline in Mudbox 2013 will help you to better integrate it into your normal workflow with more efficiency. There are several methods of working with models from other software and, once in Mudbox, utilizing the models and UV organization will help strengthen your experience.

Flattening to UV space

This recipe will show you how to flatten your model in UV space. This can come in handy while trying to paint details that are laid out in a straight line in the UV space but are curved surfaces in 3D space.

Getting ready

Once you have laid out your UVs in your preferred 3D software and have imported your 3D model, you will be able to flatten your model to UV space.

Keep in mind that sculpting in this mode will not affect the model. This option is mostly used to help you in painting textures onto the surface of your model.

How to do it...

In order to flatten your model to UV space, just go to **Mesh** in the top menu bar and select **Flatten to UV Space** as shown in the following screenshot:

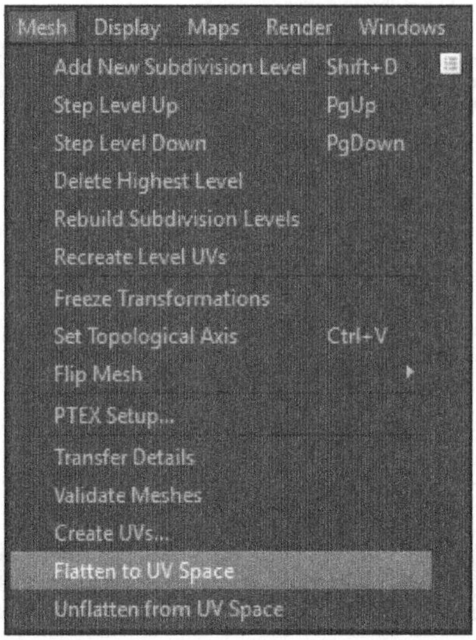

On the left in the following screenshot is the 3D model and to the right, the screenshot shows how this model looks, flattened to UV space:

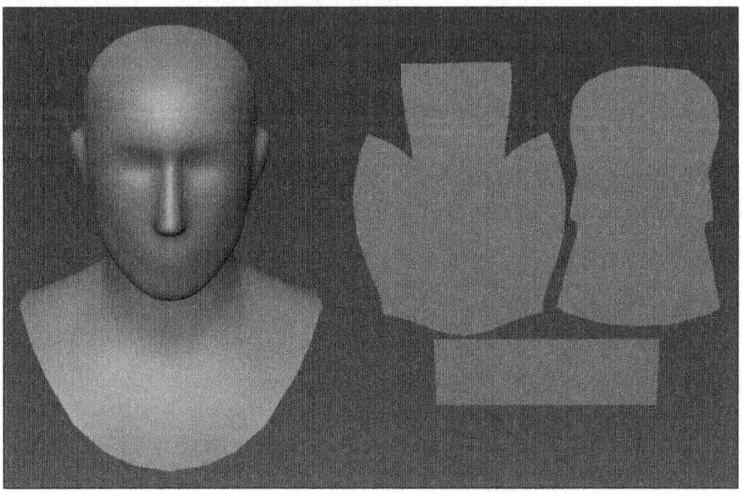

There's more

You can use this tool to help you add stripes or apply text to round surfaces. To demonstrate this, we will apply paint to the side of a missile. This recipe will add text using a stencil but you can also add stripes using curves as a guide. You can refer to *Chapter 4, Fine Tooth Comb*, in a recipe called *Tricks for painting with stamps* if you would like to learn how to use curves to apply straight lines to your mesh.

If you look into the code files of this book you will find a file called `missile.fbx`. Go ahead and import this file into Mudbox 2013 and then perform the following steps:

1. If you try to create a straight line around a cylindrical object without using the method described here, then it will take more steps to complete and it leaves room for some unnecessary frustrations to present themselves.

   So, let's start by creating a paint layer on our missile by going to the **Paint** section under the **Layers** tab in the upper-right corner of the Mudbox 2013 interface, right-clicking in the empty space below **Name**, and choosing **New Layer**. You can leave the defaults for the window that pops up and hit the **OK** button.

2. Go ahead and apply a base color by using the **Paint Tools** found in the bottom left-hand side of the Mudbox interface. I used a bluish-white color but you can use whatever color you'd like.
3. Now click on **Mesh** | **Flatten to UV Space** from the top menu.
4. Next we're going to get the camera to look straight at our flattened mesh. To do this you can right-click on the empty space in your viewport, hover your mouse over **Switch Views**, and choose **Front View**.
5. Now hit the *A* key to focus on the flattened mesh and zoom in until you are looking at the large bar on top of the UV layout.

   The UVs are sloppy on the rest of the UV shells because this top shell is the only piece needed to demonstrate this technique. The following screenshot is what you should be looking at:

6. The next thing we need to do is select the **Projection** tool from the **Paint Tools** menu, on the bottom left-hand side of the Mudbox interface.
7. Now we have to choose a stencil to use with our projection brush. Click on the **Image Browser** tab at the top of the viewport and then navigate to the folder containing the assets for this chapter.
8. Now choose the `Air Force Logo.png` image and click on the icon for **Set Stencil**. The image should look like the following screenshot:

9. Next, you can go back to the **3D View** tab and line up your stencil. By holding the *S* key your navigation tools will control your stencil. Resize and position your stencil until it matches the location shown in the following screenshot:

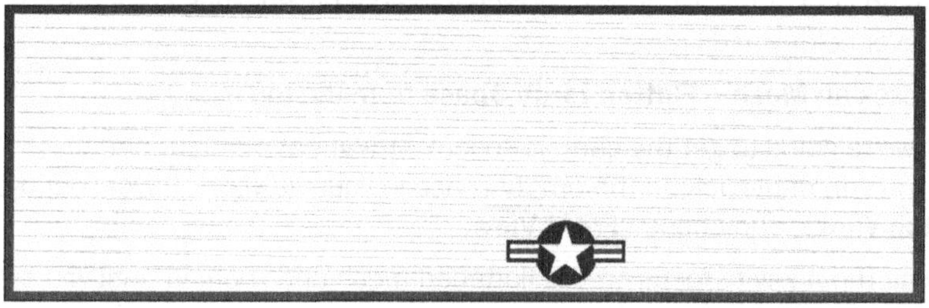

10. The last two steps are to go to the top menu and select **Mesh** | **Unflatten from UV Space** and then right-click on the empty space of the viewport and go to **Switch View** | **Perspective** to get back to the initial camera. You should see something like the following screenshot:

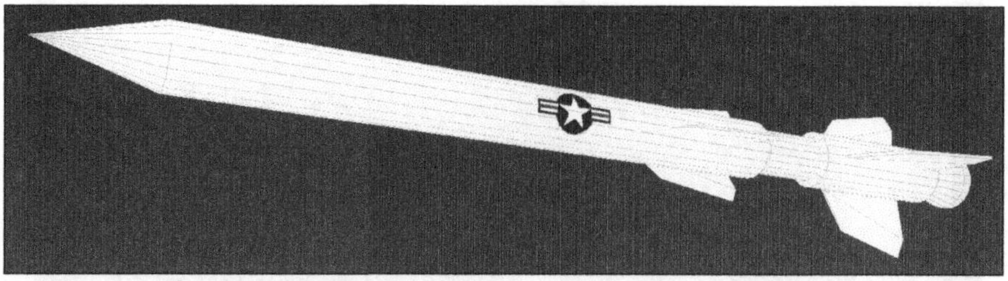

Depending on the curvature of your mesh, using this technique will save you from having distortion on your projections.

See also

- The *Tricks for painting with stamps* recipe in *Chapter 4, Fine Tooth Comb*

Deleting the highest level of resolution on your model

This recipe will show you how to delete the highest level of resolution on your model.

How to do it...

The following steps will help you to delete the highest level of resolution on your model:

1. Once you have a multiple-level mesh within Mudbox 2013, you will want to switch to the level that you would want as the highest level.
2. Now go to **Mesh** and choose **Delete Highest Level**.

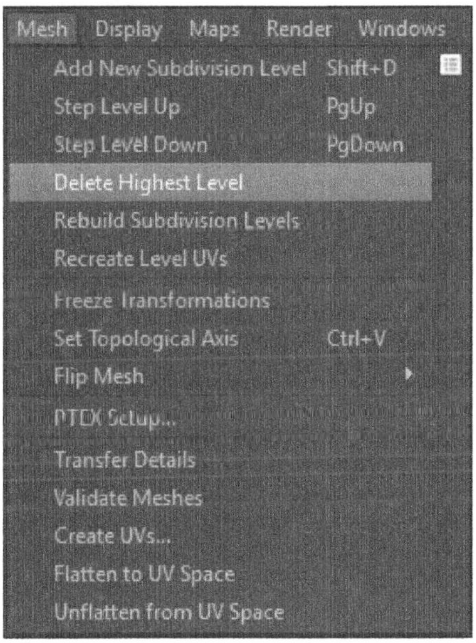

3. Repeat the previous step until it does not let you delete anymore. It will not let you delete your current level.

There's more...

The **Mesh** menu also provides other functionalities based on subdivision levels, one of them being rebuilding subdivision levels.

Rebuilding subdivision levels on an imported mesh

If you need to rebuild the subdivision levels on an imported mesh, you can go to **Mesh** in the top menu bar and go to **Rebuild Subdivision Levels**.

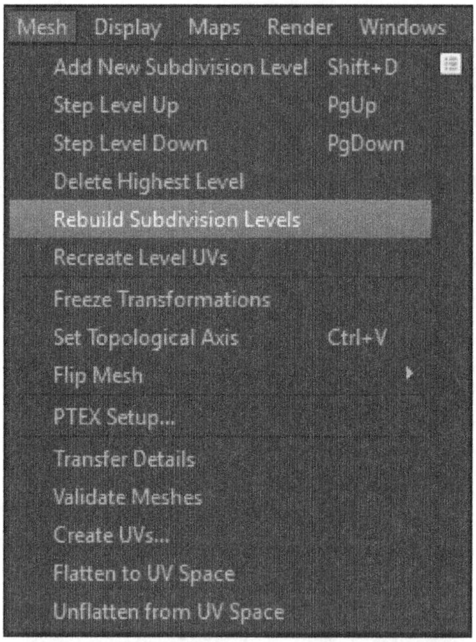

Rebuilding the subdivision levels is essentially un-subdividing a model so that you can work on the lower levels of the model while preserving the detail on the higher levels.

Keep in mind this will only work on models that have been subdivided using the Catmull-Clark method. Maya and ZBrush are just a few software that use this method to subdivide their models.

See also

- The *Importing, exporting, and working with multiple objects within Mudbox 2013* recipe

Blocking out a rough Mayan pyramid using a displacement map

This recipe will show you how to create a quick block out of a Mayan pyramid in Mudbox 2013. By learning this method, you will be able to get early shapes blocked in fairly quickly without ever *touching* a brush. When you complete this recipe, you will have a rough shape of a Mayan pyramid that you can use as a base for a sculpt or for creating a paintover.

Getting ready

First you will need a displacement map created in Photoshop or another software, such as Gimp or Corel Painter. The following points will help you to start off:

- In your preferred 2D image editing software, lay down a series of squares within the squares. Make sure that each square has an equal change in value as well as an equal change in size. In this case, I have changed the value and size of each box by 20 percent. The following screenshot shows what the image should look like:

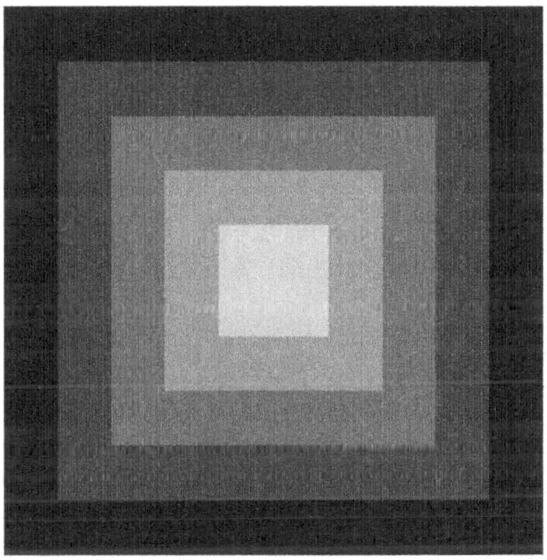

  Now all you need is a plane to sculpt on.

- Click on **File** | **New Scene** and choose **Plane** from the list of **Starting points** in the window that pops up.
- Now, boost up the subdivision levels by clicking *Shift* + *D* until you reach **Level 7**.

How to do it...

The following steps will help you to block out a rough Mayan pyramid using a displacement map:

1. To apply this displacement map to your surface in Mudbox, you will go to **Maps** and under **Sculpt using Map** you will choose **New Operation...**.

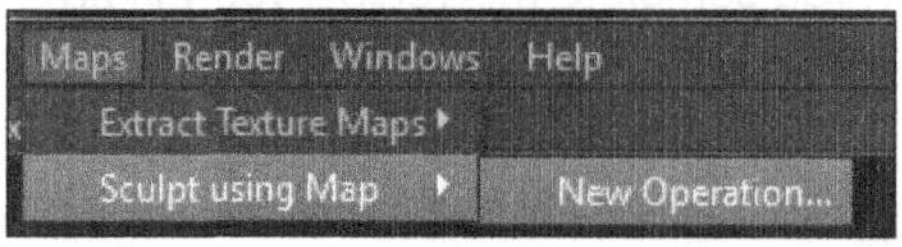

2. A window will pop up with the attributes you will need to set. First, choose the mesh you are trying to affect by going to the **Target Mesh** drop-down menu and choosing your mesh. The screenshot following step 6 shows an example of the menu.
3. Next you will choose the displacement map you plan on using on the mesh by choosing the **...** next to **Map**.
4. For your typical black and white displacement map, leave the **Map Space** setting on **Normal** (regular displacement map).
5. Under the **Advanced** section we're going to set the **Multiplier** to **80** for some more depth.
6. When all is set, choose **Go** and Mudbox will create a sculpt layer for you with the details from the displacement map. If you repeatedly press **Go** you will get more layers and the details will stack in intensity. I recommend adjusting **Multiplier** if you do not get the result you want the first time. The following screenshot shows the result:

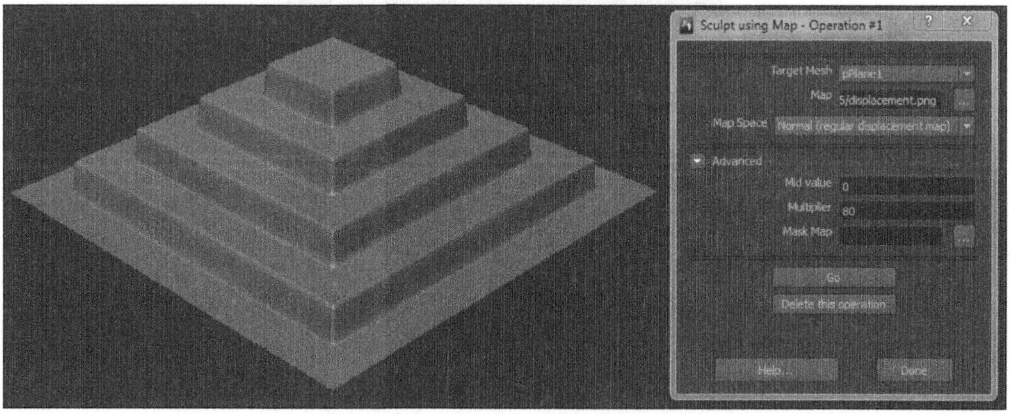

There's more

Try adding some more details to your displacement map before using the **Sculpt using Map** tool. By using a combination of the **Gradient** brush and **Posterize** within Photoshop, I added some details to the displacement map and came up with something that looks like the following screenshot:

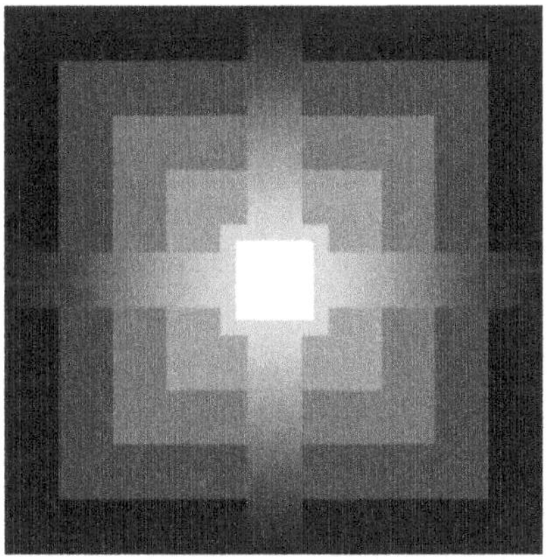

It may be hard to figure it out in this screenshot but the gradient is stepped to create a rough blockout for the pyramid's stairs. The following screenshot shows what the **Sculpt using Map** tool produced:

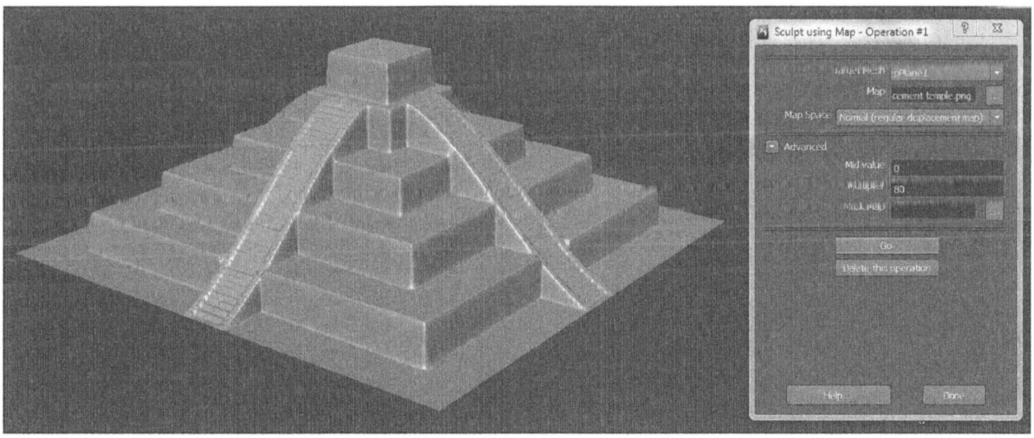

Now you can use this as a base mesh to sculpt onto.

Share your base mesh

Whenever you create a new base mesh you should consider sharing it with the community. Doing this takes very little time and will help the community to grow and become a greater resource for you and other artists like you.

1. First thing you're going to need is a `.obj` file of the mesh you would like to share. To obtain this you will need to select the object you want to share from the **Object List** window in Mudbox.
2. Then click on **File** | **Export Selection...** and save your file to your computer as a `.obj` file.
3. When you upload your base mesh, the Mudbox Community website will ask for a `.zip` file. So, the next step is to create a ZIP file using a program such as WinZip available at `http://www.winzip.com/downwz.htm` or PeaZip available at `http://www.peazip.org/`.
4. The other thing the Mudbox Community site will ask for is a thumbnail for your object. For this you can take a screenshot of your object and save it as a low resolution `.jpeg` file.
5. Now that you have your thumbnail and your base mesh zipped up and ready to go, you're going to click on the **Mudbox Community** tab at the top of your viewport. Alternatively, you can go to `http://area.autodesk.com/mudcom` to reach the same page.
6. Next, you will login to the Mudbox Community. If you do not have an account yet, you can click on the **register** link found at the top of the page. Just follow the instructions and enter your information. Don't worry, it is free to sign up.
7. The next step, after signing in, is to click on **Upload** on the far, left-hand side of the website which should open up a drop-down of choices. You are going to click on **Upload Base Mesh**, at the bottom of this list. The menu should look like the following screenshot:

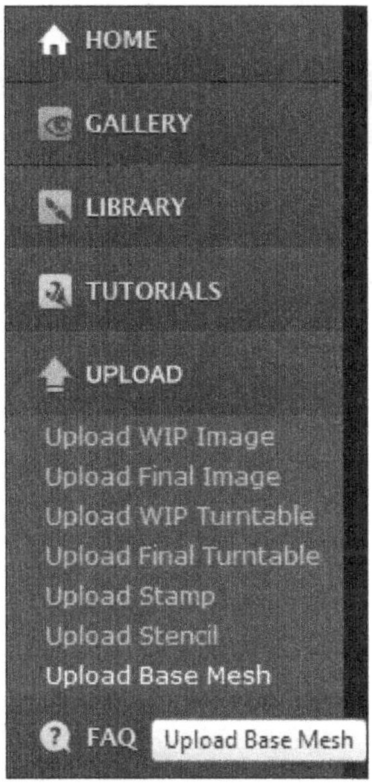

8. Once you click on **Upload Base Mesh** you should see a window that looks like the following screenshot:

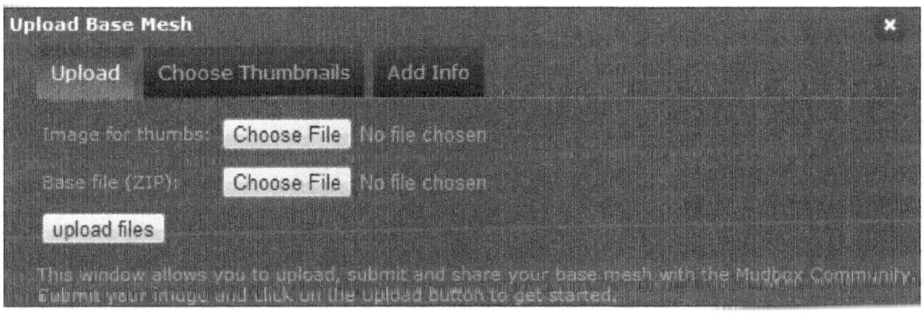

Now you are going to click on the buttons that say **Choose File** and choose the files you created in the previous steps. Follow the onscreen instructions and you will have your base mesh uploaded in no time.

See also

- The *Downloading and enabling stamps, stencils, and base meshes from the Internet* recipe in *Chapter 1, Ready? Set...*

Importing, exporting, and working with multiple objects within Mudbox 2013

This recipe will show you how to bring an object into Mudbox 2013 with textures applied so that you can add details to an existing asset. We will also go over how to work with multiple objects within Mudbox and then export the objects for use with another software.

Getting ready

For this recipe, we will be importing a textured casino die and then we will duplicate it and add some dirt to the dice. If you would like to follow along with the same die that I will be using in this recipe, you can find the `dice.mud` file and the dice-files folder available in the code files of this book.

How to do it...

The following steps will help you to import, export, and work with an object within Mudbox:

1. First thing we are going to do is open up the `dice.mud` file with Mudbox 2013. In your viewport, you should see something that looks like the following screenshot:

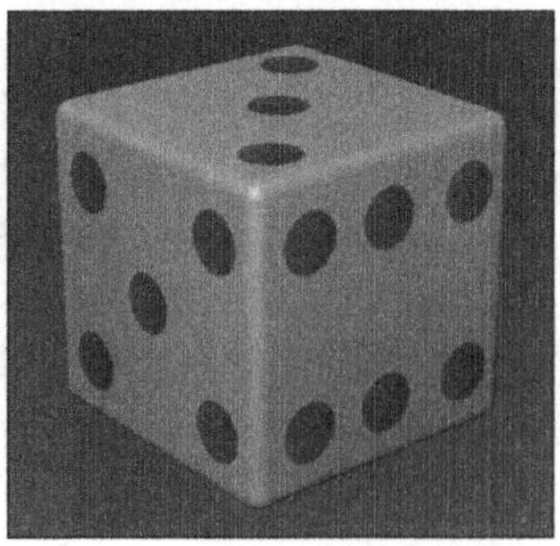

2. Next , you will go to **File** | **Import...** and select the same `dice.mud` file that you just opened.
3. You may notice that the die got brighter. That's because we imported a duplicate light along with our die. To delete the extra light, you can go into the **Object List** in the upper-right side of the Mudbox interface, and right-click on **Light01** and click on **Delete Light**.
4. You may also notice that there seems to be only one die in the viewport. This is because the two dice are sitting right on top of each other. In order to move one of the dice we will need to select which die we would like to move. Go into the **Object List** in the upper-right side of the Mudbox interface and select either **pCube3** or **pCube4**.

5. Now, go into the **Select/Move Tools** menu, in the bottom-left side of the Mudbox 2013 interface, and select the **Translate** tool.
6. You should be able to see a gizmo with an arrow for each axis. Grab the blue arrow (*Z* axis) and drag the die next to its partner.
7. Next we're going to rotate the die using the **Rotate** tool under the **Select/Move Tools** menu. Instead of using the gizmo to rotate the dice, we will go to the **Rotate Properties**, on the right-hand side of the Mudbox interface, and manually type in our rotation. The properties for the rotate tool should look like the following screenshot:

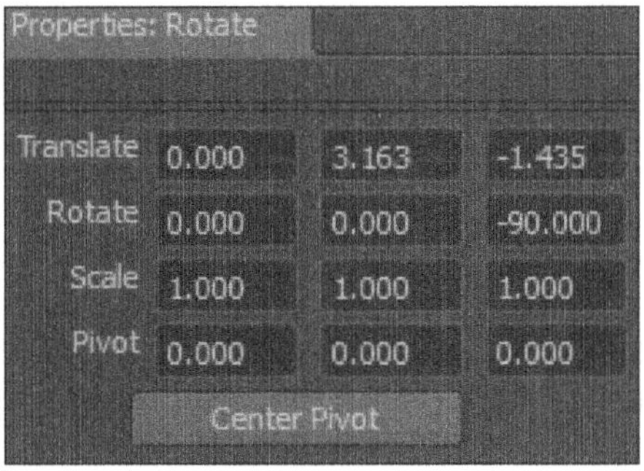

The three values next to **Rotate** stand for the degrees in *X*, the degrees in *Y*, and the degrees in *Z* in that order. So, to change which side of the die is facing you, you can type in any multiples of 90 for the *X*, *Y*, or *Z* values.

8. Now that the dice are showing different sides of each other we can use the rotation gizmo to give each die more of a natural rotation. How often do dice land exactly lined with each other? Actually often, considering their shape and how frequently the dice get rolled. But, it will still feel a little more real if your 3D objects are not lining up on a grid.

   After rotating and translating your dice into a position, you should be viewing something that looks like the following screenshot:

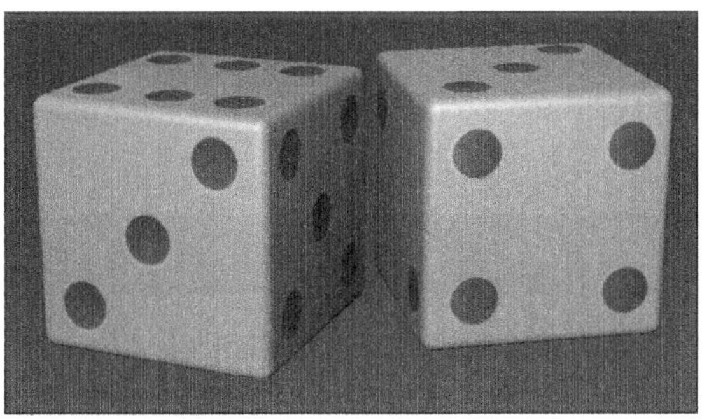

9. Next, you can paint some dirt on the dice. Take a look at *Chapter 4, Fine Tooth Comb* for a handful of good painting techniques if you need help laying down some dirt.

10. Now, that your dirt has been added you'll need to select the dice for exporting. To do this you will go back into the **Object List** and first select one die and then *Ctrl* + click the other die. Both of your dice should be showing up yellow in the viewport, as shown in the following screenshot:

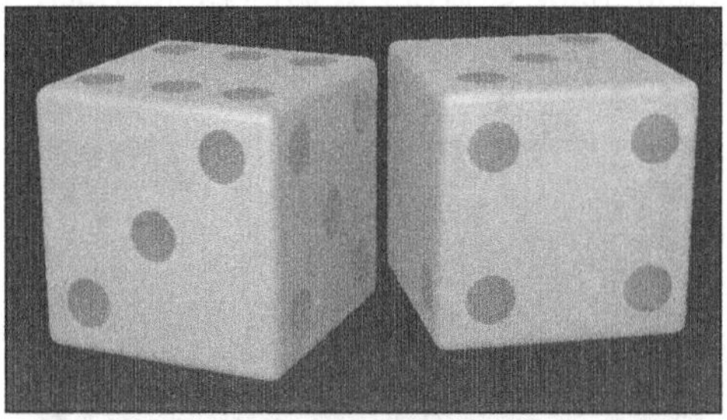

11. The last step is to go to **File** | **Export Selection** and save your file in a `.fbx` format. This will ensure that the textures will be exported along with the model. The following screenshot from Maya shows the dice after importing the `.fbx` file that was saved in Mudbox:

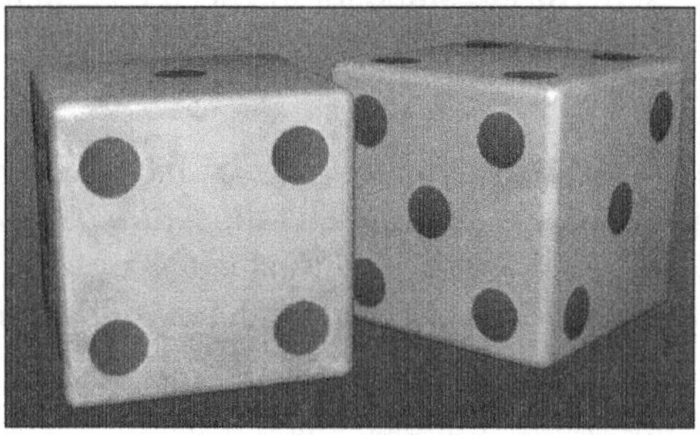

Once you go through the process once or twice, you'll start to realize how easy it is to go from one piece of software to the next. Take note that you can duplicate your object, instead of reimporting the object, if you do not need to bring a new object into the scene. If you would like to duplicate your object all you need to do is right-click on the object in your viewport and choose **Duplicate Object** from the right-click menu.

Creating a terrain

This recipe will cover how to quickly create a large area of terrain using displacement maps.

How to do it...

The following steps will help you to successfully create a terrain:

1. The first thing you will need to do is create an appropriate displacement map using Photoshop or another software package. I created this displacement map using **Filter** | **Render** | **Clouds** in Photoshop and multiplied a **Filter** | **Sketch** | **Stamp** version of the clouds render on top of it for the higher raised areas. This is shown in the following screenshot:

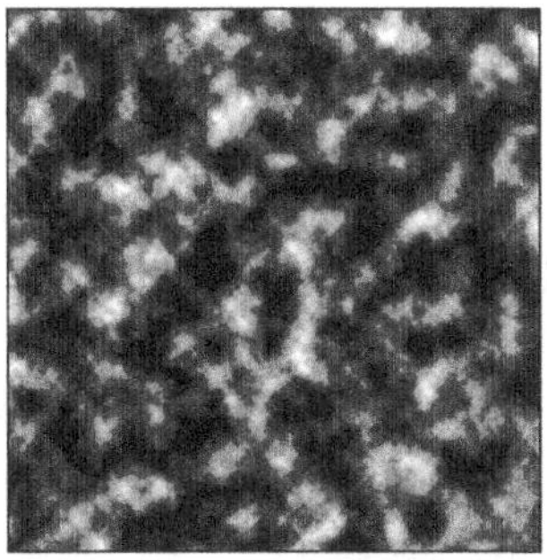

2. Once you have a displacement map you are happy with, you can go into the top menu of Mudbox and explore the **Maps** drop-down menu. Here you will mouse over **Sculpt Model Using Displacement Map** and find **New Operation...**. Click on this for further options.

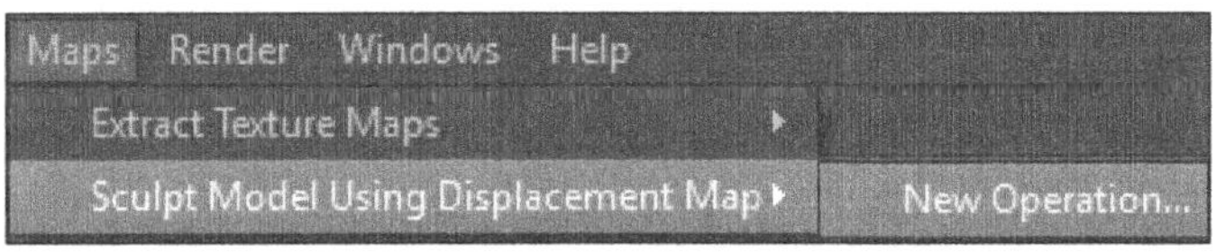

3. Now you will see this menu, where you will choose a **Target Mesh** for the displacement map to be applied to, as shown in the following screenshot:

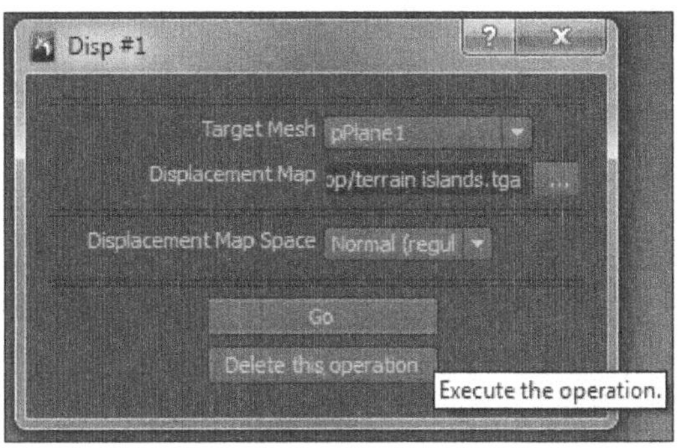

4. The next option is where you will set your displacement map file by clicking on the **...** button and browsing to your displacement map file.
5. **Displacement Map Space** can be left set as **Normal** and now all you need to do is click on **Go** to execute the operation.
6. Now a new sculpt layer will be created on your object so that you may adjust the intensity of your newly displaced mesh. This is shown in the following screenshot:

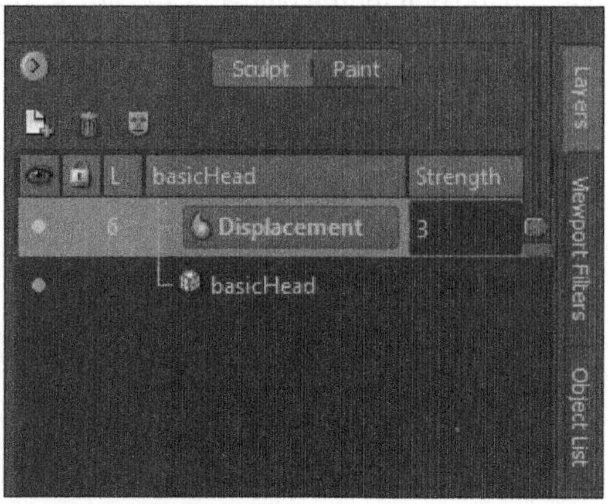

7. The following screenshot shows the sculpt that this displacement map produced:

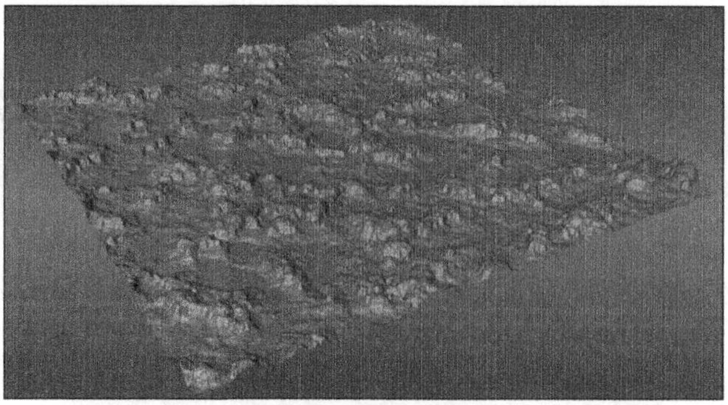

How it works...

Displacement maps use values of an image to determine the height of geometry where pure white is the highest point and pure black recedes the furthest.

See also

- The *Blocking out a rough Mayan pyramid using a displacement map* recipe

6
Shine On

In this chapter, we will cover:

- Creating a Blinn material
- Using a simple Blinn material
- Using Lit Sphere as a reflective material
- Creating a gold bar
- Creating a glass sculpture

Introduction

This chapter will cover various ways to customize materials within Mudbox 2013. It will go over the basics of creating a material in Mudbox as well as creating some more advanced materials using the reflection and specular channels. With the knowledge gained from this chapter you will be able to create believable materials to bring more realism into your sculpts.

Creating a Blinn material

This recipe will show you how to create a new material. This allows the personalization of the visual look that a model will attain by interacting with lights and texture maps.

How to do it...

The following steps will help you to create a new Blinn material:

1. To create a material for your model, click on **Create** in the top menu bar, hover over **Materials** and select **Simple Blinn Material**.

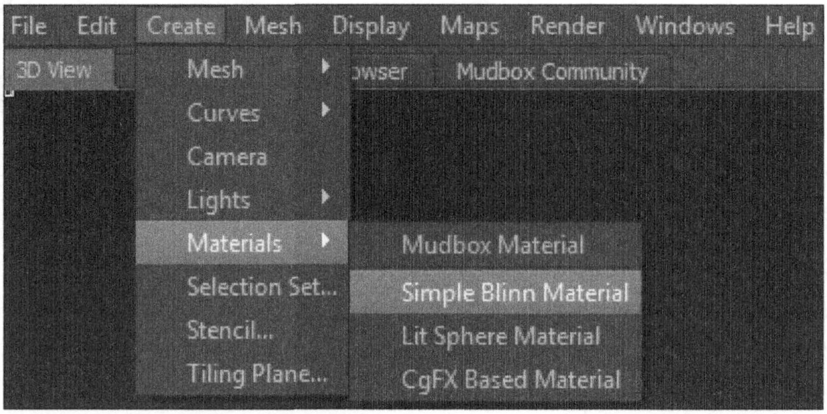

2. The options such as **Diffuse**, **Specular**, **Ambient**, and **Shininess** will appear in a prompt after your selection. Additionally, **Object List** will display your new material as **Material**. You can rename your material by right-clicking the material in the **Object List**.

   You can utilize these options to change how your object reacts to light. The following screenshot shows the different options:

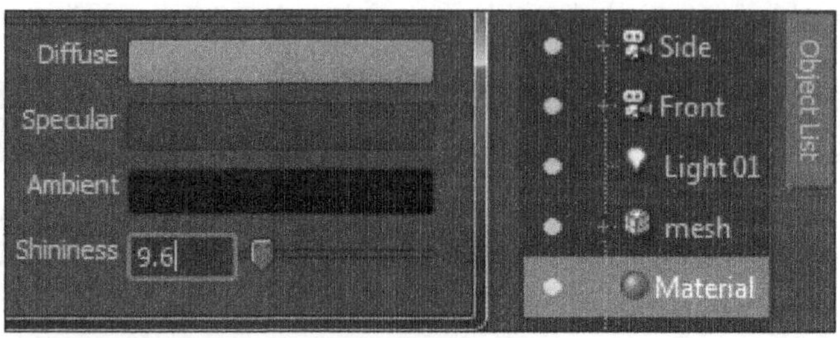

- The **Diffuse** color is the reflected light that bounces in all directions off the surface of your object. This is the color that we would define objects with.
- The **Specular** color is what you might call a *highlight*. These are rays of light that bounce off the surface in only one direction. This is an attribute that is most apparent in shiny objects.

- The **Ambient** color is the color of the shadow areas in your model. The colors that usually make up this area come from bounced light. Ambient light does not come from a direct light source.
- The **Shininess** slider refers to the size of the specular highlight on your object.

See also

- The *Using a simple Blinn material* recipe

Using a simple Blinn material

This recipe will show you how to customize the simple Blinn material to achieve different looks.

How to do it...

The following steps will help you to customize the simple Blinn material:

1. Once you have a simple Blinn material created, you will want to apply it to your model by right-clicking on your model, selecting **Assign Existing Material**, and then clicking on **Material**.

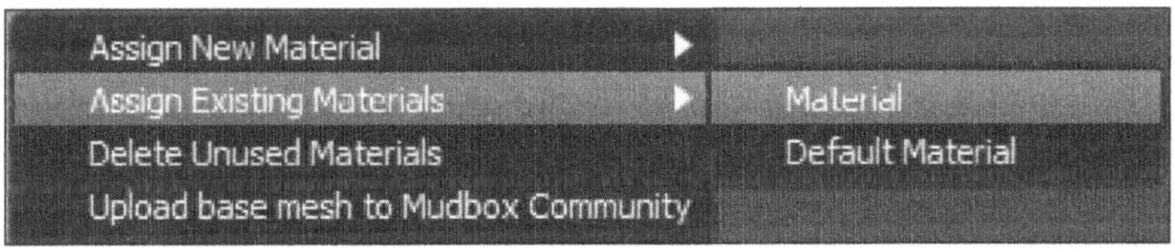

2. Under the **Properties** tab you will see the color options for **Diffuse**, **Specular**, **Ambient**, and **Shininess**.

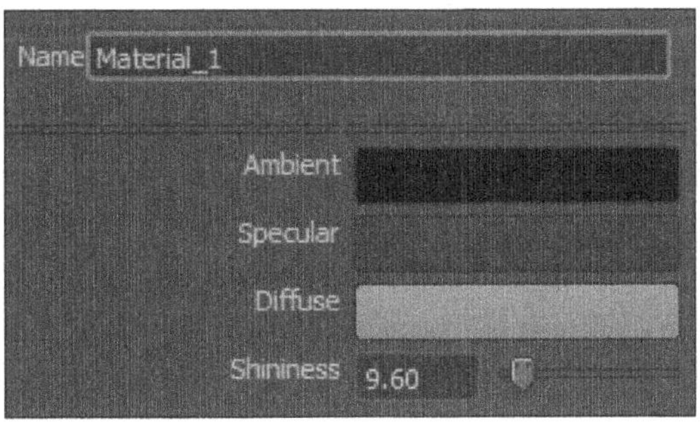

- **Diffuse**: This specifies the base color of the material which in essence is a combination of the colors that bounce in all directions off the surface of an object. The colors that are absorbed by the object are not seen by the human eye.
- **Specular**: This specifies the color of the specular highlight on the material.

  Non-metallic objects, such as skin, should be given a hue that is the opposite of the diffuse color so that the highlight will show white. The reason for doing this is because, in RGB, grays and whites have all colors in them and when you add these to your diffuse color, you will get a slightly metallic look. By using the inverse color you will neutralize the diffuse color so your highlight will stay white.

  Metallic objects, such as gold, will include some of the bounced light from the diffuse color. For this reason you will want your specular colors to be similar to those of your diffuse colors. You can adjust this slightly for different types of metals but for the most part you will want a similar hue.
- **Ambient**: This specifies the color of light that comes from the environment around an object and is usually known as the shadow area of your material.

  Ambient light can be described as any light rays that have bounced off from multiple surfaces. For example, light that has reflected off from the atmosphere, or sky, may provide a blue color when it hits the shadowy area of a tree. These light rays will have reflected off from the moisture in the air and then off the bark of the tree before it meets your eyes.
- **Shininess**: This specifies the size of the specular highlight. The higher the value, the more acute the highlight. The lower the value, the wider the highlight.

  This attribute determines how flat a surface is compared to the light rays' wavelength. The more flat a surface is, the more specular will show while the more rough a surface is on a light wave scale, the more the specular will scatter and become a part of the diffuse color. This option allows the artist to fine-tune the falloff of a highlight for more accurate representations of different materials.

3. Choosing the correct colors for the bounced light coming off your model is essential to make your sculpts believable. Begin with choosing the diffuse color of your object.
4. Next, adjust the specular using the guidelines previously mentioned. When using images in your specular channel, you are able to add things, such as smudges and dirt by paint in different values and colors for different locations on your model.

5. The next thing you will want to adjust is the ambient light. If your model is set outside on a sunny day you may want to add a little bit of blue to the ambient color. This will represent the bounced light from the blue sky. If it is dusk or dawn, you may want to add a pink, orange, red, or purple tint for the bounced light.
6. Finally, the shininess can be adjusted for a more intense light source or just a larger light source that is creating larger highlights.

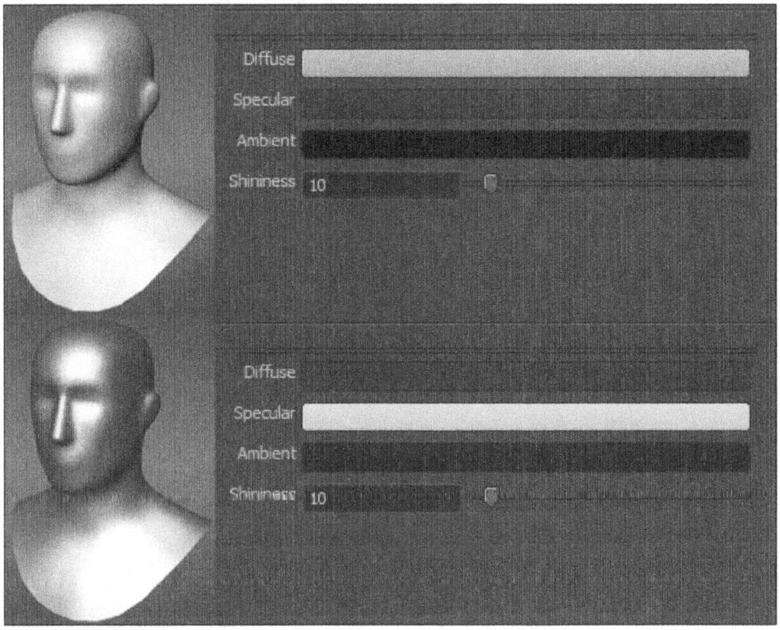

See also

- The *Creating a gold bar* recipe

Using Lit Sphere to mimic other materials

This recipe will show you how Lit Sphere materials can mimic materials from other 3D programs. Using this material you will be able to use materials from other software by rendering out a sphere and applying it to a Lit Sphere material in Mudbox. This material uses the shading information, within the rendered sphere, to determine the shading of the Lit Sphere material.

Getting ready

The following steps will help you get ready to be able to use Lit Sphere materials:

1. First you will need to render a sphere with the material of your choice from another 3D program as shown in the following screenshot:

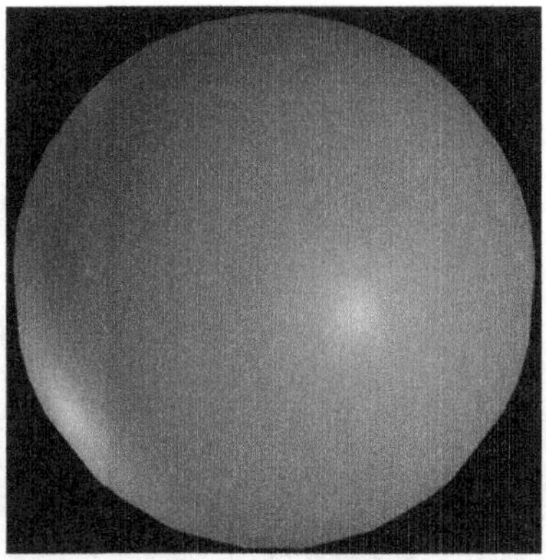

2. Next, you should extend the color on the edges of the sphere out to the edges of the texture and save it. I've added some color to the light sources of this texture so that you can easily see what is going on.

3. Now that the texture is created, we can start building our material.

How to do it...

The following steps will help you to mimic other materials using Lit Sphere:

1. Right-click on your model, select **Assign New Material**, and click on **Lit Sphere Material**.

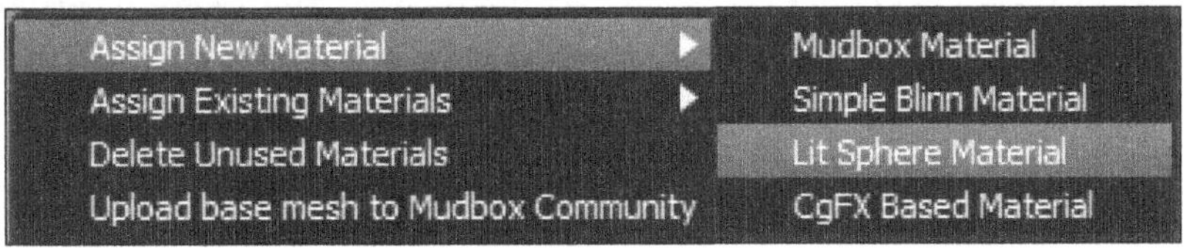

2. Now you will browse for the texture through the **Lit Sphere** attribute.

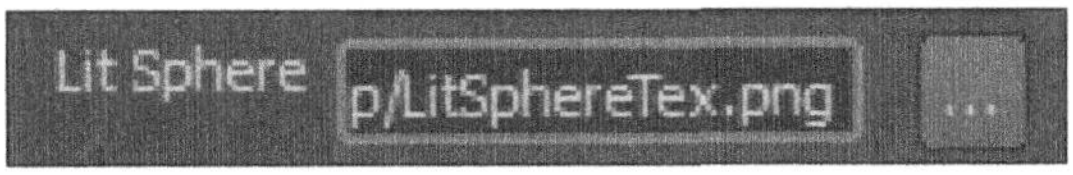

3. Now that your material is ready you can throw it onto one of your models or one of Mudbox's default models. In this case, I used Mudbox's default torso.

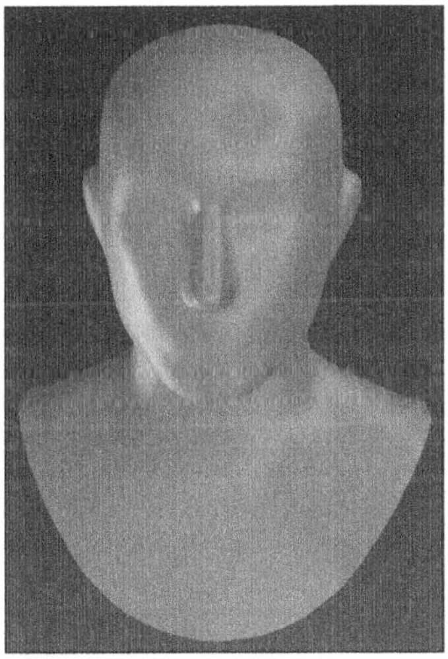

If you look closely you will notice how the lighting corresponds with the location of the colors within the texture.

4. This material allows your object to react to the perceived lighting information offered by the Lit Sphere image.

See also

- The *Creating a gold bar* recipe
- The *Creating a glass sculpture* recipe

Creating a gold bar

This recipe will show you a fast way to utilize the Mudbox material to make a gold material on a gold bar.

Getting ready

First you will need to import the gold bar model that is included in the code files of this book. The file is named `Gold_Bar.obj` and should be imported into a new Mudbox scene.

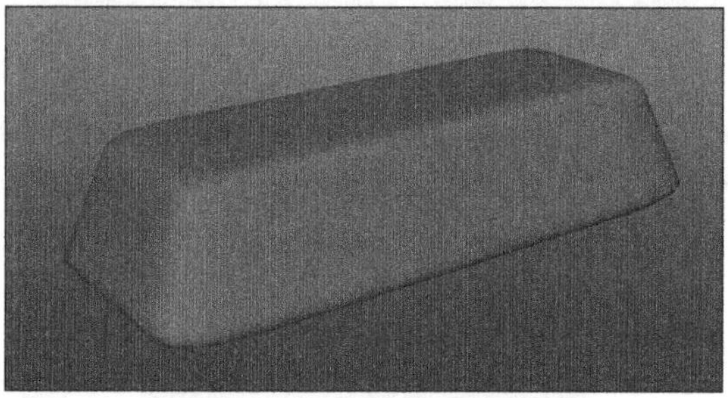

How to do it...

The following steps will help you create a gold bar:

1. We will start by adding a new material. Right-click on your model, select **Assign New Material**, and click on **Lit Sphere Material**.
2. Apply a new shader to the gold bar by right-clicking over the object, hovering over **Assign New Material**, and then clicking **Mudbox Material**.

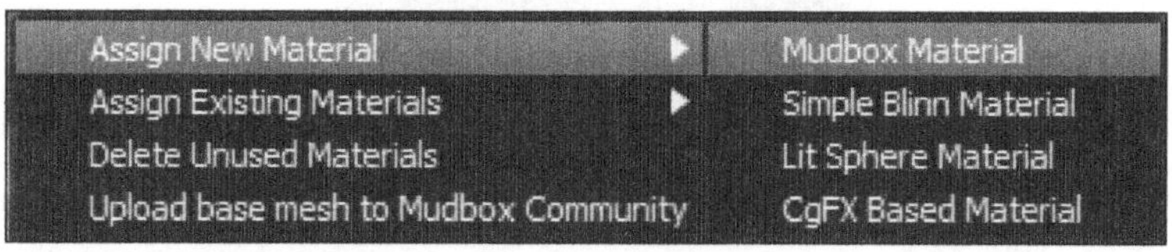

3. A series of options will come up to customize the look of the shader. Experiment with these options to achieve the gold look you desire.

4. Set the RGB values for **Diffuse** to `128, 100, 0`.
5. Set the RGB values for **Specular** to `180, 130, 0`.
6. Set the RGB values for **Gloss** to `30, 30, 30`.
7. Import a reflection map, an image of your choice, to allow interesting reflections in the shader.

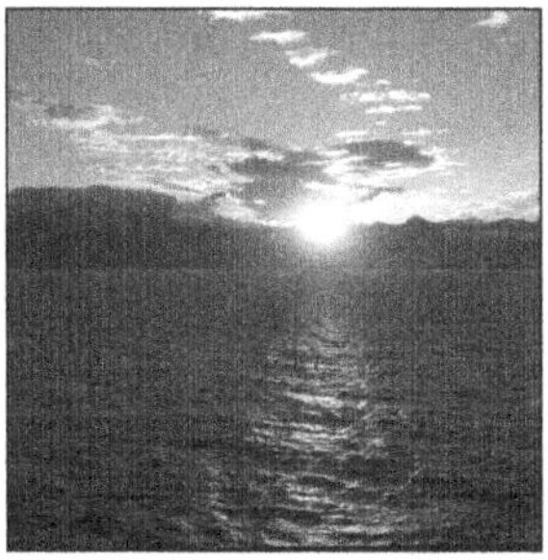

8. Set the RGB values for **Reflection Strength** to `0.5` for a solid visibility of reflection.
9. For added vibrancy set the **Fresnel Scattering Strength** to `0.75` and **Fresnel Refractive Index** to `1.5`.

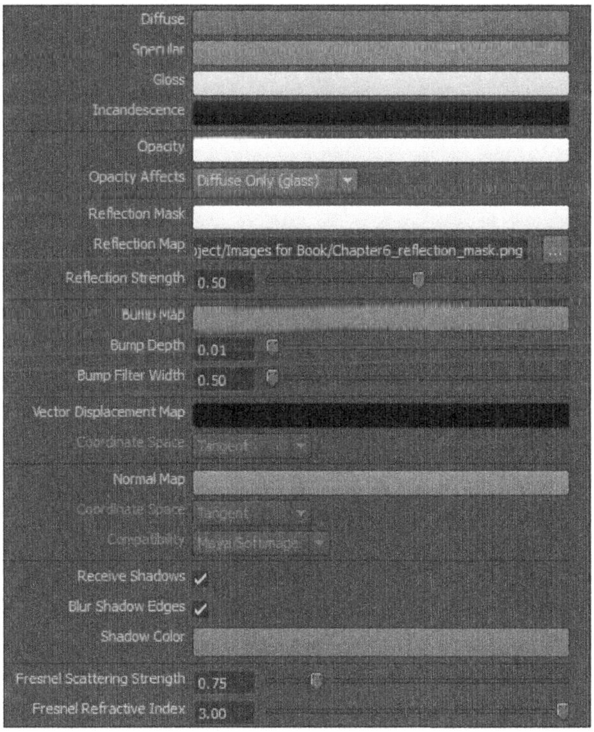

10. This will result in a shiny gold material.

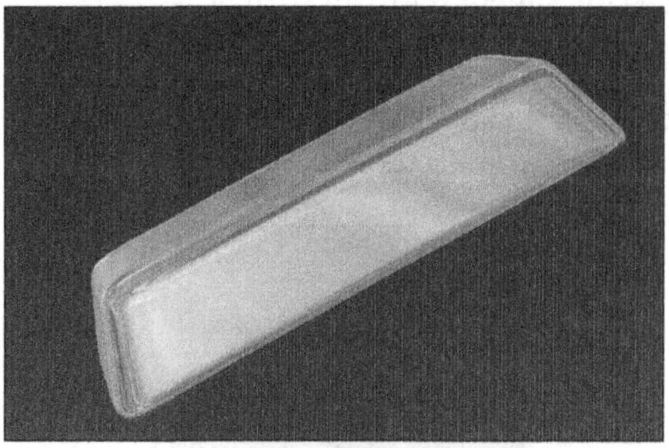

11. For added effect, try applying a **Bump Layer** by right-clicking in the **Layers Paint** tab and selecting **New Layer**, as shown in the following screenshot:

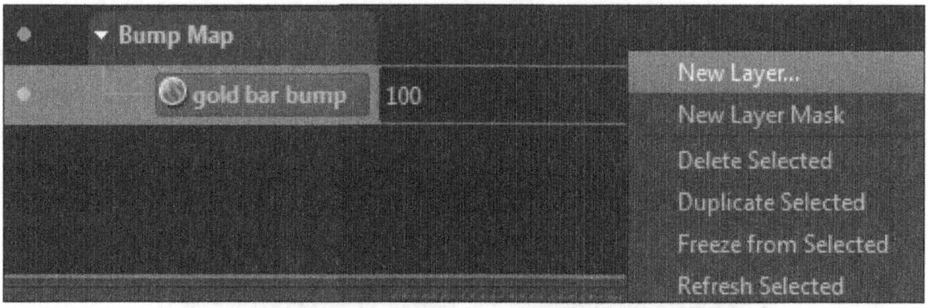

12. Set the **Size** to **2048**, **Save As** file type to **Photoshop [8 bit, RGBA]**, and **Channel** to **Bump Map**.

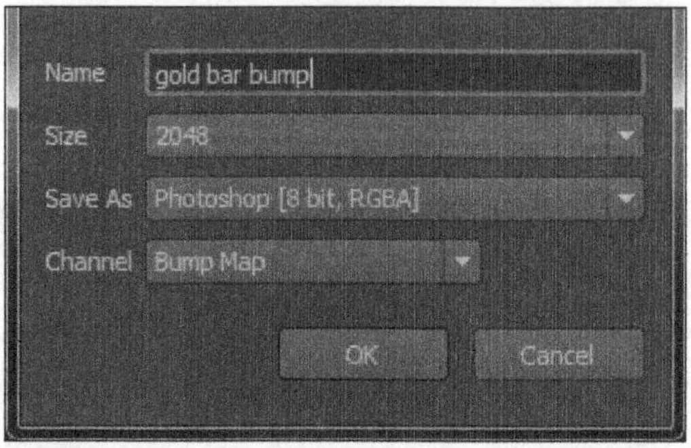

13. Select **Projection** under the **Paint Tools** tab and choose a black and white image under the **Stencil** Tab.

14. Your stencil will be superimposed over the model in the viewport. Stroke the brush over the object and create the desired bump effect you desire.

15. Set the **Bump Depth** to **0.01** and **Bump Filter** width to **1.00** for a subtle bump appearance.

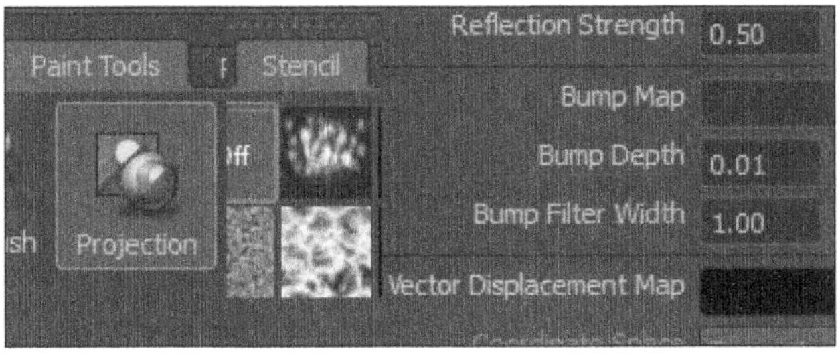

You will see the projection as shown in the following screenshot:

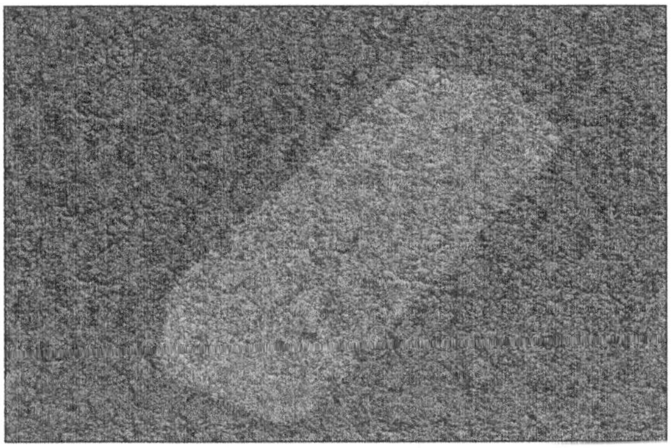

16. This will result in a vibrant gold shader.

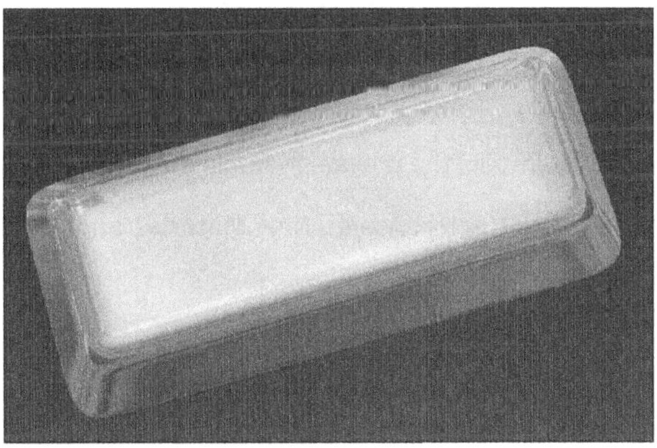

Creating a glass sculpture

This recipe will show you a fast way to utilize the Mudbox material to make a glass shader. This will be demonstrated using a model of a glass sculpture with a complex shape.

Getting ready

First you will need to import the `Glass_Sculpture.obj` file, which is included in the code files of this book.

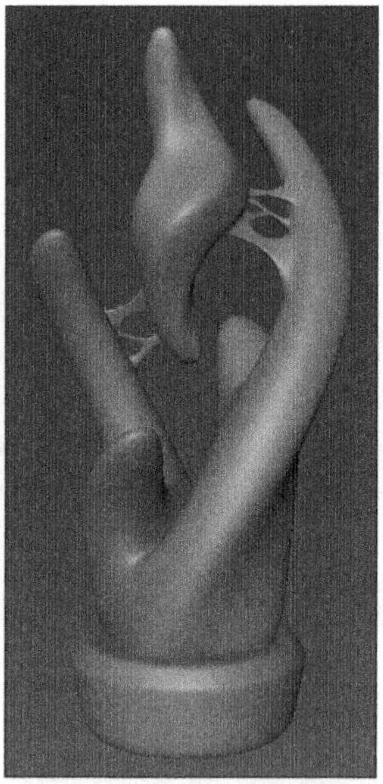

How to do it...

The following steps will help to model the previously depicted sculpture into a glass sculpture:

1. Right-click on your model, select **Assign New Material**, and click on **Mudbox Material**.

2. Apply a new shader to the glass sculpture by right-clicking over the object, hovering over **Assign New Material**, and then clicking **Mudbox Material**.

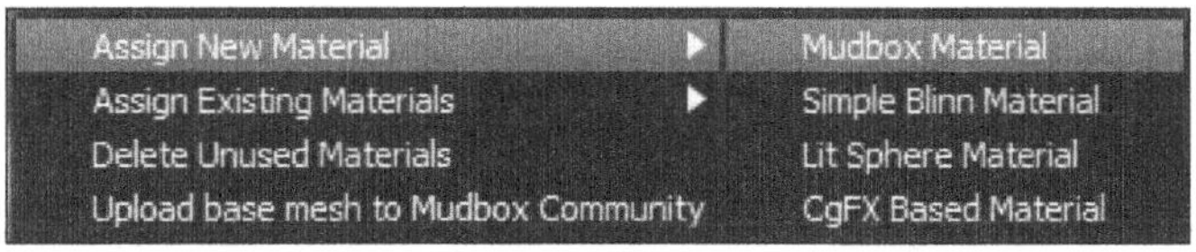

3. A series of options will come up, as shown in the following screenshot, to customize the look of the shader. Experiment with these options to achieve the gold look you desire.
4. Set the **RGB** values for **Diffuse** to `40`, `40`, `40`. Before setting these values you will need to change the **Range:** drop-down menu to **0 to 255** as shown in the following screenshot:

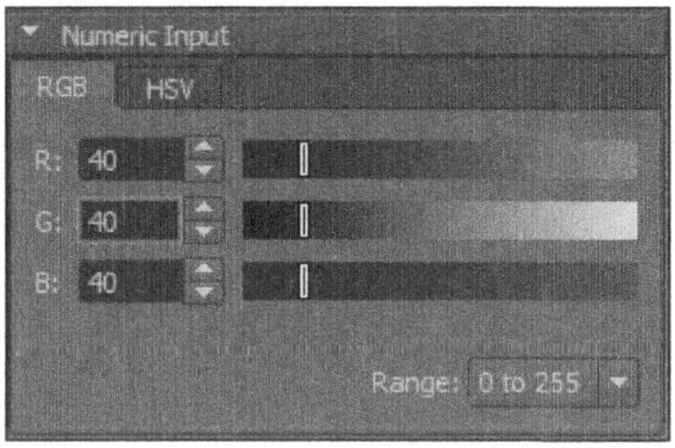

5. Set the **RGB** values for **Specular** to `255`, `255`, `255`. This determines the color and strength of your highlights.
6. Set the **RGB** values for **Gloss** to `255`, `255`, `255`. This setting determines how sharp or diffused the highlight is.
7. Now change the **RGB** values for the **Opacity** to `50`, `50`, `50` for a semi-transparent look.
8. Import a reflection map and an image of your choice to allow interesting reflections in the shader.
9. Set the **RGB** values for **Reflection Strength** to `0.5` or slightly higher for a solid visibility of reflection.

10. For added vibrancy set the **Fresnel Scattering Strength** to `1.19` and **Fresnel Refractive Index** to `1.76`.

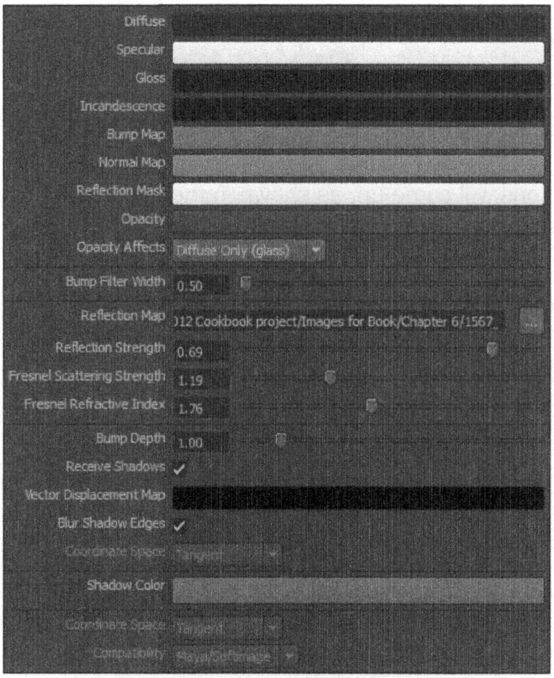

11. This will result in a transparent and shiny glass material.

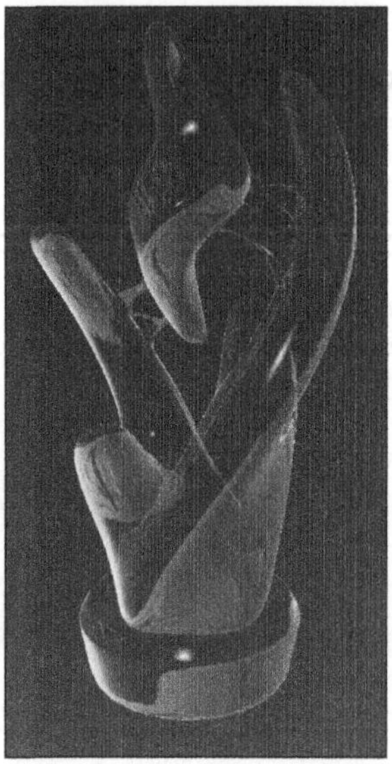

7

Time to Paint

In this chapter, we will cover:

- Painting a rock texture using projections
- Painting out seams on a rock using the Clone brush
- Painting a rock Specular map
- Painting a rock Bump map
- Adding text to a cape using Flatten UV mode
- Adding dirt to a cape using a layer as a mask

Introduction

This chapter will cover proper practices to aid in mesh painting within Mudbox 2012. You will learn how to create a variety of texture maps that can be used to add details that react in similar ways to the real world. This results in textures that look more realistic and interesting to look at. You will also learn tools such as the layer mask, which will give you more control over your layers and textures.

Painting a rock texture using projections

This recipe will show you how to paint an image projection onto your model. This is a very useful tool that is revolutionary in the way artists can apply their textures to their models. By using this technique you can add complex details in a fraction of the time by using an image to apply details in a single stroke, directly onto your model.

Getting ready

Once you have created or imported a model into Mudbox, you will be ready to project an image onto it.

Make sure that your model is UV mapped to allow the use of texture maps as you develop your model.

How to do it...

1. First apply a new material by right-clicking on the object and assigning a new material.

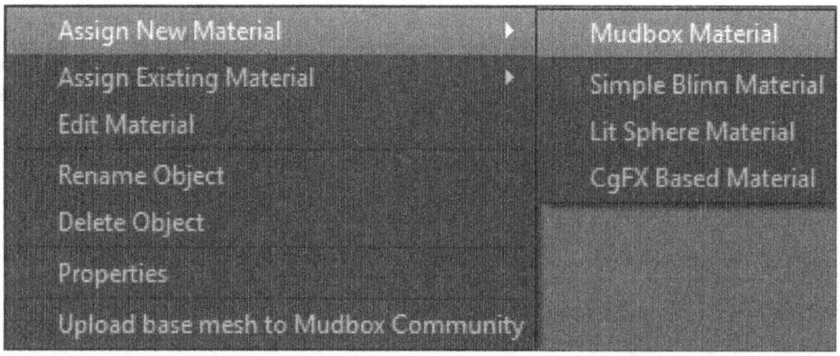

2. Then, click on the **Paint** button under the **Layers** tab and right-click to select **New Layer**. The **Create New Paint Layer** options will offer options to customize the name, size, format, and texture channel of the new layer. Select the **Diffuse** channel to start with, as shown in the following screenshot:

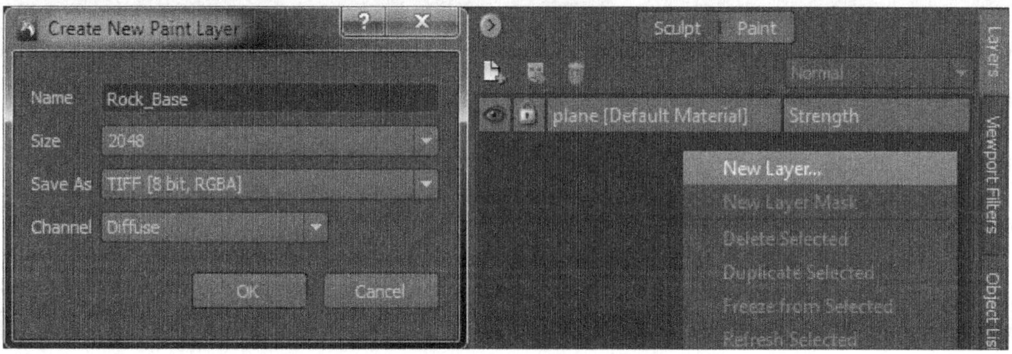

3. Click on the **Paint Tools** tab, on the bottom left side of the interface, and select the **Projection** brush.

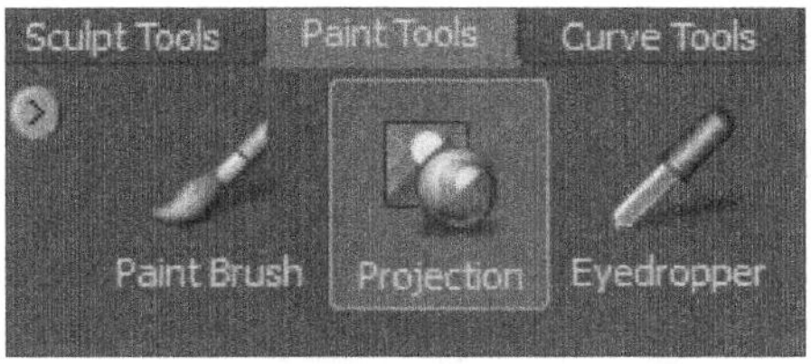

4. On the bottom right, go to the **Stencil** tab and click on the small arrow. Now go to **Add Stencil** (as shown in the following screenshot) and choose your rock texture.

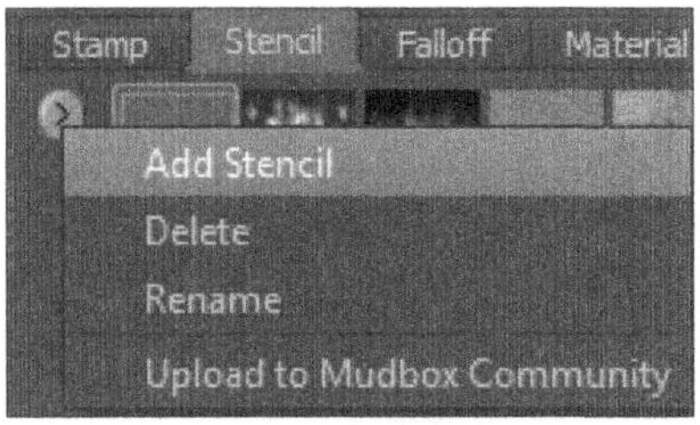

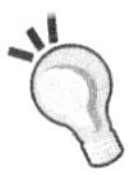

> If you do not want to create your own rock texture painted or photo sourced, then you can always grab one online. One place I sometimes go for textures is `www.cgtextures.com`. They have a wide variety of textures, both tileable and non-tileable. They also offer very high resolution textures for members.

5. The stencil will now be added to the list of thumbnails in the **Stencil** tab.
6. Once you choose the thumbnail of your stencil you will see a semitransparent overlay of your stencil in the viewport

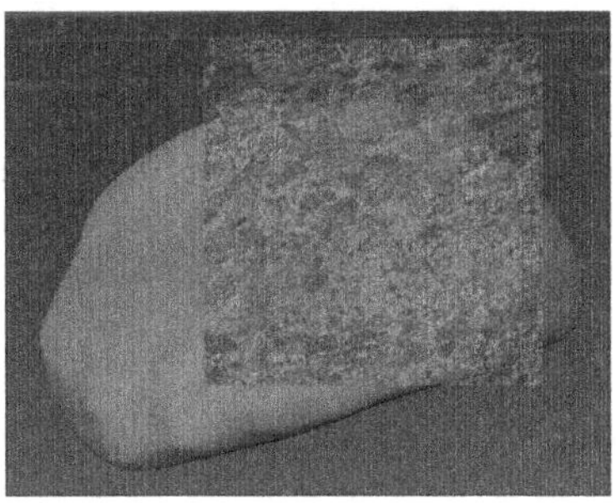

7. If you have a tiling image, you can turn on **Use Tiles**, found in the stencil's properties. The following screenshot shows the checkbox for **Use Tiles** and **Show Tiles** (mentioned in the next step):

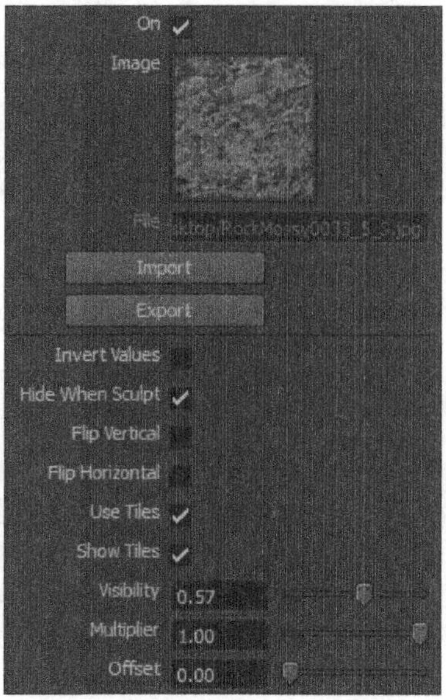

8. You can also turn on **Show Tiles** if you want to make the tiled images visible. Once this option is checked off your stencil should look like the following screenshot:

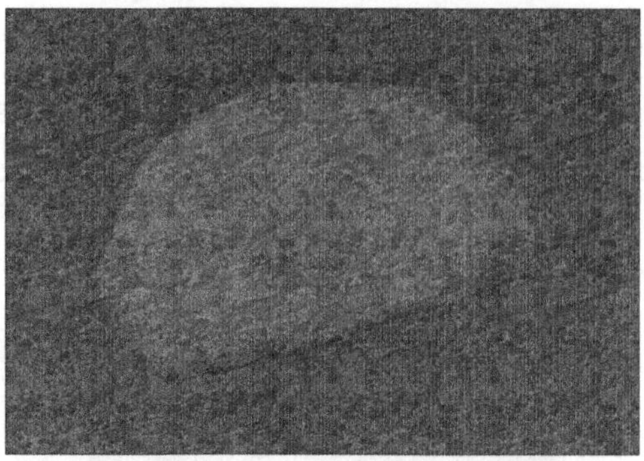

9. Once you have painted your rock using the stencil, you can set your viewport to **Flat Lighting**, to better see any stretching or seams that need to be painted over. This can easily be found in the right-click menu, or you can use the hotkeys, *Shift* + *L*. This will help you to see the diffuse texture without any highlights or shadows getting in your way. In the following screenshot you can see the flat lit version on the right and the default lighting (with specular turned down) on the left:

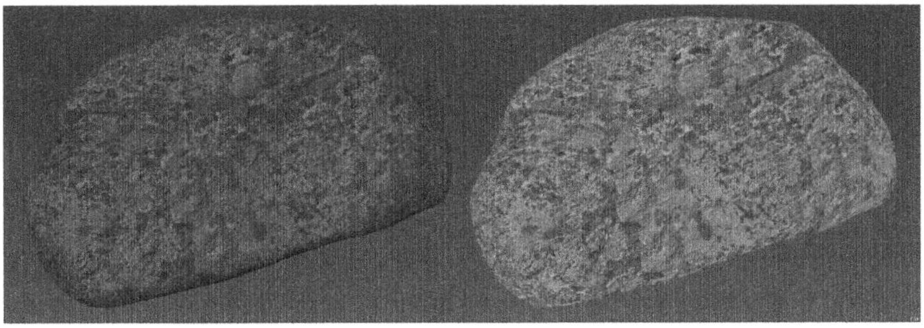

10. Now you can use other stencils or brushes to add any extra details to your rock.

How it works...

The **Projection** brush allows you to place a texture where you would like it, before actually applying it. This can be very helpful in adding details to your model.

Traditionally, you would have to paint your details in Photoshop, save your file, then go into your 3D software and see how the updated texture looks on your model. Sometimes it would take some tweaking to get the placement of the details correct. With this new method, you can add complex detail with one stroke, while eliminating the need to switch back and forth between your 2D and 3D software.

The following is a list of controls used for placing your stencil:

- Hold *S* + *left-click* + *drag* to rotate your image
- Hold *S* + *right-click* + *drag* to scale your stencil
- Hold *S* + *middle-click* + *drag* to move your stencil
- To hide the stencil you can hit the *Q* key

See also

- The *Painting out seams on a rock using the Clone brush* recipe

Painting out seams on a rock using the Clone brush

This recipe will show you how to paint out seams using the Clone brush. The Clone brush is a very powerful tool that can copy details from one part of the texture to another part in one stroke. This makes it very useful for getting rid of hard edges where your UV shells end.

Getting ready

If your imported model's texture has seams, this will show you how to easily rid yourself of them.

How to do it...

1. Select the **Clone** brush under the **Paint Tools** tab at the bottom left.

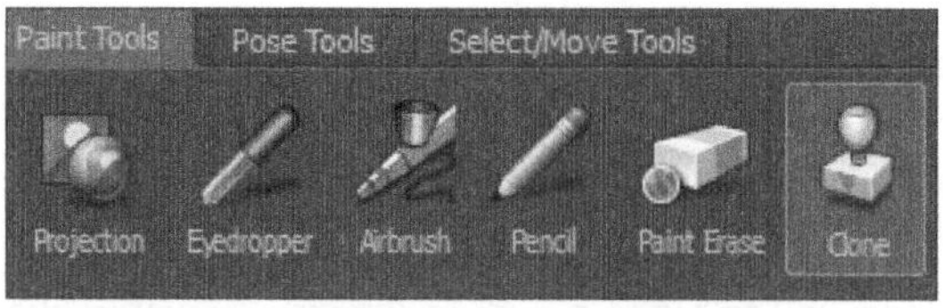

2. Now, *Ctrl* + *left-click* on your model to select the area your brush will clone from, as shown in the following screenshot:

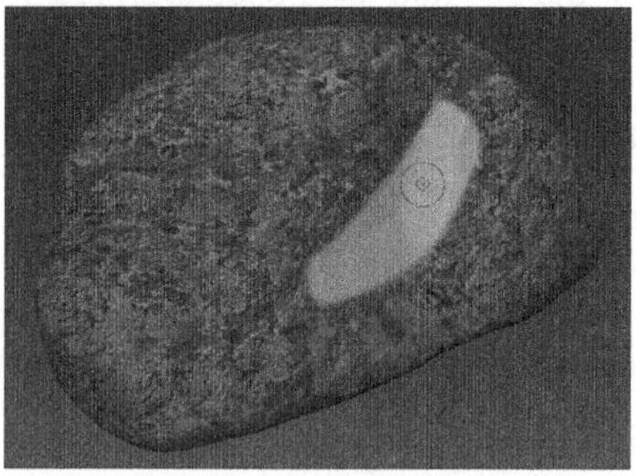

3. After selecting the area to clone from, start stroking the brush along the seam in your viewport and watch as the seam is easily reduced. The following is a screenshot showing the rock after the Clone brush was used to eliminate most of the green area:

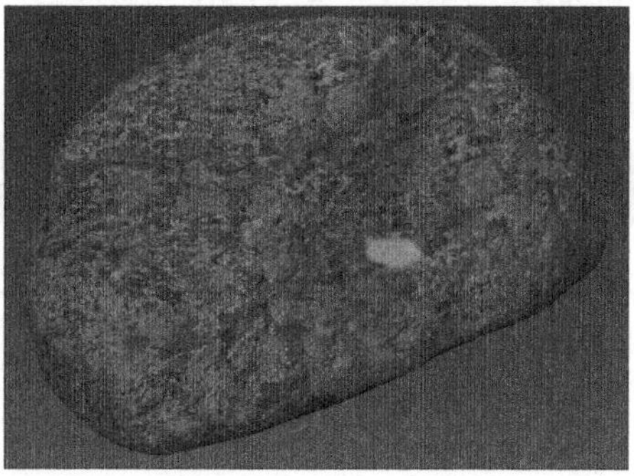

Painting a rock Specular map

This recipe will show you how to paint a rock Specular map onto your model. The Specular map plays a large part in how an object reacts to light, by controlling the highlights that are revealed when light hits the object. The type of object you are creating will guide you in how to handle the Specular map. For example, if you are creating a dielectric material (such as plastic, clay, and other nonelectric conductors), then your highlights will be a neutral value, lacking color. If you are creating a conductive material (such as bronze or other metals), then the specular highlight will be altered by the material.

Getting ready

We will start by importing the `Rock.obj` file present in the code files of this book.

If you are using a model of your own, then you need to make sure that your object is UV mapped, so that what you paint is not stretched or inconsistent with its resolution.

How to do it...

1. Click on the **Paint** button under the **Layers** tab, and right-click to select **New Layer**. The **Create New Paint Layer** option will offer options to customize. Next to **Channel**, choose **Specular**.

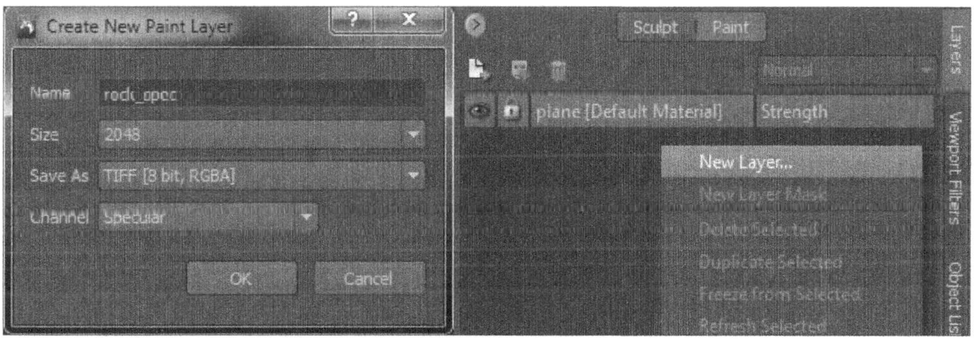

2. Click on the **Paint Tools** tab and select **Projection** at the bottom left of the screen. On the bottom right, click on the **Stencil** tab and import an image of your choice to project over the model. We will be using the next screenshot for this recipe. This stencil is one of the default stencils that come with Mudbox.

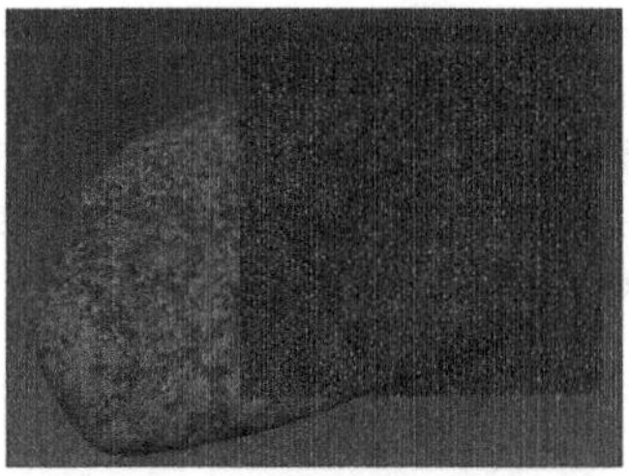

3. Make sure to paint over the model to see the projection work. This will cause different highlight values to appear on your model to further bring out the desired effect.

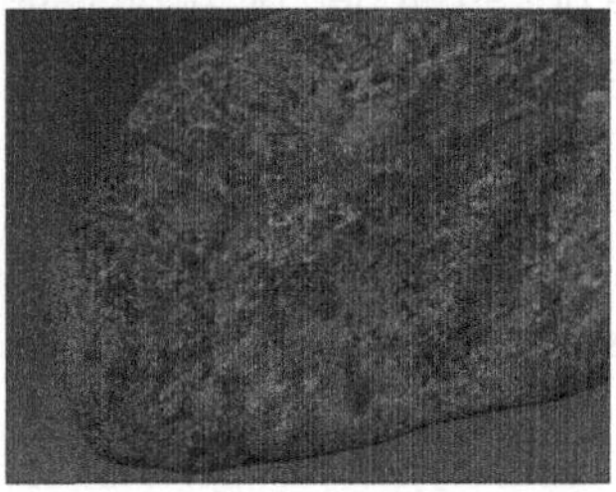

There's more...

The technique we just discussed is the most straightforward way to add specular with an image. Another helpful technique is to use the diffuse map that you have already created as a starting point for your Specular map. The following are the steps you will need to follow for this technique:

1. Make a duplicate of your diffuse texture in the **Layers** tab. The following screenshot is what you should see:

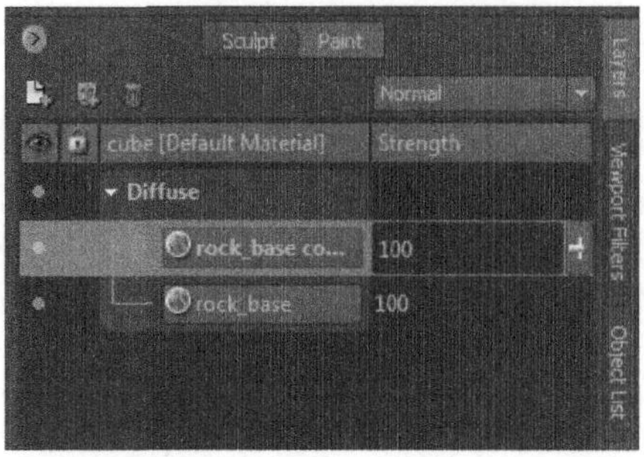

2. Now you can rename this layer as `rock_spec` so that it is easier to identify. Just double-click on the name of the layer and it should allow you to rename it.
3. The next step is the real trick. What we are going to do now is change the hue of this texture to its opposite hue, and then apply it as a specular layer. What this is going to do is neutralize the light as it hits the diffuse texture as well as keep the variations of value that you have established in your diffuse channel.
4. To adjust the hue of the copied layer, you can right-click on the copied layer and choose **Adjust Color** from the menu that pops up.
5. Now, you will adjust a few settings in the **Adjust Color** menu. First, choose the preset called **More Contrast** from the **Presets** drop-down menu. This will add some more variation to our specular highlights. Next, slide the **Hue** bar all the way to the right, or the left, so that the highlights will be neutralized. The diffuse color and the specular color will cancel each other out and produce a white highlight. Lastly, you will bring the **Value** down to about **-60** so our highlights are not too strong. The following screenshot is what you should see:

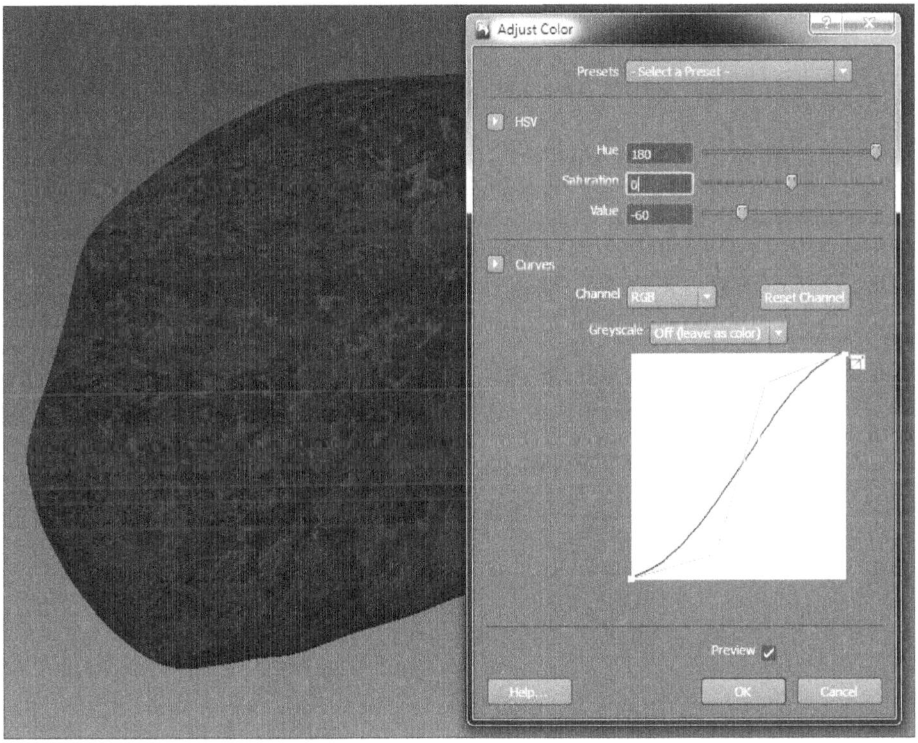

6. Now, you will create a new layer using the method learned earlier in this recipe. Make sure you set it as a specular channel. This layer can be used to add any hand-painted specular details after completing this technique.

7. Next, you will take the layer that we adjusted the colors of, and middle-mouse drag the layer into the **Specular** group, within your layers.

8. Now, you should have a specular that matches up with your diffuse texture. If the **Specular** is not strong enough, try duplicating the specular layer and setting its blend mode to **Screen**. This will lighten up the details in this layer. The following screenshot shows where the blend mode is located:

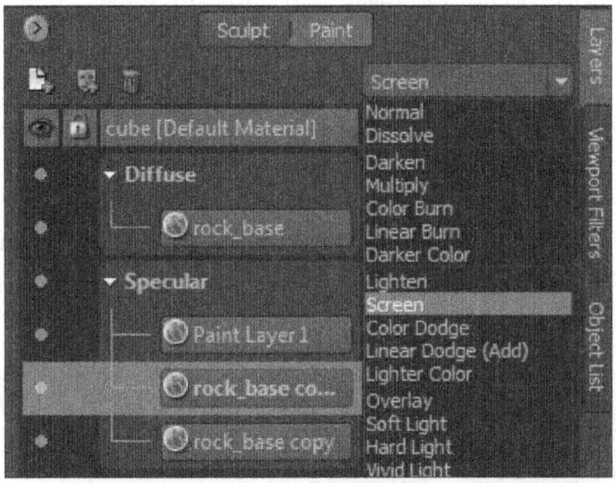

9. Now you can adjust the **Strength** slider on the **Screen** layer to fine-tune the intensity. You can also paint into another layer if you would like to add any details to your specular channel, such as wet spots or any other adjustments needed, based on details that have been added to your rock texture. In the following screenshot you can see that the specular is causing details to "pop" with higher contrast as the light hits the surface fom certain angles:

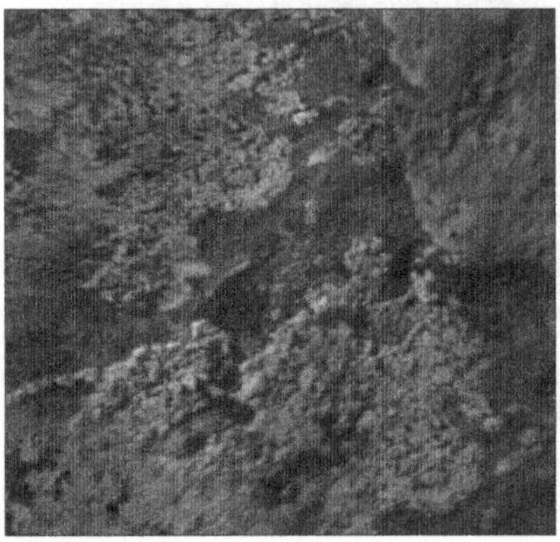

Painting a rock Bump map

This recipe will show you how to paint a Bump map onto your model. Bump maps can be used to create smaller details that don't call for a normal map. This type of map uses a black and white image where darker values represent surfaces that are farther away, and lighter values represent surfaces that are raised up, relative to the other values.

Getting ready

First off, you will want to import the `Rock.obj` file present in the code files of this book. This is the model that we will be using to demonstrate this technique. If you are planning on using your own model for this recipe, then make sure you have your UVs laid out nicely, or you may have stretching and/or resolution inconsistencies. Please note that I used the default Mudbox cube to create this rock, so the UVs are not the best on this model, but do the trick for our purposes.

How to do it...

1. Click on the **Paint** button under the **Layers** tab, and right-click to select **New Layer**. The **Create New Paint Layer** window will offer options to customize. Select the **Bump Map** channel.

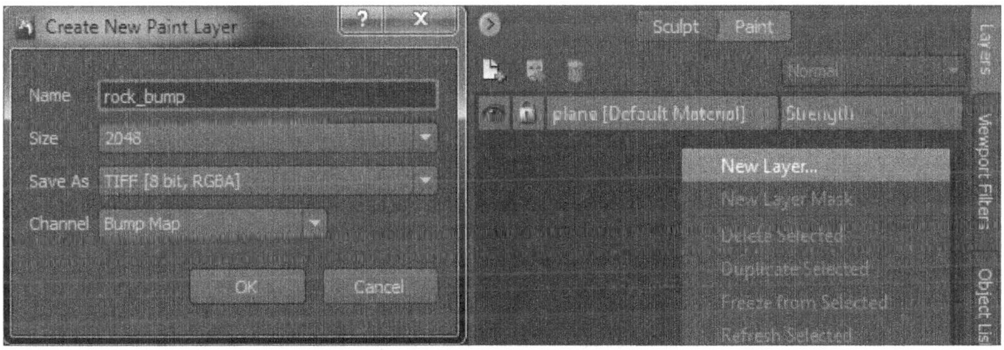

2. Click on the **Paint Tools** tab, and select **Paint Brush** at the bottom left of the screen. On the bottom right, choose **Stamp** or import an image of your choice to use as a stamp. The following `Bump Map.png` image is used for this recipe, which is present in the code files of this book:

3. Keep in mind that when you create a bump layer, in Mudbox, the layer is filled with black. This will not be obvious since there are no color indications, nor details, to inform you of this.

   This just means that, when you begin painting on your bump layer, you will need to consider the value of your brush. If you want very intense contrast on the details you are painting, then you will be using values close to white. If you would like to paint subtle details as we will be doing with this rock, then you will set your brush's value to something a lot closer to black.

   So, with that in mind, you should set your brush to dark gray and randomize your stamp. The following screenshot shows the settings that were used for this rock:

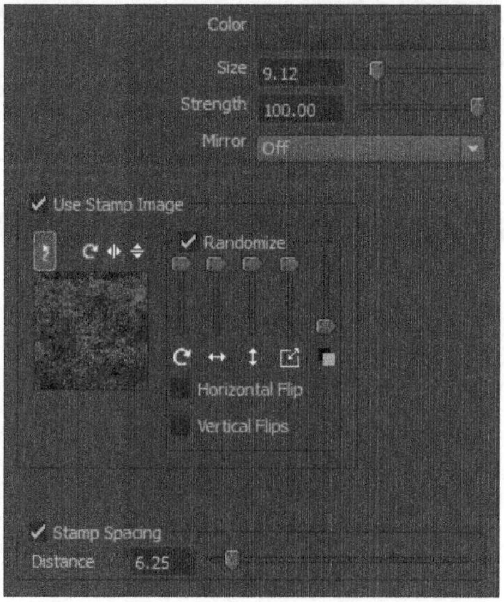

4. The last step is to paint your rock! In the following image, I added a touch of specular to the material, so that you can see the details a little better. The details that you put into this layer will react to the light, similar to a normal map.

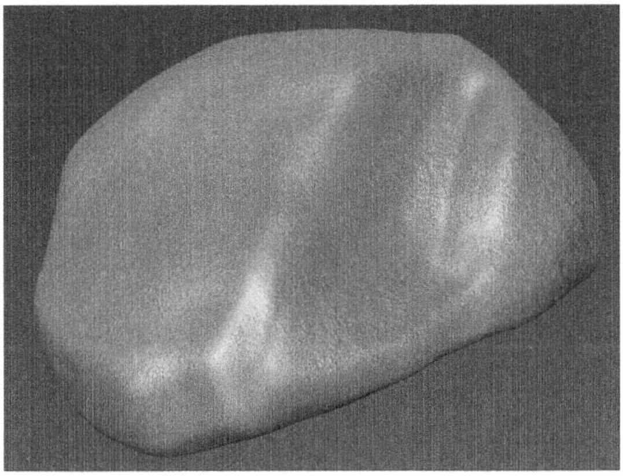

How it works...

Wherever you paint white it will give the appearance of a raised surface. Any area that is closer to black starts to recede. So if you were to start with a 50 percent gray image and then paint a white area and a black area, you would notice that the light is reacting as if there is detail there. In the following image you will see the sculpt on the left and the values painted on the right:

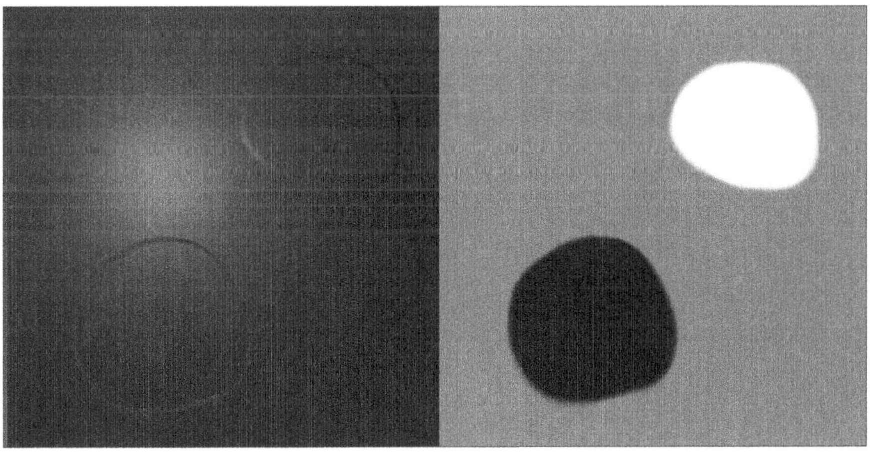

If you were to rotate the sculpt, you would notice that there is no depth in the geometry of the object.

Adding text to a cape using Flatten UV mode

This recipe will show you how to project an image onto a model in Flatten UV mode.

Getting ready

Once you have created or imported a UV mapped model into Mudbox (as shown in the next screenshot), you will be ready to project an image onto it.

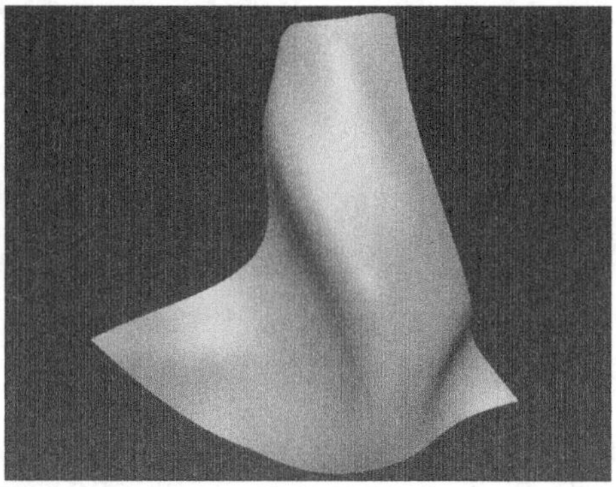

How to do it...

1. Apply a new material by right-clicking on the cape and assigning a new material.

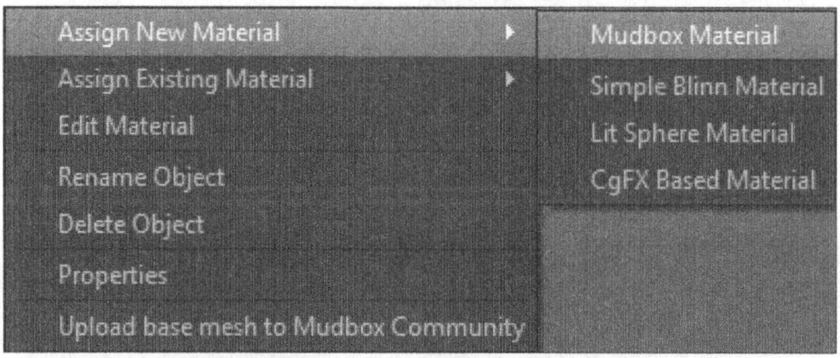

2. Create a new **Diffuse** layer in **Paint** under the **Layers** tab. This will be the base texture for projecting the text onto your cape.

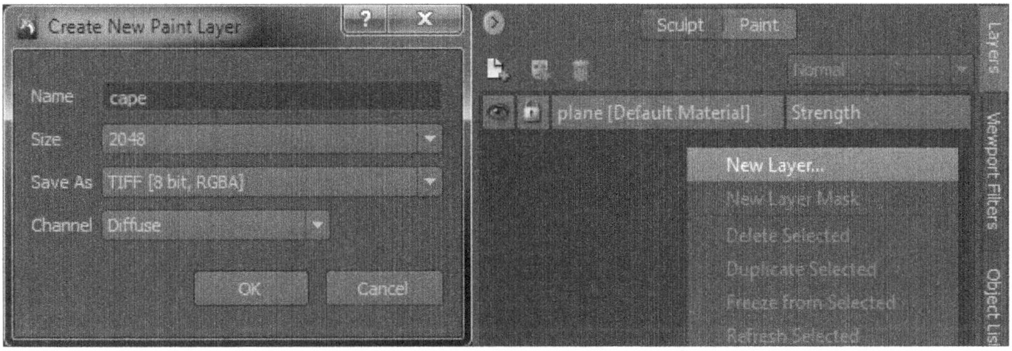

3. Select **Flatten to UV Space** under the **Mesh** tab, and your model will be temporarily flattened to its UVs. Now, you will be able to project an image onto the cape without it distorting as it would in the 3D view.

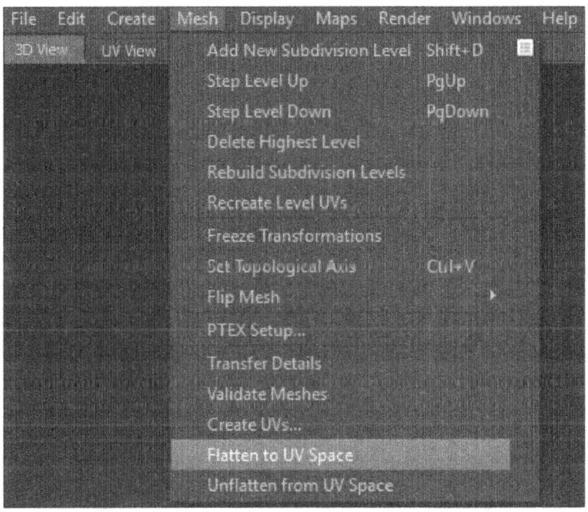

4. Click on the **Paint Tools** tab and select **Projection** at the bottom left of the screen. On the bottom right, click on the **Stencil** tab and import an image of your choice to project over the cape.

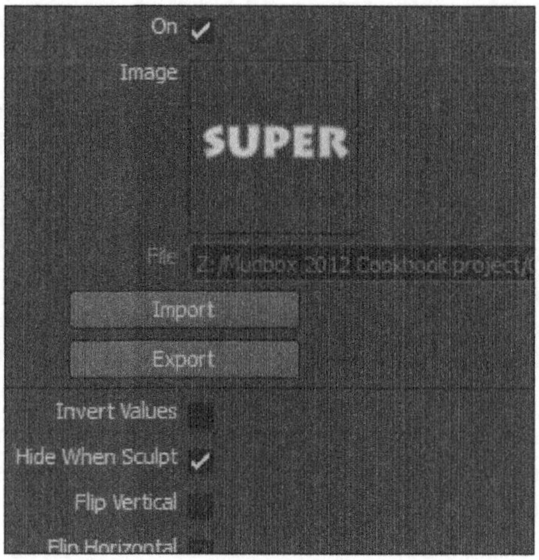

5. For text with transparency, consider creating an image in Photoshop and leaving the background empty to create an alpha.

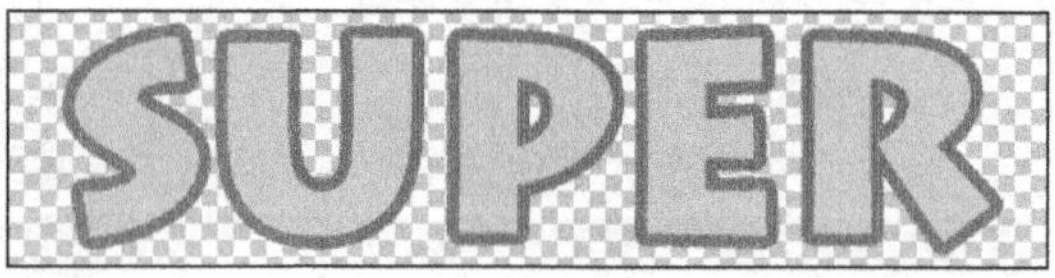

6. Position the text over the part of the cape in its UV space you wish to project it over. Stroke the brush over the text. Your image will project over the UVs without being distorted by the actual shape of the cape.

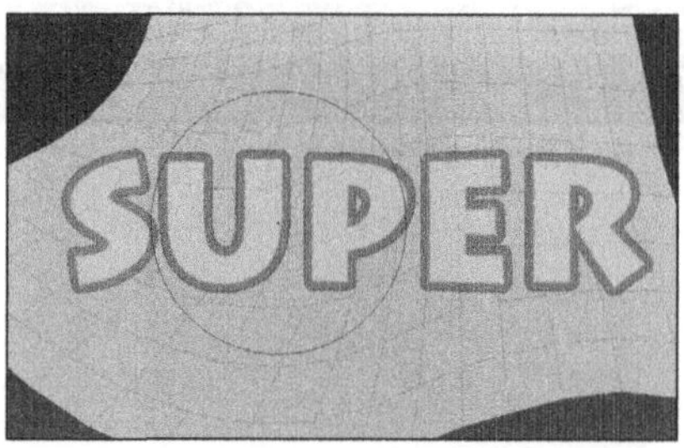

7. Select **Unflatten from UV Space** under the **Mesh** tab and your cape will be returned to its normal shape.

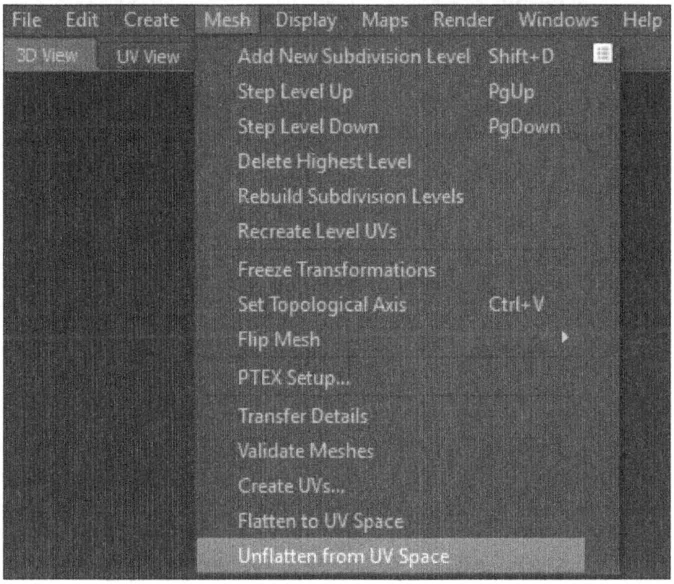

8. Now, you have the image or text you projected showing on the cape without distortion.

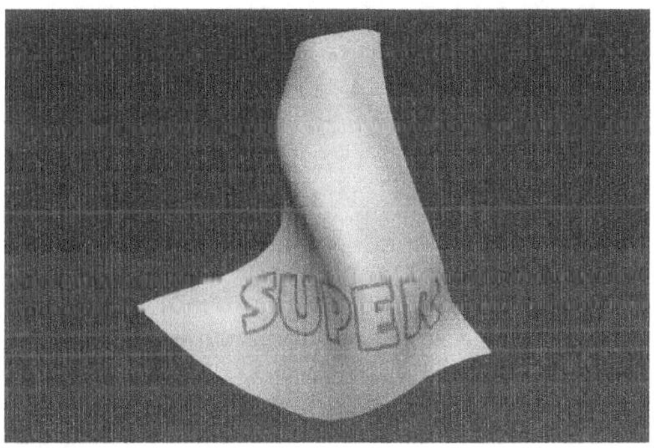

See also

- The *Adding dirt to a cape using a layer as a mask* recipe

Adding dirt to a cape using a layer as a mask

This recipe will show you how to create a mask from an existing layer. This can be very helpful in using details that you have already painted, to single out details on another layer. Layer masks can also be painted into, in order to reveal or hide textures that you have created on the surface of your model.

Getting ready

Once you have created a painted layer on the cape, paint a dirt layer in the same manner.

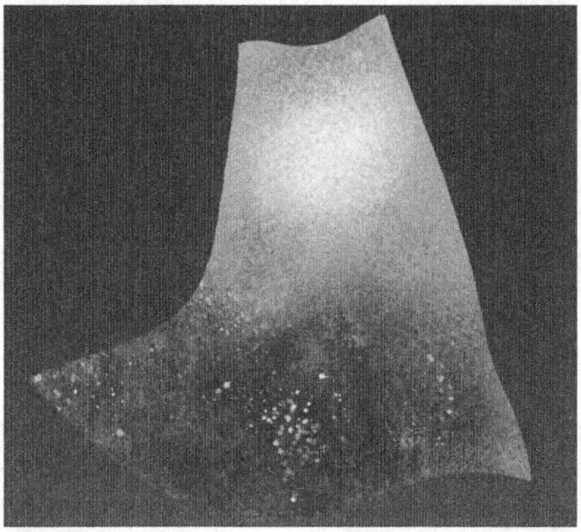

How to do it...

1. In **Paint**, under the **Layers** tab, right-click on your dirt layer and click on **Duplicate Selected**.

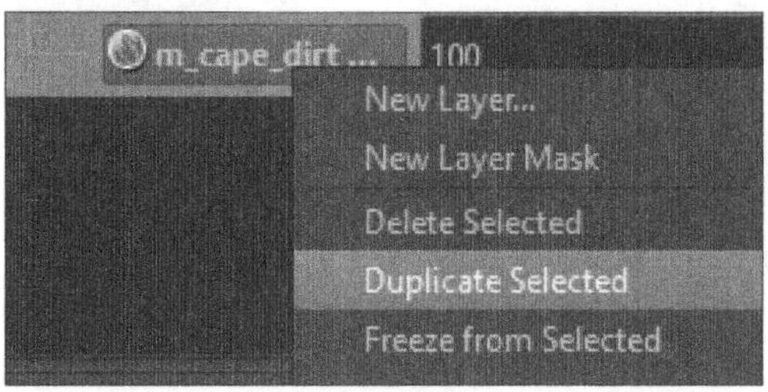

2. Click-and-drag the newly duplicated dirt layer onto the image or text layer until it turns yellow, and let go of the middle-mouse button. This will apply the dragged layer as a mask, allowing the dirt layer to show through.

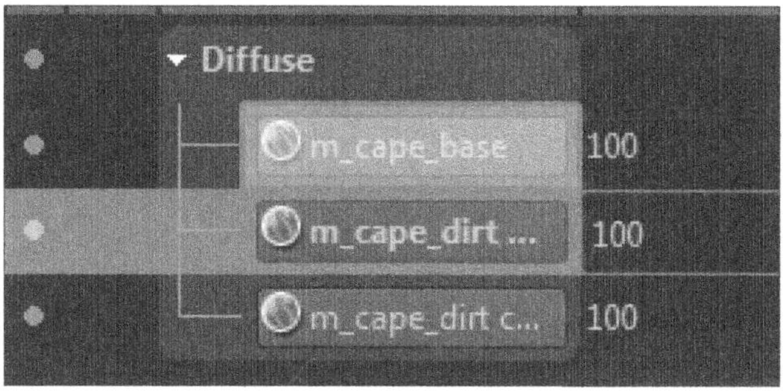

You can use this kind of mask to reveal areas that correspond to the details painted on another layer. The following screenshot shows an example of the dirt masked onto the cape:

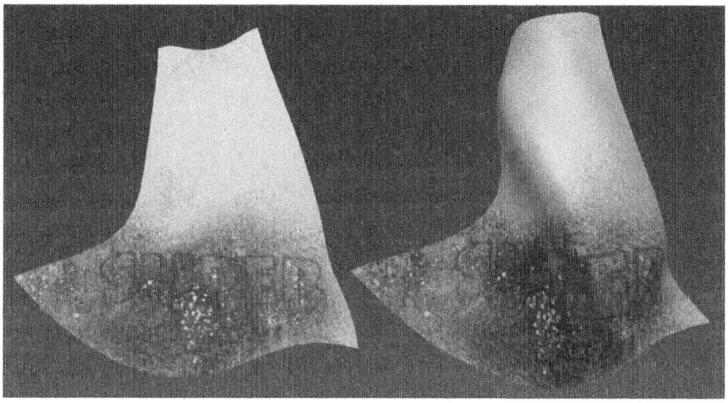

See also

- The *Adding text to a cape using Flatten UV mode* recipe

8

Ready for My Closeup

In this chapter, we will cover:

- Creating a light
- Creating a three-point lighting preset
- Lighting an indoor scene with a simple light setup
- Enhancing your scene with viewport filters
- Creating a rock normal map using a normal map filter
- Creating a turntable

Introduction

This chapter will cover proper, useful lighting and rendering practices in Mudbox 2013. We will go over several techniques for lighting objects and scenes, to establish the mood and present your models in a clear and interesting manner. Viewport filters will be covered to enhance the scenes that you create and to provide other methods of creating normal maps. This chapter will also cover how to create a turntable for presenting your sculpts on your demo reel or website. You will benefit greatly by learning these tools and techniques. There are a lot of things you can pull of by using this knowledge on your own projects.

Creating a light

This recipe will show you how to create a light and modify its settings. Lighting is a very important part of presentation, whether you are working in games, movies, television, or just want to make something nice to look at. It is easy to spot a beginner by looking at the lighting of a particular object or scene.

The following is a list of a few things you should think about when setting up your lighting.

- You almost never want your shadows to be pitch black. Try adding a low intensity blue light in your shadow areas to let some of your hard earned details show through the darkness. Keep in mind that the light color is situational. If you are in a cave with lava all around you, it might be more appropriate to boost the shadows with an orange light instead of blue.
- Use lighting to draw the eye of the viewer. Restrict your full intensity lights to the areas of your model or scene that have been defined as your focal point. Other areas where light hits can still be lit brightly, just not as brightly.
- Another trick to draw the eye is to add some texture to the light. Try breaking up the light with tree leaf shadows or other obstructions. If you break the light up into interesting shapes near your focal point, then people's eyes will surely be drawn to it. Just make sure it is not too distracting. It should work well with the focal point you are trying to present.
- Pay attention to cool and warm light. Also, pay attention to the way sunlight reacts within an environment at different times of the day. For instance, at dusk the sun looks more orange. This is because the light rays have to travel through more atmosphere. This causes a lot of the bluer light rays to scatter throughout the air, which is also why the sky is blue.

Getting ready

First off, you will want to import one of your assets to add some lighting to. If you do not have an asset to light then you can either import a default model from Mudbox or open `Rock.mud` from the code assets of this book. Then delete the lights that are currently in the scene. No cheating!

How to do it...

The following steps will help you to create a light and modify its settings:

1. By default, Mudbox will already have a single directional light in your scene. This light should be used before inserting another light. To add more lights, select the **Directional** light under the **Lights** tab in the **Create** menu as shown in the following screenshot:

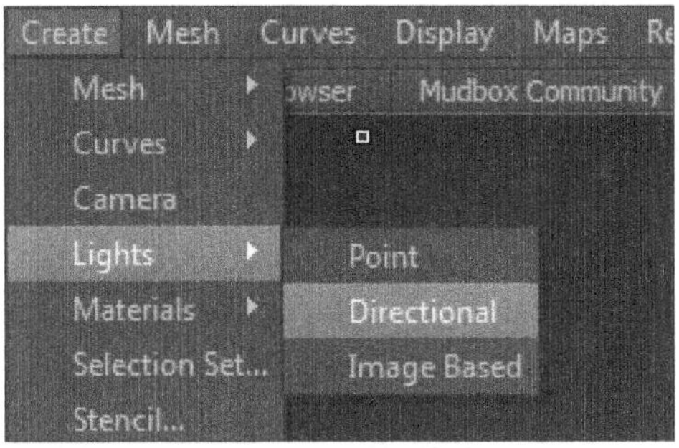

2. This will create a light in the scene. To see the light in your viewport, check the box for **Show Light**. Additionally, check the box for **Show Grips** if you want to rotate the light. This is shown in the following screenshot:

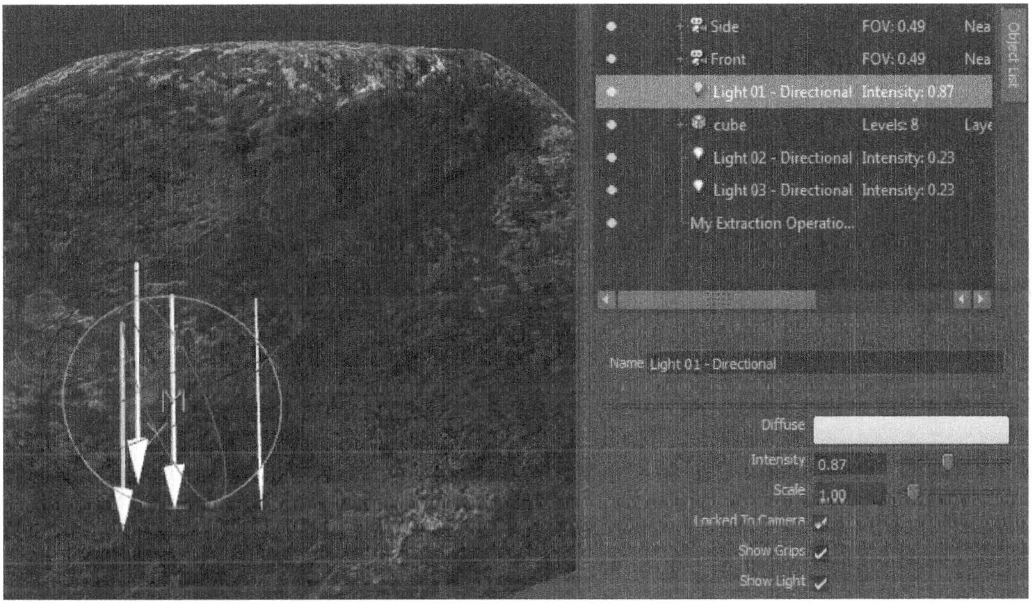

3. **Diffuse** will change the color of the light while the **Intensity** will increase or decrease its effect on the objects in your scene.
4. Using the rotational grip, you can change the angle of your light and how it hits your object.
5. Now, try adding a few lights, adjust these properties, and see what kind of lighting schemes you can come up with. Also, see how close you can match the lighting as shown in the following example.

> The following example is using three-directional lights. One is orange, simulating the sun, while the other two are blue, to fill in the shadows with diffused light from the atmosphere.

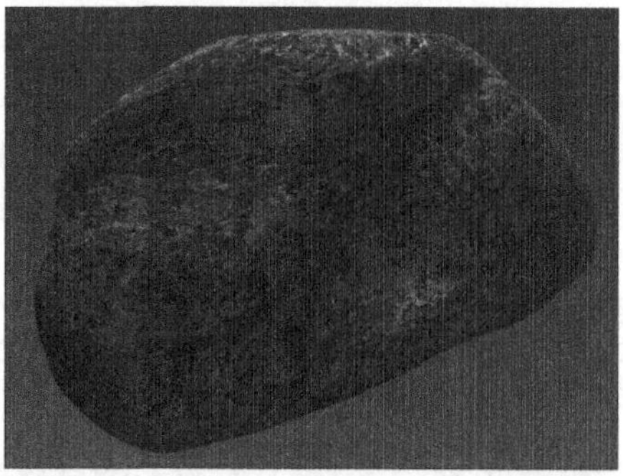

See also

- The *Creating a three-point lighting preset* recipe
- The *Lighting an indoor scene with simple light setup* recipe

Creating a three-point lighting preset

This recipe will show you how to create a three-point light setup and save it as a preset. This setup is a standard light setup that is used by all industries. This recipe will explain the purpose of the three individual lights and how they work together to light your characters or assets.

Getting ready

To start, you will want to import an asset that you would like to light. Otherwise, you can use one of the default Mudbox meshes or open up the `Rock.mud` file from the code assets of this book. Then delete the lights that are currently in the file.

How to do it...

The following steps will help you to create a three-point lighting preset:

1. Rotate Mudbox's main light to address the lighting of the object by an offset of one side, aimed downward at the object. This will be the starting point of your three-point lighting.

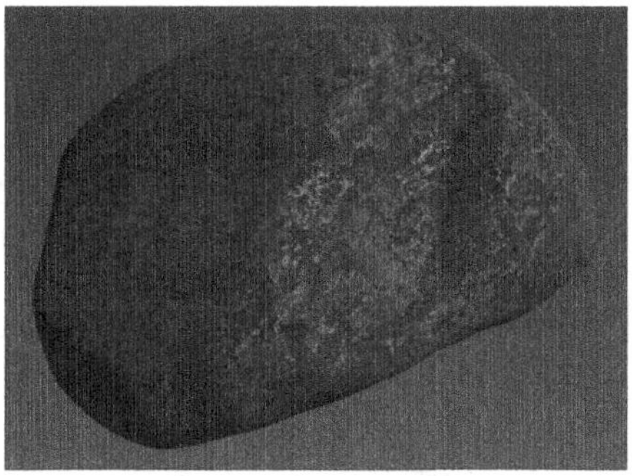

2. Create a second light and rotate it to affect the other side of the object, similarly at a downward angle toward the object. This will illuminate the opposite side of your first light. Also bring the intensity down on this light. This light will fill in the shadows on the other side of your object or character.

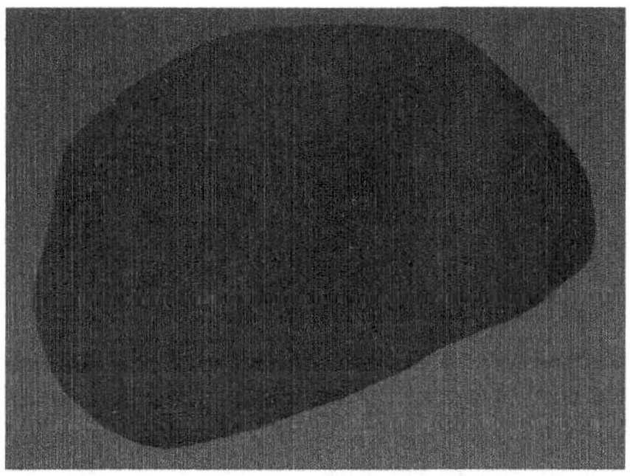

3. Create a third light and rotate it to affect the rear of the object, opposite the camera. Typically this light is aimed downward at the object. This will illuminate the silhouette of your object and help the character or asset to *pop* from the background.

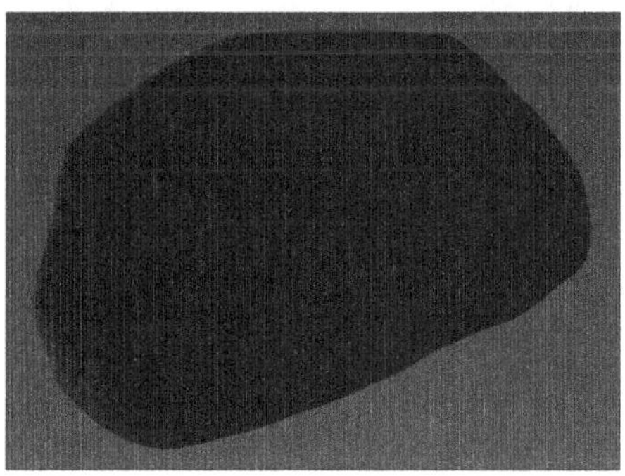

4. All three lights in the scene will offer a lighting scheme that easily helps the object to pop out to show off your work.

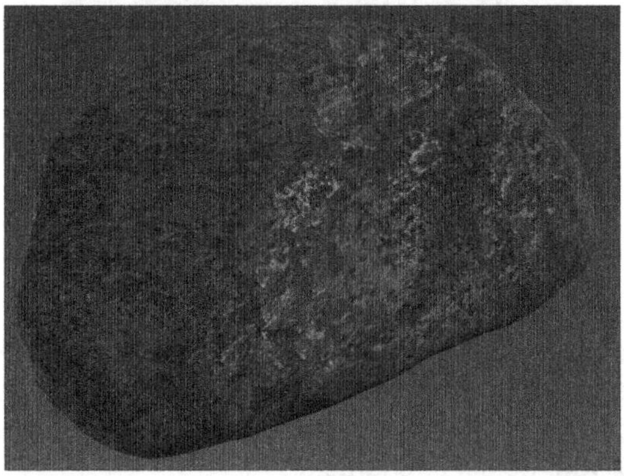

5. To save your current lighting in the scene, click the **Lighting Presets** tab on the bottom right-hand side of the Mudbox interface.
6. Now, click the arrow and then click on **Add Lighting Preset**. This will create a lighting preset from all the lights in your scene so you can use it in future projects. Once this is done, Mudbox will create a small thumbnail in the **Lighting Presets** tray showing the lighting scheme that you have created, as shown in the following screenshot:

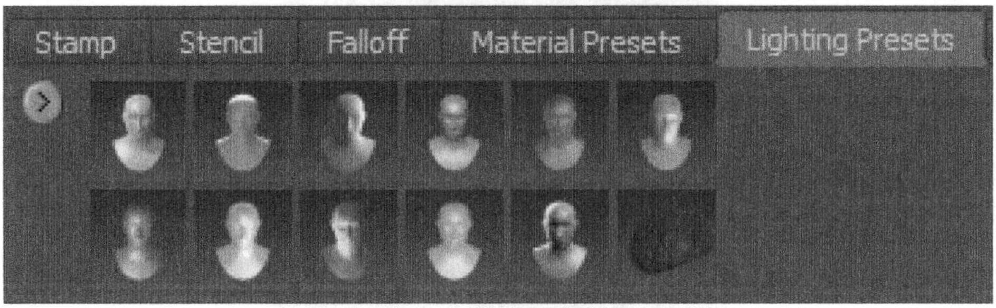

Keep in mind that using a lighting preset from the **Lighting Presets** window will erase all lights previously present in your scene.

How it works...

There are a couple of things being taught in this recipe. One of them is the lighting preset feature which allows you to save the lighting scheme that you create, so that you can easily light feature assets with the same, or similar lighting setup.

Another thing this recipe is teaching is how to set up a three-point lighting scheme. This lighting scheme is the most widely known lighting setup, especially when lighting characters. This is because it does a great job of separating the character or object from the background while giving a pleasing light setup void of harsh shadows. You can still have harsh shadows, if you would like to use that effect for the mood you are setting, by adjusting the intensity of your fill light. If you are wondering which light is the fill light, I have listed the roles of the three lights, within the three-point lighting setup, as follows:

1. First, there is the **key light**. This is the first light we went over. This is the light representing your main light source, for example, the sun or a candle. This light is the attention getter. It is typically set to an intensity between 0.75 and 1.5, though this is not an absolute rule. What is an absolute rule is that it remains at a higher intensity than the fill light.
2. The second light is the **fill light**. This light usually has an opposite angle from the key light and has a lower intensity than the key light, usually half the intensity. The purpose of this light is to fill in the shadow areas on a character's face or the shadow areas of your asset. Sometimes, you may require more than one fill light to boost the shadow areas of your model. Also, the color of this light is usually the color of the bounced light within your scene or it could be a secondary light source. For example, you may have a bright full moon being used as a key light while a distant candle is filling in the shadows as the fill light.
3. The third light is the **rim light**. This light's main purpose is to pop the figure or asset from its background. Let's say you have a character standing outside in the dark. You have a candle as a key light and a low intensity blue light as the fill light. Some of those low intensity blue shadow areas may blend in with the background. To fix this, we can add a high intensity light coming from the moon above that is only hitting the shoulders and the top of the character's head. This bright highlight will pop the character out from the background and give some depth and focus to our subject.

Lighting an indoor scene with a simple light setup

This recipe will show you how to easily light an indoor environment. We will go over some things you need to consider when lighting an indoor scene. With the knowledge you gain from this recipe, you will be able to plan your lighting for your scenes more effectively.

Getting ready

First things first. Open up the file named `Interior Demo.mud`.

This is a quick hallway that could easily be made modular. This means that it could be broken down to smaller pieces that can be reused over and over. You may notice this scene is not created modularly. For the sake of speed, I have combined all the elements and thrown an automatic map onto the hallway.

How to do it...

The following steps will help you to light an indoor environment:

1. When you open up the file, you should see something that looks like the following screenshot:

   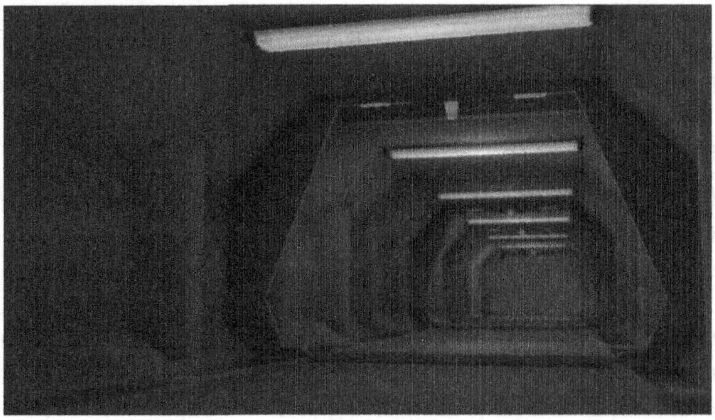

   This file has come already lit with viewport filters enabled. I'm going to go over the steps you need to go through to get to this point. So, the first thing you need to do is identify your light sources.

   For anything that is self-lit, you will want to first paint an incandescent map for that object. If you are using your own interior model then you will want to make sure you have your UVs laid out the way you want them.

2. In the example, you can see that the overhead lights and the emergency lights seem lit up. These are the areas where an incandescent map was painted. To do this you can simply right-click in the empty space of your Paint layer toolbar and select **New Layer...**. The following is a screenshot of what it should look like:

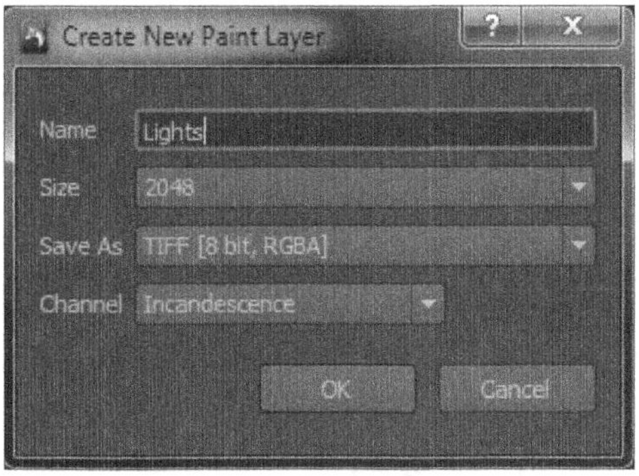

3. When the **Create New Paint Layer** window as shown in the previous screenshot pops up, you will need to choose **Incandescence** from the drop-down menu. The previous screenshot shows an example of what your new layer's properties should look like.
4. Now with your incandescence layer created, you can begin painting in your light sources. The color that you paint will represent the color of the light that the object is giving off. The following screenshot shows a few strokes of paint on one of the overhead lights:

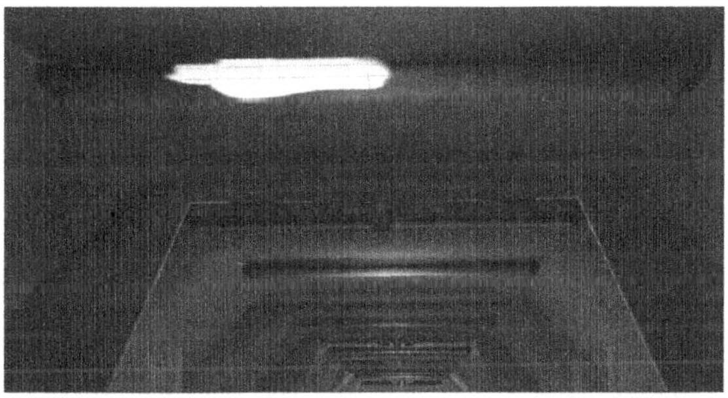

5. After you paint in your designated light sources, you will want to start placing lights.

One thing you need to consider when lighting within Mudbox is that there is an eight-light limit. If you want lighting beyond what eight lights can provide, then you will need to paint that lighting into an incandescence layer.

So, for this example we will only be placing eight dynamic lights for the overhead lights. If you want lighting for the emergency lights, you will need to paint that in.

In game development, a lot of the lights are baked into light maps, meaning the lighting was captured into a texture map that is set as an overlay to the other texture maps in the scene. This allows the use of fewer dynamic lights which can eat up more resources and slow down the frame rate in a game. **Dynamic lights** are lights like the ones that are placed in this example. They can be moved and adjusted where a light map would be considered as static lighting, since you cannot move the light source without creating a new render.

Now, let's take a look at how these lights are placed. In the following screenshot you can see where I have laid out the dynamic lights for this scene:

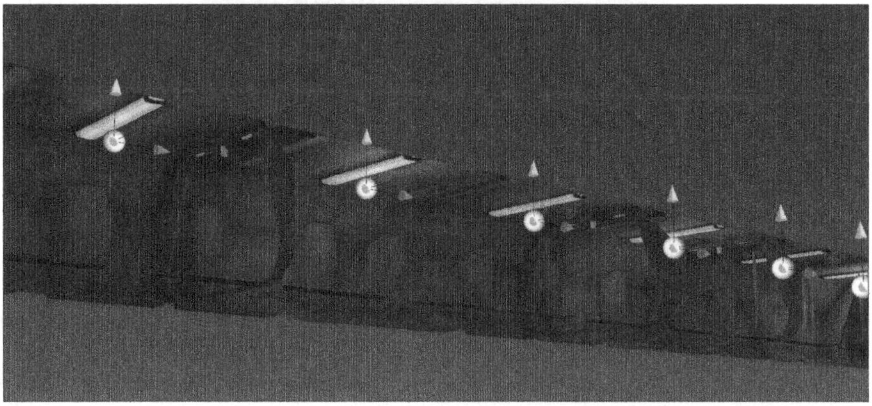

Once you have rotated your camera view, in the example file, you can always return to the framed shot by clicking on the camera bookmark that I have created in the **Camera Bookmarks** tab, located on the bottom right-hand side of the interface.

1. For this lighting setup, I used point lights that were created by going to **Create** | **Lights** | **Point**. The following is a screenshot of what the menu looks like:

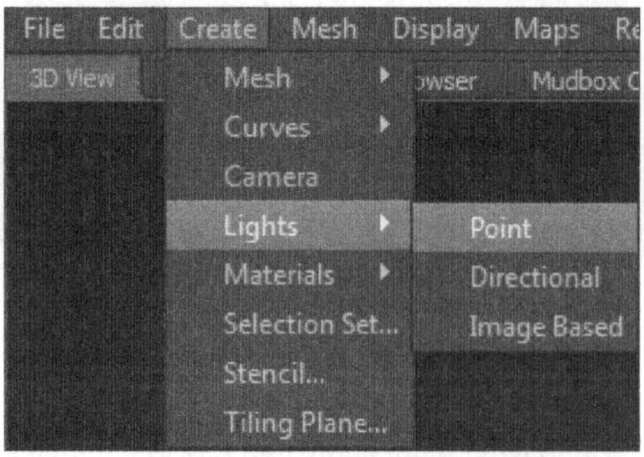

2. Once you have the light in your scene you will need to place it. In order to see your light's location and to move your light, you will need to go into the light's properties and check the boxes for **Show Grips** and **Show Light**. The following screenshot shows the properties of one of the lights in this scene along with the intensities of the other lights in the scene, as shown in the **Object List** section:

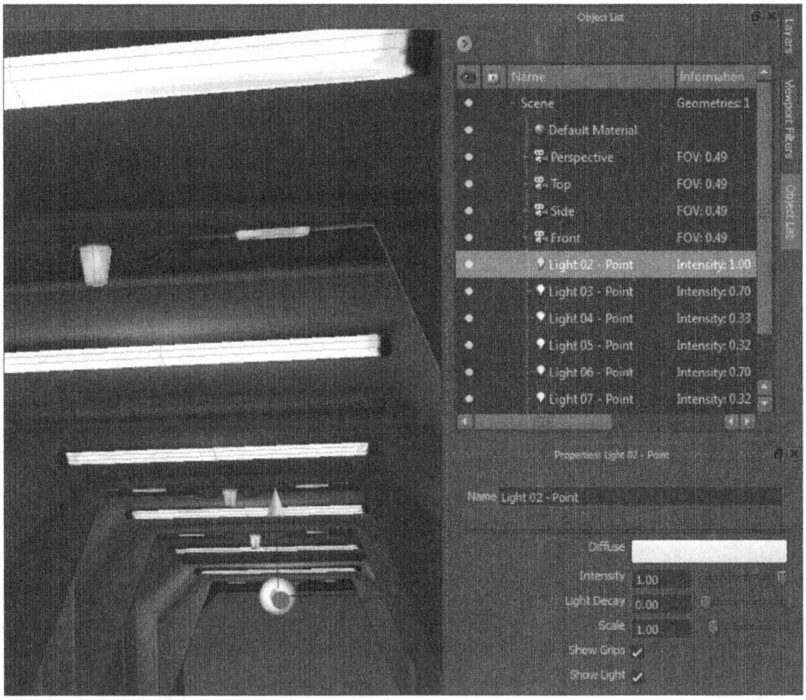

3. Following the previous steps, you can then create the rest of the lights in your scene. You will notice that the light intensities are varied. This is to show that the scene is not flatly lit and you can vary the lights a little to show that some of the lights have become slightly dimmer over the years.

See also

- The *Enhancing your scene with viewport filters* recipe

Enhancing your scene with viewport filters

This recipe will show you how to improve the believability of your scene using viewport filters. These filters allow a nice variety of post process effects to be applied within the viewport. This just means you can add some nice qualities to your view that are typically only seen when you render out the view in other software packages, which takes longer.

Getting ready

Once you have lit a scene and enabled shadows, you can apply **Ambient Occlusion**, **Cavity Ambient Occlusion**, **Depth of Field**, and **Tonemapper** filters to further improve the dynamics of your scene. For this recipe you can follow along using the `Interior Demo.mud` file that is present in the code files of this book, or you can set up your own scene.

If you are using the example that comes with the code assets of the book, then the viewport filters are turned on to begin with. Go ahead and turn these off before starting this recipe. Your scene should look like the following screenshot:

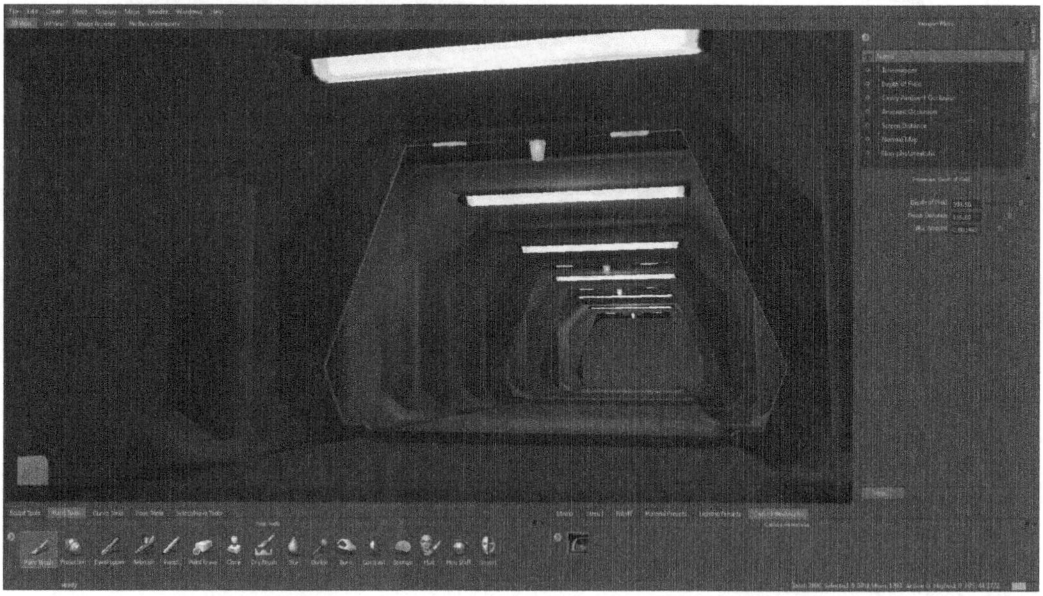

How to do it...

The following steps will help you to use viewport filters in order to enhance your scene:

1. Click on the **Viewport Filters** tab at the top-right of the screen and a list of available filters will appear. You can see the menu in the following screenshot:

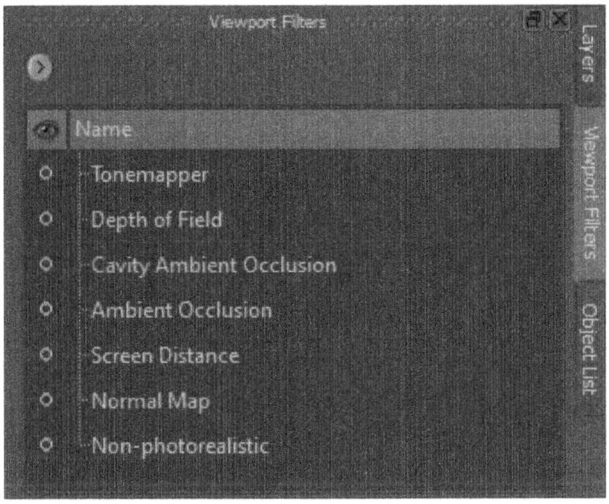

2. First, click on the **Ambient Occlusion** filter. This will add shadows, based on surface proximity and normal direction, on all the objects in your scene.
3. Now you can tweak your settings depending on the scale of your scene and your desired effect. The following screenshot is an example of the settings used in the scene that is provided. Try sliding the values around to get comfortable with what they affect:

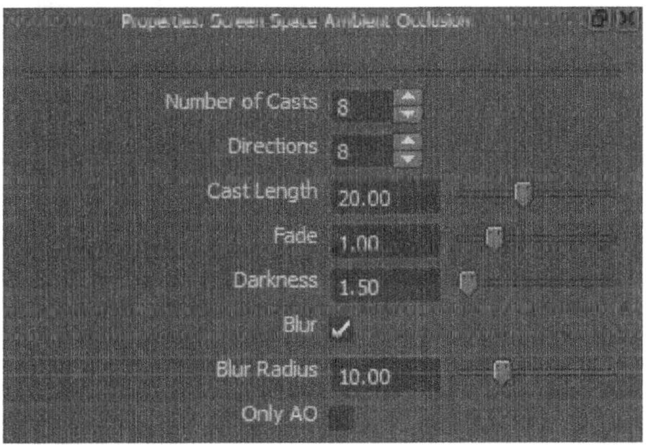

- By adjusting the **Number of Casts** and **Directions** values, you will basically be able to control how much noise or smoothness the ambient occlusion creates with its light rights and the direction of those rays.
- **Cast Length** will determine how far the shadows will reach out from the corners of your objects.

- **Fade** controls the falloff of the shadows coming out of the corners. This will give a more subtle change to the way the ambient occlusion is affecting the scene.
- **Darkness** affects how dark the dark areas will become. This will have a stronger effect on your scene.
- **Blur** will help smooth out the noise to a great extent. Every ambient occlusion ray will be blurred so that you don't see each individual ray.
- **Blur Radius** will adjust the extent of the blur for fine-tuning.
- If you check the box for **Only AO** then you will only show the ambient occlusion, which consists of only black to white values without any other texture map detail. This can be useful if you are going to composite your ambient occlusion onto other renders outside Mudbox.

4. The next viewport filter is the **Cavity Ambient Occlusion** filter. This filter is similar to the **Ambient Occlusion** filter, except it is more geared towards finer details. This setting is to help define cracks, crevices, and places where objects meet. The following screenshot shows the settings used in the example:

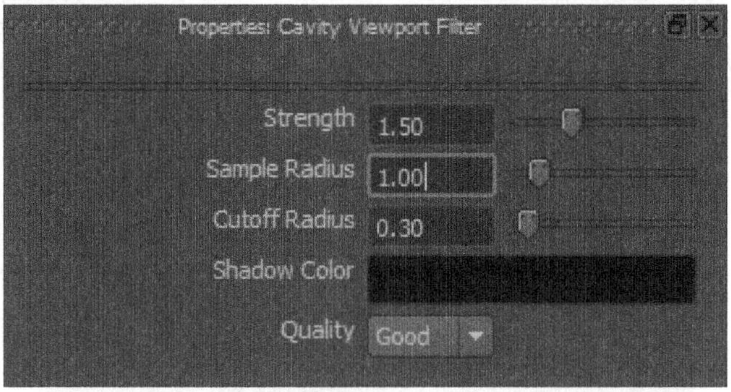

- The **Strength** attribute will control the intensity of this effect.
- **Sample Radius** defines the amount of screen space that is sampled to determine the filter's effect. This may need some tweaking to make sure you get the details you want out of small and large objects. This setting can make things look wrong if you do not set it correctly.
- The **Cutoff Radius** settings adjust how far the effect extends from the cavities, crevices, or corners of your models.
- **Shadow Color** will define the color of the dark areas that are added. I recommend not setting this to pitch black. Give a little bit of color depending on what kind of ambience (bounced light) is in the room.
- The **Quality** drop-down menu will just let you choose how crisp it looks.

5. Next thing that is added is the **Depth of Field** filter. This filter will mimic a camera's focal length. This is most apparent in macro lens cameras. Macro lenses tend to have very little depth of field. This means that only objects that are at a certain distance from the camera are sharp looking. As you get away from the focal point, the image will get blurry real fast. The following screenshot shows the settings for this example:

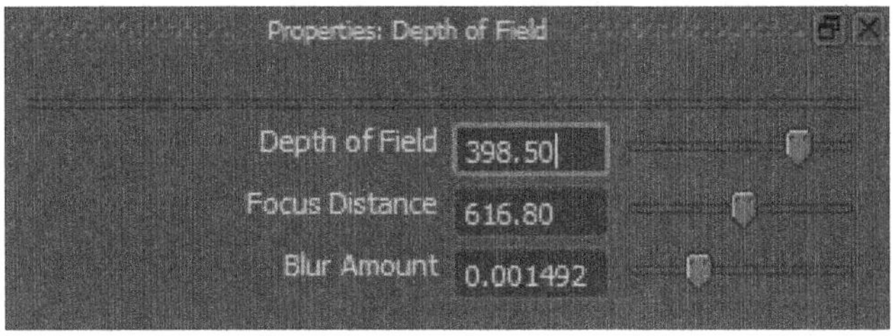

   - The **Depth of Field** attribute controls how fast the image gets blurry as you get away from the focal point.
   - **Focus Distance** is the setting for how deep into your scene you want the focus to be. Outside this area, the scene will start getting blurry depending on your settings.
   - **Blur Amount** determines just how blurry the image gets as you get farther away from the area under **Focus Distance**.

6. Keep in mind that setting up **Depth of Field** is reliant on your camera position.
7. Lastly, click on **Tonemapper** under the **Viewport Filters** tab. **Tone mapping** is often used to simulate a higher dynamic range of color and values in a scene, which can improve the contrast and color quality. The following screenshot shows the settings used in the example:

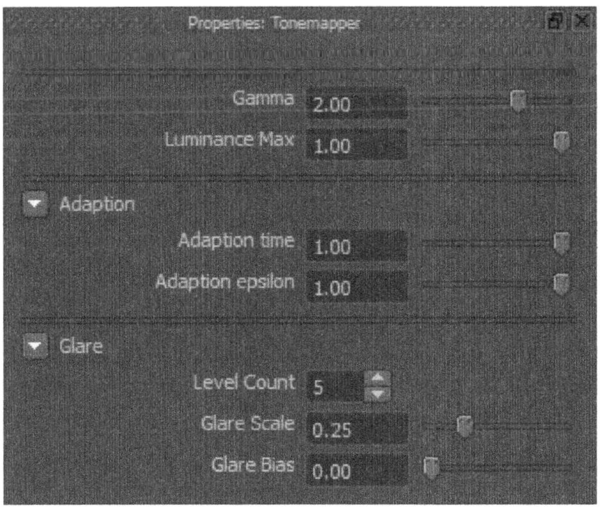

- **Gamma** will control the brightness of your viewport while **Luminance Max** will alter what color value is used as *white*.
- A higher *gamma* will result in a brighter image while a higher *luminance* will increase the value considered white and thus, darken the scene.
- Click the **Glare** arrow to see the **Glare** options. **Glare Scale** will increase the amount of glare or bloom that is in the viewport while **Level count** will blur the glare. **Glare Bias** will limit how far the glare will spread where it exists on screen.
- A higher **Glare Scale** will result in more glare softened by a higher **Level Count**. A higher **Glare Bias** will spread the amount of glare over a larger distance. Glare creates a simulated effect of reflected light; more glare means more light reflecting back at the camera. This can help enhance your scene but can also lead to a blown out image.

See also

- The *Creating a turntable* recipe
- The *Lighting an indoor scene with a simple light setup* recipe

Creating a rock normal map with a normal map filter

This recipe will show you how to create a normal map from your scene using the normal map viewport filter. This technique can be very useful in creating a large variety of textures with multiple map outputs. Not only will this recipe teach you how to get a normal map, based on your viewport, but it will also show you how to use that in combination with other viewport renders.

Getting ready

First thing you need to do is import some rocks that you would like to make a normal map out of. If you do not have rocks of your own, than you can open up the file named `Rock_Layout.mud`, in the code files for this book.

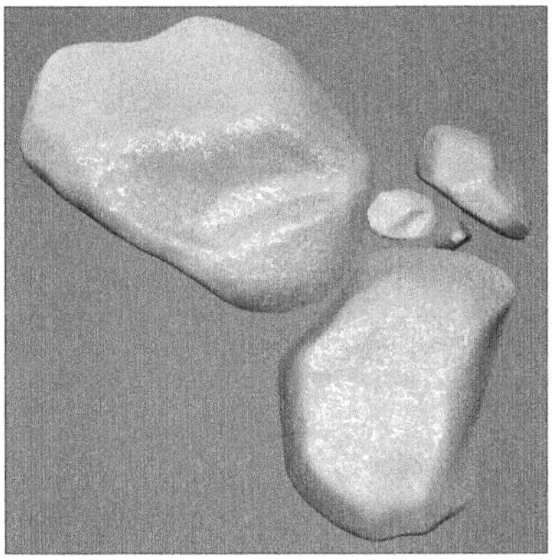

This was created by duplicating and arranging the rock that we used in the earlier recipes of this chapter.

How to do it...

The following steps will help you to use normal map filters to create a rock normal map:

1. Click on the **Viewport Filters** tab, on the top right-hand side of the Mudbox interface.
2. Now, click on the **Normal Map** filter, as shown in the following screenshot:

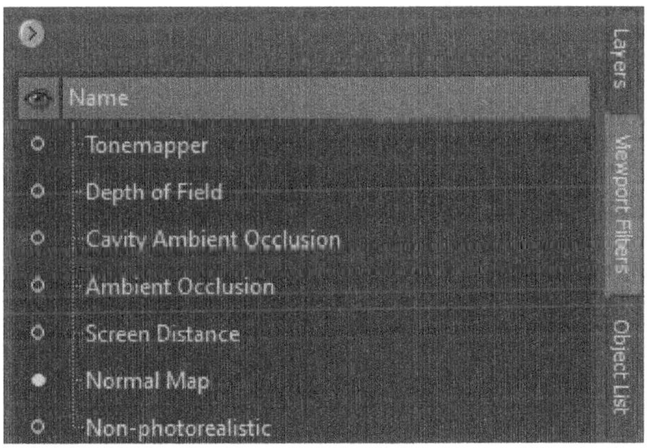

Notice the viewport change to the spectrum of normal map colors.

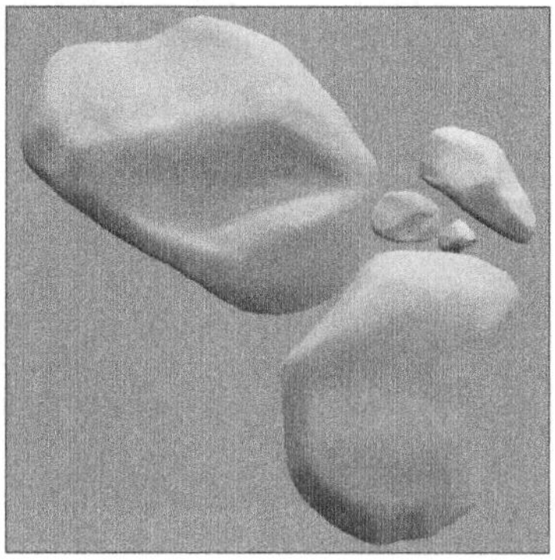

3. Next, we should switch to the top camera angle. While you can save the screen image from any camera angle, it is suggested that you organize your scene for one of the perpendicular cameras such as **Top** in the **Object List** tab.

   The easiest way to switch to the top view is by clicking on the **Top** plane of the view cube in the corner of your viewport. The view cube should look something as shown in the following screenshot, before you click on **Top**:

   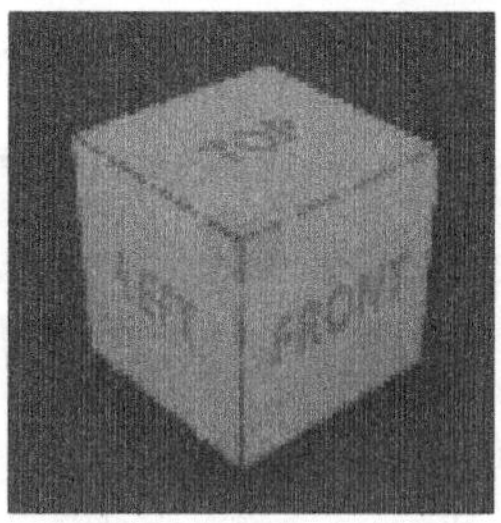

   By looking through the top view you can rearrange your rocks easier, if needed, as well as get rid of any angles from the flat plane that the rocks are sitting on. If you'd like you can add some texture by sculpting onto the plane itself. Otherwise, you can combine this normal map with other normal maps using software like CrazyBump or nDo.

4. The last thing we need to do is render out a high resolution screen render of our normal map.

   One nice feature that Mudbox offers is its ability to take very high resolution screen captures of its viewport. If you want a screen grab from most other software, you would have to use the *Print Screen* button, which limits the resolution to the size of your desktop resolution.

   To get a high resolution screen grab from Mudbox, you need to go to **Render** | **Save Screen Image...**. It should look like the following screenshot:

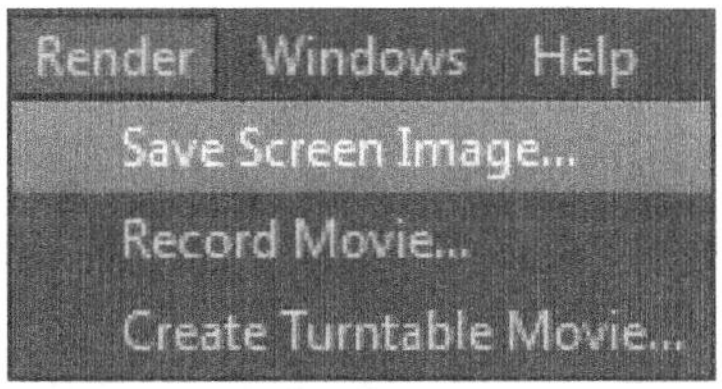

5. Now, you can adjust the settings to your liking. It is best to get a higher resolution render than you need. This is a good idea because you can always shrink your map down later, but you can not scale it up. Your image is limited to the resolution that the image was created at. The following screenshot has the settings that I used for this example:

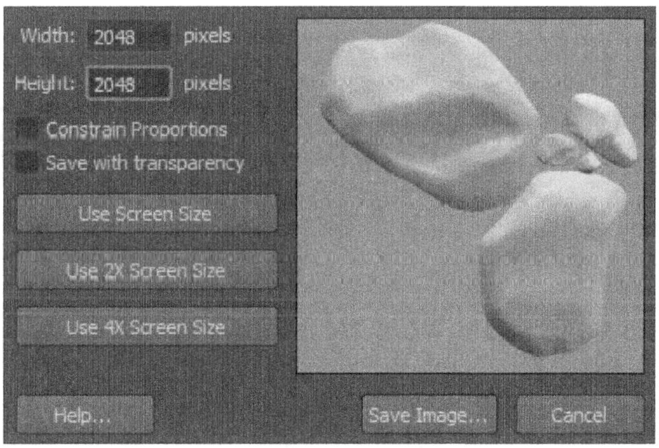

Also, keep in mind that if you are creating a texture for games, then the image needs to be saved in a resolution that is a power of 2. Some examples of this would be 64 pixels, 128 pixels, 256 pixels, 512 pixels, 1024 pixels, and so on.

Another thing you could do is remove the plane from the scene and check the box labeled **Save with transparency**. This will create an alpha channel for your rocks so that you can combine it with other normal maps within a program, such as Photoshop, more easily.

The following screenshot is of the normal map that was created, applied to a plane in Autodesk Maya, consisting of only two triangles:

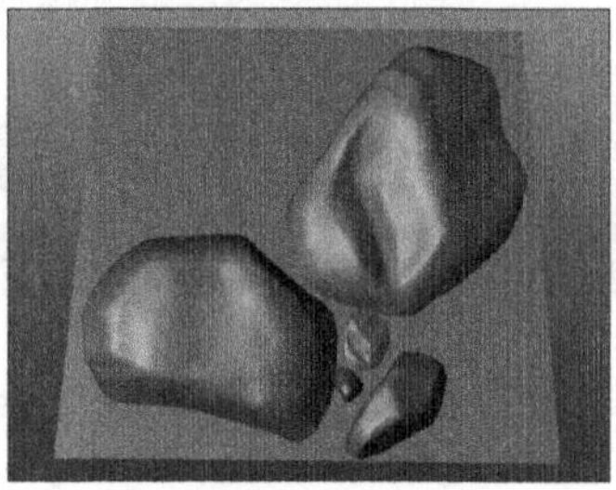

See also

- The *Creating a light* recipe
- The *Creating a three-point lighting preset* recipe

Creating a turntable

This recipe will show you how to create a turntable in Mudbox 2013, and save it to a movie file. Creating a turntable of your model is a very good method of showing off an asset that you have created. You get to see the model from all sides and you can let it loop for as long as you want.

Getting ready

For this recipe we are just going to use the default cow model that comes with Mudbox. Just open up Mudbox, choose **File** | **New Scene**, and choose the cow from the **Starting points** window that pops up.

How to do it...

The following steps will help you to create a turntable:

1. First, choose **Render** | **Create Turntable Movie...**.

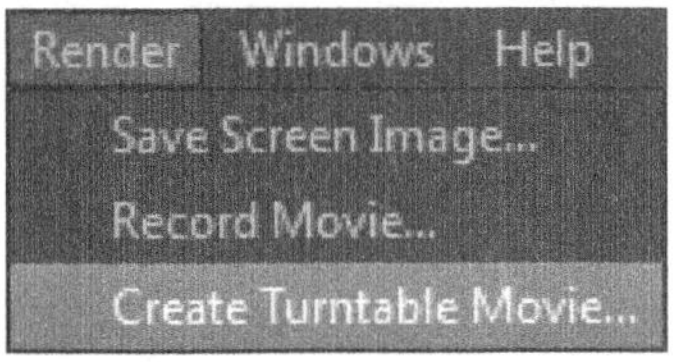

2. Adjust the settings to the output size and frames per second you desire. Recording at a larger resolution and higher frame rate will require more computing power. The following screenshot shows the settings for an HD sized render of the turntable:

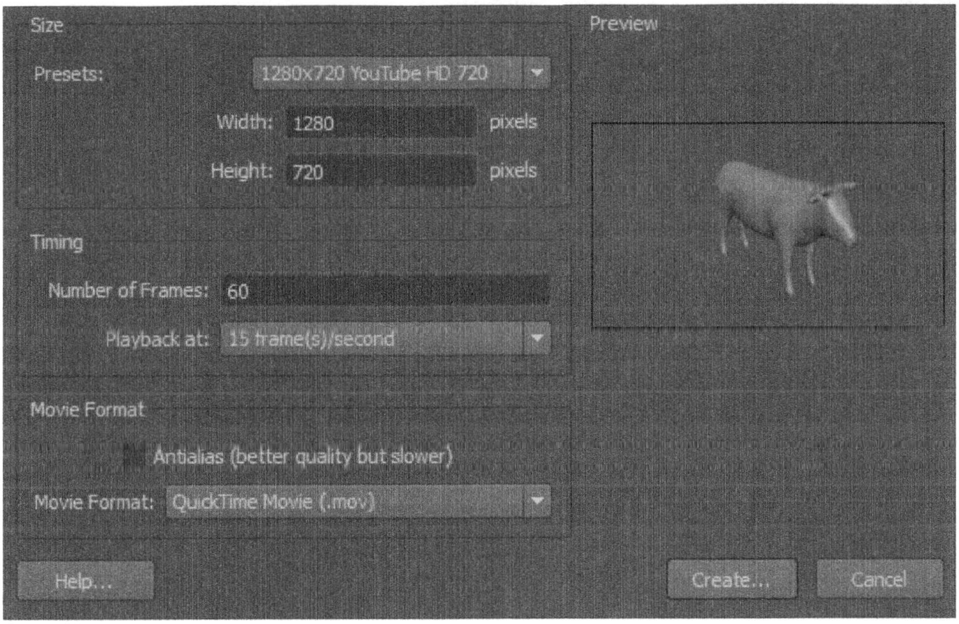

You have to do a little math when setting up your timing. In the previous example, we are rendering out **60** frames of video, total, with a playback speed of **15 frame(s)/second**. This means that the turntable, which is created with these settings, will last 4 seconds long.

In the **Movie Format** section, you will need to choose between rendering a `.mov`, a `.swf`, a `.flv`, or a sequence of images.

3. Lastly, click on **Create...** when you are ready to record the turntable and indicate where to save the movie.

   The turnaround movie will automatically open after Mudbox has completed rendering.

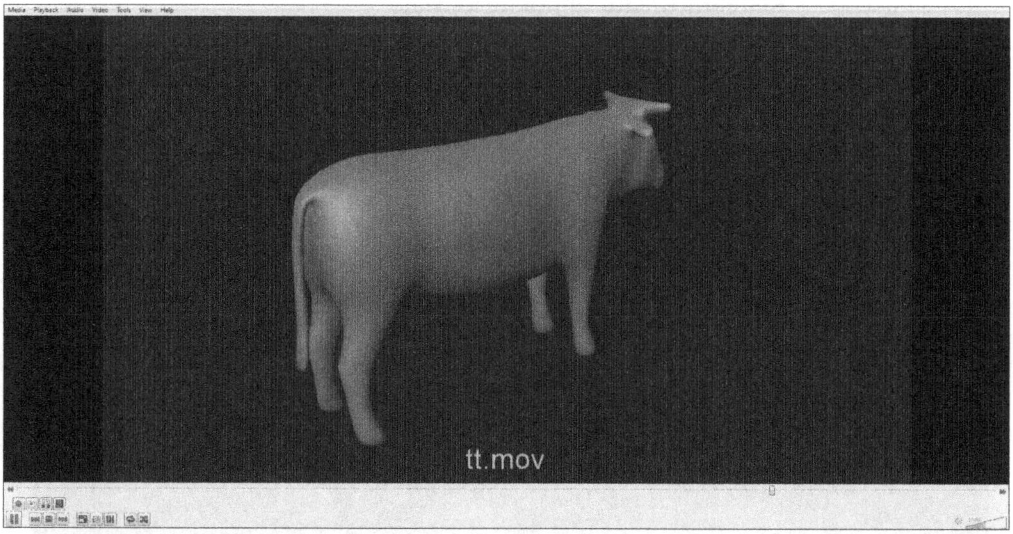

See also

- The *Creating a light* recipe
- The *Creating a three-point lighting preset* recipe

9

One Step Forward

In this chapter we will cover:

- Posing a lamp cord by adding joints to your mesh
- Posing multiple objects at the same time
- Adjusting joint pivot and painting weights
- Creating a human rig by importing joints

Introduction

This chapter will cover proper joint creation and posing practices in Mudbox 2013. The techniques and tools you will learn in this chapter will help you in presenting your sculpts. By giving a dynamic pose to the characters you create, you will add more emotion to your sculpt. When you pose your character you should always be thinking about how your adjustments are affecting the silhouette of your character or object from all angles. A more interesting silhouette will make a much more interesting pose. When looking at the silhouette, you not only want to look at the shapes your model is creating, but also the shapes that the negative space is creating. This means you want to have interesting shapes that fit your theme within the empty space that surrounds your character or object. By paying attention to these details, you will be able to affect the viewer in subtle ways. For example, if you give your silhouettes positive and negative space, and a lot of sharp angles, it may support the theme of a villain, of anger, energy, or danger. Sharp angles tend to bring up similar emotions to these and therefore can infuse a deeper emotional impact into your sculpts and poses.

Posing a lamp cord by adding joints to your mesh

This recipe will go over the process of adding joints and posing a lamp cord using Mudbox's posing tools. In this recipe, we will be using the basic posing tools **Create Joint** and **Pose**. These tools will allow you to define an area of influence so you can rotate and/or move these areas of your mesh into your desired position.

Getting ready

To begin, you will need to import the `Lamp.obj` file from the code files of this book. If you would like to see the finished product you can open up the `Lamp.mud` file.

Once you've opened the `Lamp.obj` file, you will get a couple of dialog boxes that you can ignore. For example:

- The first one will say that **There are t-shapes in this mesh**. When this pops up you can just hit **OK**.
- Next, you will see a window saying there is a **High-valence vertex** and **Non-manifold topology** in the mesh. To ignore this message, just click on **Keep this Mesh**.

The reason we can ignore these messages is because we will not be subdividing this mesh within Mudbox. If you try to subdivide this mesh without cleaning it up first, in another program, then you will just get an error and Mudbox will not allow the subdivision to happen.

After importing the mesh, you should be left with the model shown in the following screenshot:

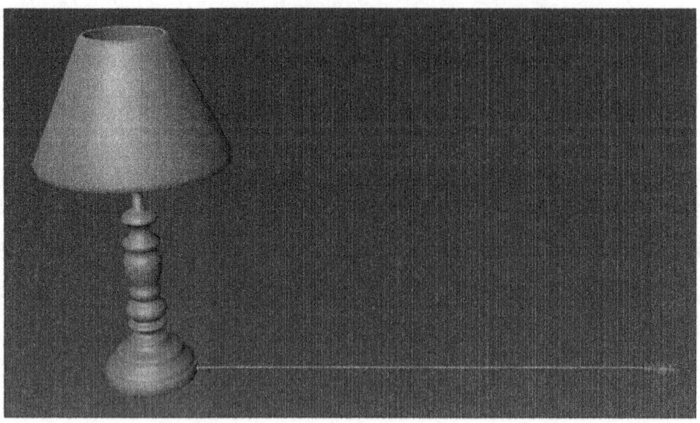

How to do it...

The following steps will help you to add joints and pose a lamp cord using Mudbox's posing tools:

1. First thing you are going to do is change the view that we have of the object. By switching to the top view we will be able to move the wire around in the *X* and *Z* directions but not the *Y*. This will help you to pose the wire more accurately without having to worry about whether the cord is lying flat or not. The easiest way to do this is to click on **Top** located on the view cube on the corner of your interface.
   The following screenshot shows what the view cube looks like:

   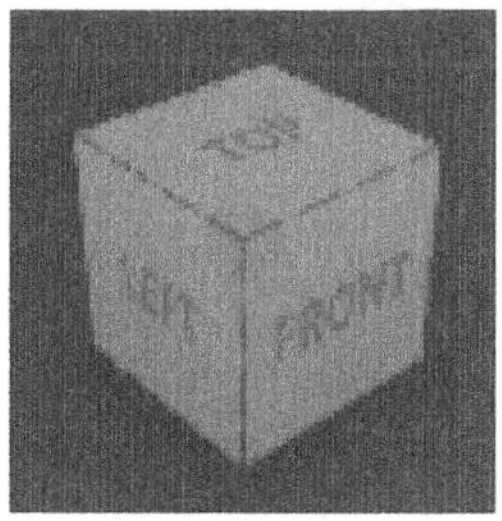

2. Now that you are looking from the top view, which should look like the following screenshot, you can add a joint to the lamp's power cord:

   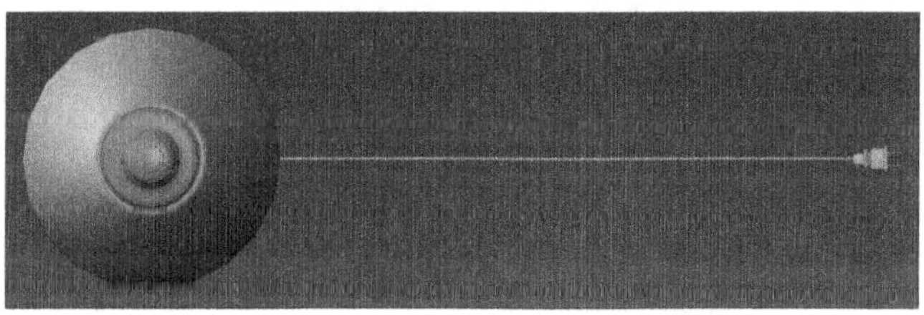

   To do this you will need to select the **Create Joint** tool from the **Pose Tools** toolbar at the bottom left-hand side of the Mudbox interface. The toolbar should look like the following screenshot:

   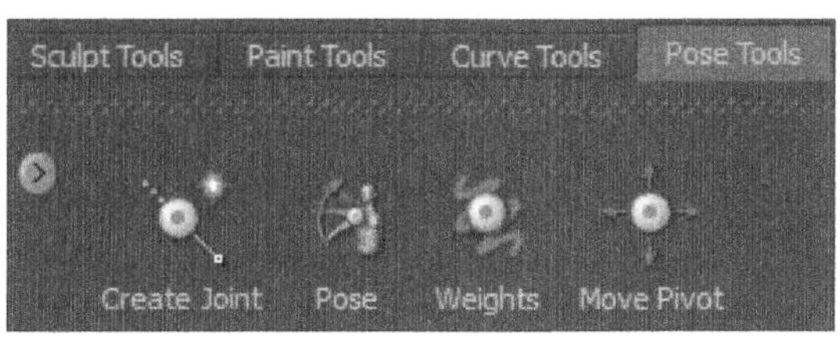

3. Now, you are going to left-click and drag on the part of the mesh that you would like to influence. The way in which this tool works, you will start your drag in the location where you would like your mesh to bend, while posing, and end your drag in the direction that you would like influenced. Also, take note that the length of your drag defines the falloff of the bend. This means, a short drag will create a sharper bend while a longer drag will allow a more gradual bend. Try creating a joint using a short drag using the **Create Joint** tool. The following screenshot is an example of a drag in progress:

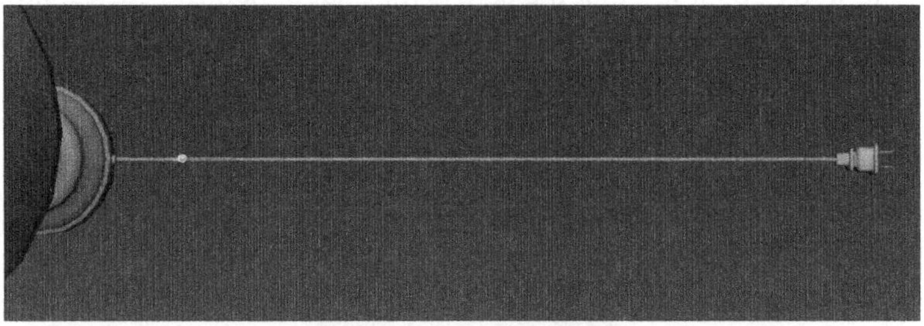

4. Once you have done this, you will be switching over to the **Pose** tool. This can be found in the same toolbar as the **Create Joint** tool. With this tool you are going to grab the end of your lamp's power cord and left-click and drag to bend the cord. The following screenshot shows this tool in action:

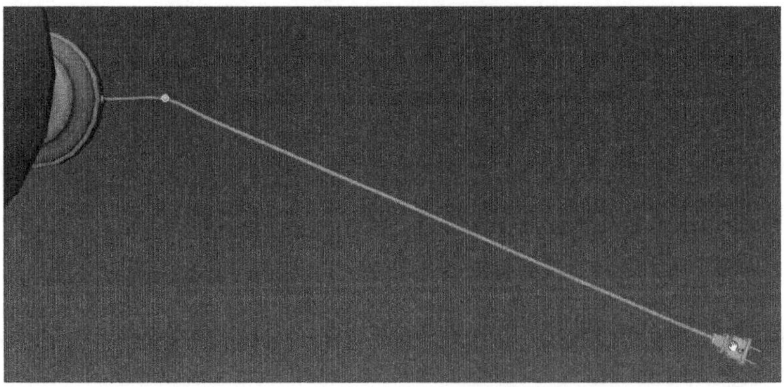

5. Now, just repeat steps 2 to 4, while trying out different drag distances, until you end up with something like the following screenshot:

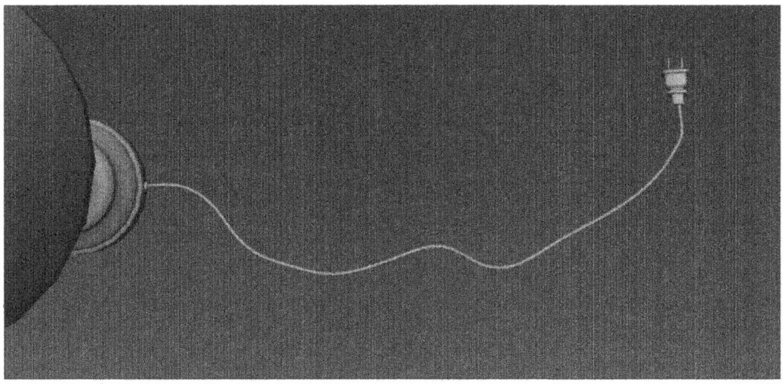

If you would like to see the finished version, you can open up the `Lamp.mud` file to see the final project, as shown in the following screenshot:

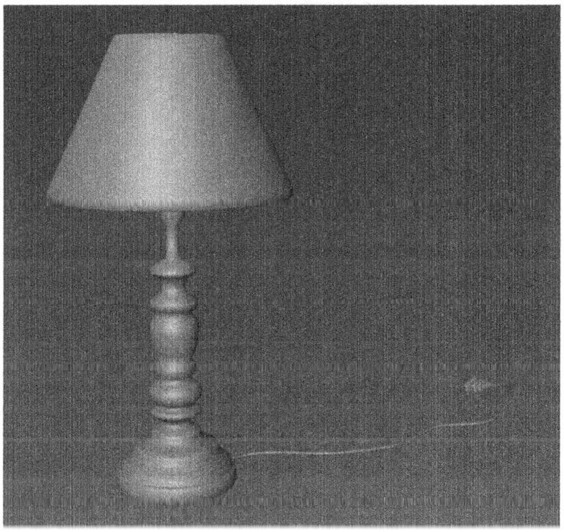

See also

- The *Adjusting joint pivots and painting weights* recipe

Posing multiple objects at the same time

This recipe will demonstrate how you can create joints and pose multiple objects using the **Weights** tool. What you learn here will be used over and over again, especially if you are a character artist for games or films. Most of the time, your characters will have many accessories that they will be wearing, such as hats, shirts, armor, weapons, jewellery, and so on. In order to have all these objects stay with the body part they are attached to, you will need to follow the steps listed in this recipe.

Getting ready

To start with, you can either bring in your own objects and work along with the recipe or you can open up the `Hand.mud` file that is present in the code files of this book. When you open up the `Hand.mud` file, the following screenshot is what you should see:

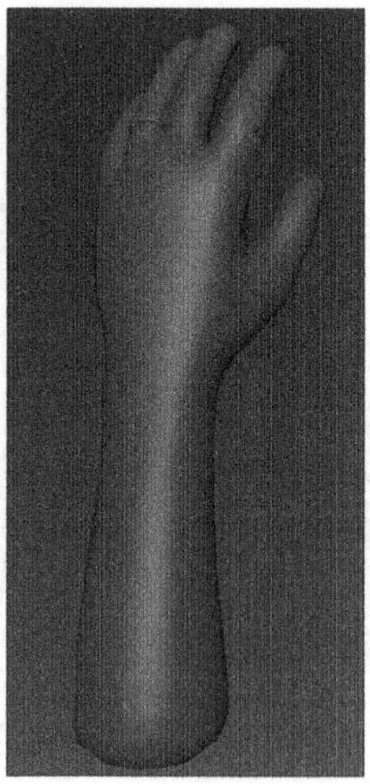

As you can see in the previous screenshot, there are two objects in this scene, part of an arm and a ring. This recipe will show you how to pose this hand while having the ring follow along.

How to do it...

The following steps will help pose multiple objects at the same time:

1. First, you are going to select the **Create Joint** tool located in the **Pose Tools** toolbar in the bottom left-hand side of the Mudbox interface. It should look something similar to the following screenshot:

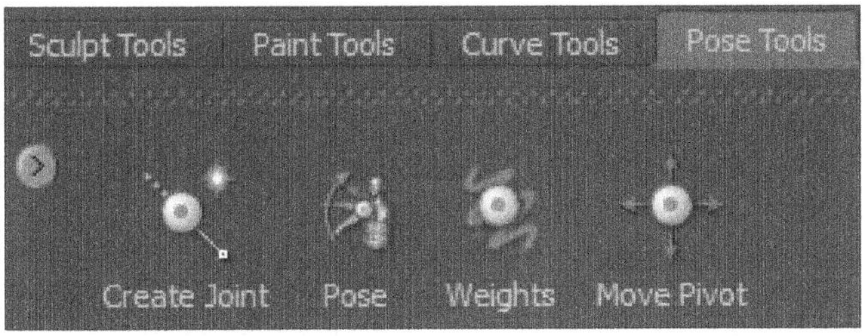

2. Next, you can click-and-drag a short distance on the wrist to create a joint with a short falloff. The following screenshot shows what your joint should look like. If you would like more information on how the joint tool works you can read the recipe *Posing a lamp cord by adding joints to your mesh,* found in this chapter.

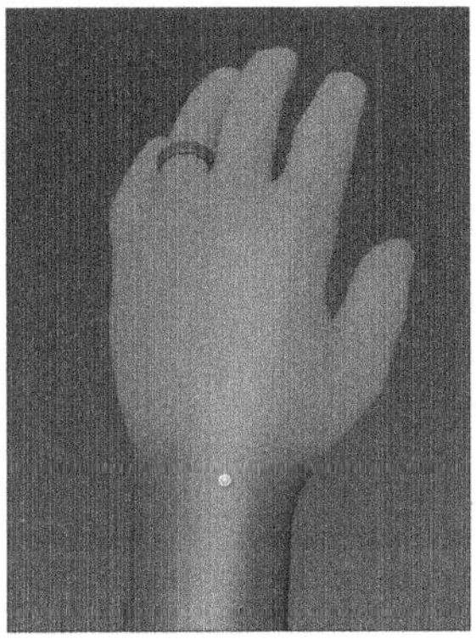

3. You will notice in the previous screenshot that the ring is not green like the rest of the hand. This is because the **Create Joint** tool only works on one object at a time. If we were to pose this hand in its current state, it would turn out looking something like the following screenshot:

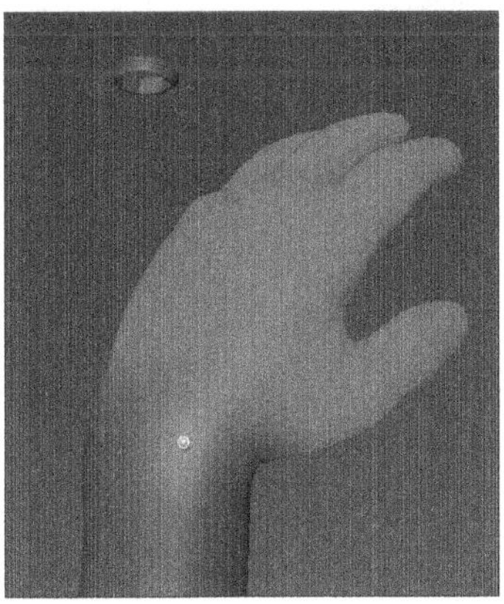

Notice that the hand moved but the ring did not. To fix this we are going to have to add weights to the ring.

To do this you will need to select the **Weights** tool from the same toolbar where you found the **Create Joint** tool, in the **Pose Tools** toolbar on the bottom left-hand side of the Mudbox interface.

4. Now, you can paint the weights in by using the tool like a brush. Paint the ring until it is all green. Once you have done this, your ring will now be influenced when you pose the hand. The following screenshot shows what the hand should look like after adding weights:

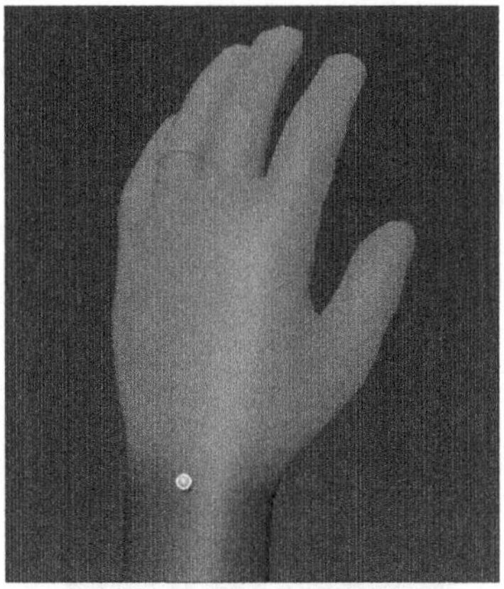

5. Next, try posing the hand with the weights painted on the hand. By using the **Pose** tool, found in the same toolbar as **Create Joint** and **Weights**, you can now grab the tips of the fingers and pull the hand down to bend it. The following screenshot shows an example:

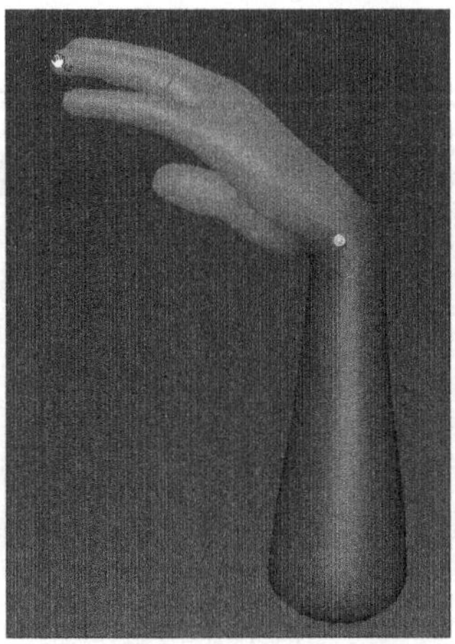

By knowing this, you will be able to pose as many objects as you need by using the **Weights** tool. The following screenshot is what the hand looks like posed with the ring. Notice, none of the geometry is cutting into the other geometry, leaving you with a nice clean pose:

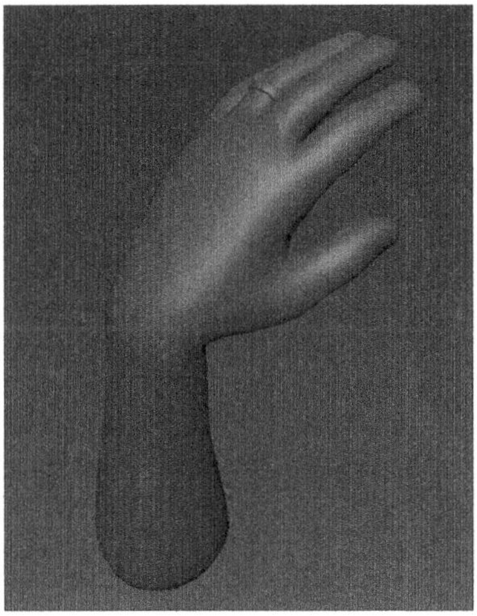

See also

- The *Posing a lamp cord by adding joints to your mesh* recipe
- The *Adjusting joint pivots and painting weights* recipe

Adjusting joint pivots and painting weights

This recipe will show you how to create and adjust joint pivots, and paint weights. **Joints** are the bones of the skeleton, which will let you pose your model. **Weights** allow you to specify what portions of the model a joint will influence.

Getting ready

Once you have imported a model to pose, like the one shown in the following screenshot, you will be ready to create joints:

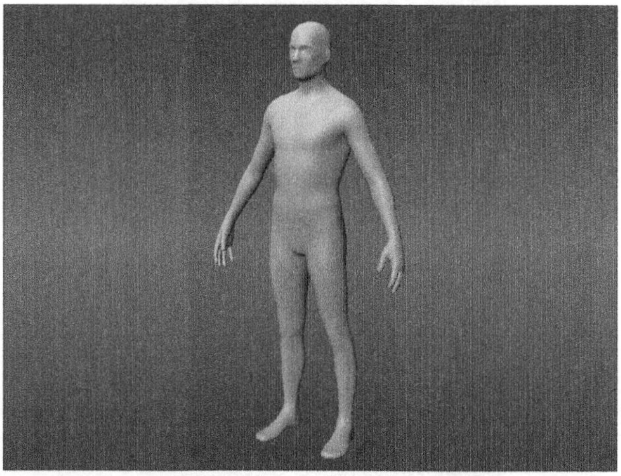

How to do it...

The following steps will help you to create and adjust joint pivots, and paint weights:

1. Click on the **Pose Tools** tab at the bottom left-hand side of your screen and select the **Create Joint** tool. This will allow you to pick the starting anchor of the joint for your model.

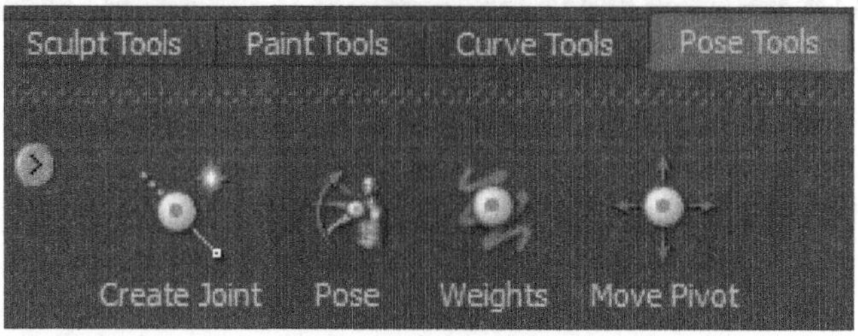

2. Click on the area of your model you wish to start the joint from and drag the joint out to where you want it to end. In the case of a human, try creating a simple arm joint to affect the arm, as shown in the following screenshot:

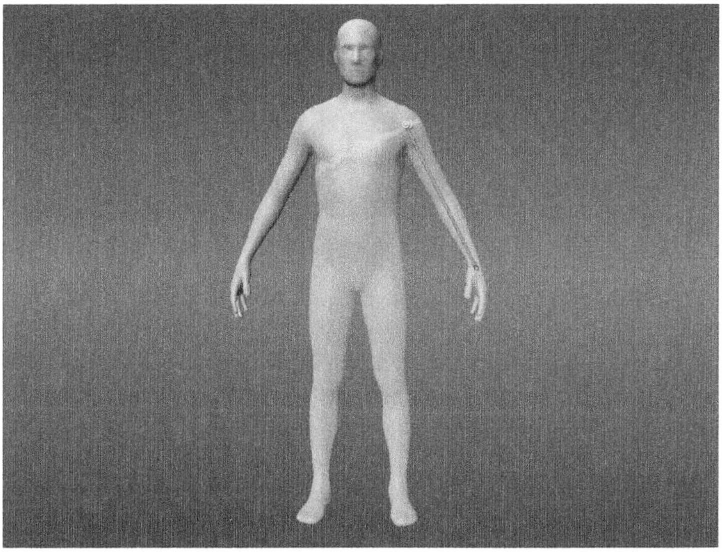

Notice a bright green gradient emanating from the initial pivot. This is the weighted area of your model that will be affected by the joint.

3. By rotating, *Alt* + left-clicking and dragging the camera, you will also notice that the pivot you just created needs some adjustment.

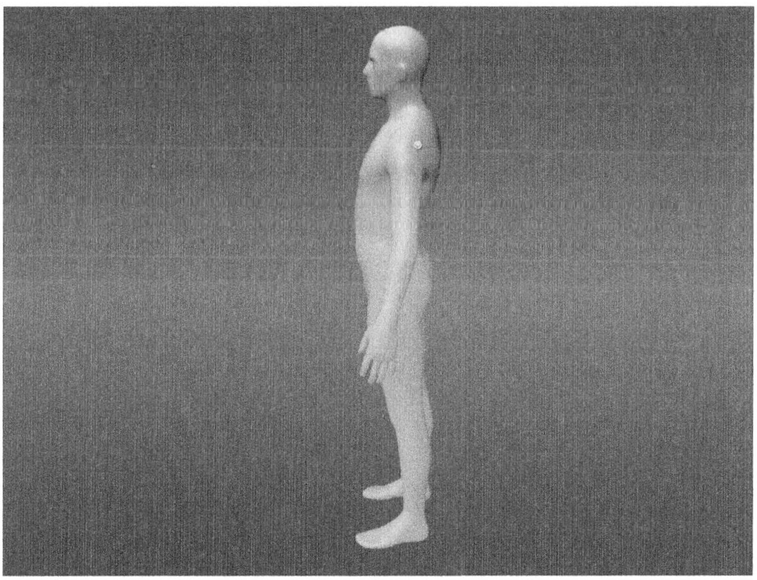

4. Click on the **Pose Tools** tab at the bottom left-hand side of your screen and select the **Move Pivot** tool. This will allow you to freely drag the pivot in the viewport.

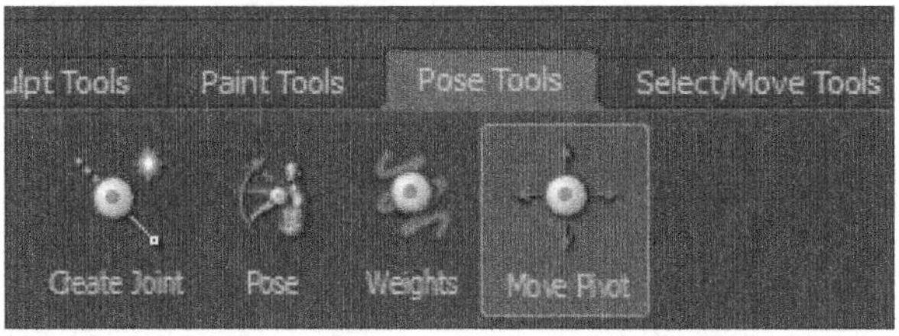

5. Drag the pivot to adjust it and set it in the proper position. Think of this as a real human. Locate the shoulder joint and that is where you will want to place your pivot. This is shown in the following screenshot:

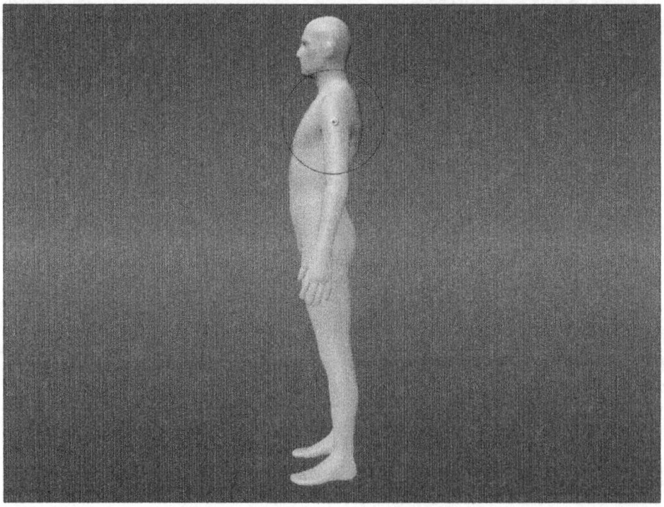

6. Now that the pivot of the joint is in the right place, you will need to adjust the weighting of the joint to have it affect the proper areas of your model.

   To do this, click the **Pose Tools** tab at the bottom left-hand side of your screen and select the **Weights** tool, as shown in the following screenshot:

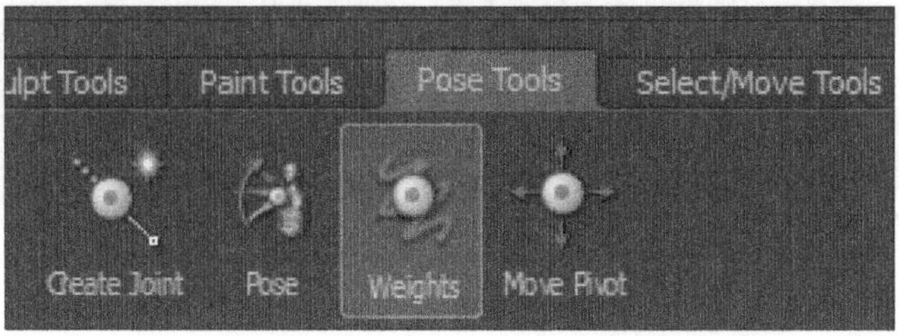

This will allow you to paint a gradient, from clear to bright green on your model. The joint will fully influence areas with solid bright green and, will have no influence on areas which are clear.

7. Drag the brush along areas you want to influence and *Ctrl* + left-click and drag your brush to paint out the influence, as shown in the following screenshot:

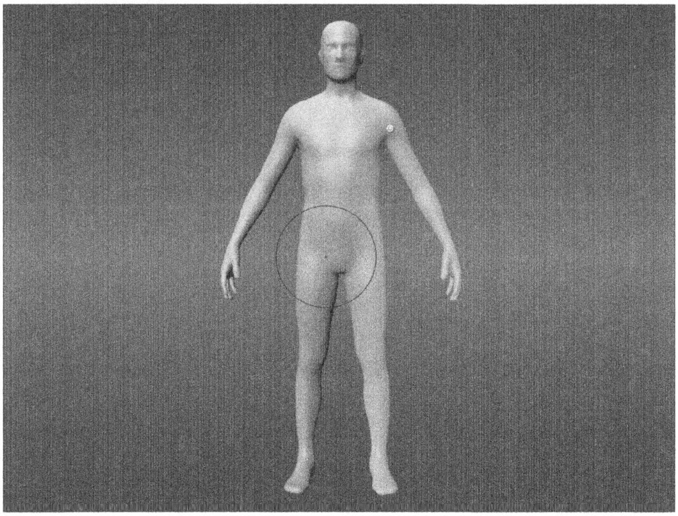

8. Adjust your brush size by pressing *B* + left-clicking and dragging the brush. This will allow you to affect larger or smaller areas easily. This is shown in the following screenshot:

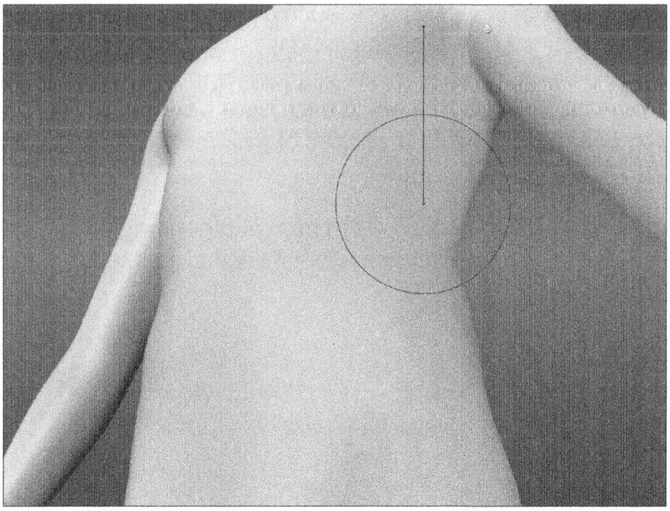

9. Adjusting weights of joints is the key to achieving the desired effect of a joint on your model.

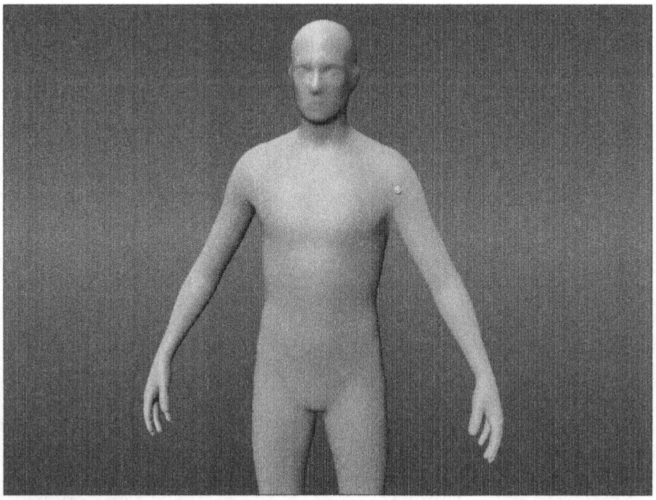

How it works...

When you are applying joints to your model you are basically creating bones that make it easier for you to position your model. Each joint is a location that can be rotated and moved while every piece of mesh around these joints is given a certain percentage of influence.

In Mudbox, the way this works is, everything with solid green is influenced by 100 percent, by the joint you have created. As this green falls off, so does the influence. Another thing that is different about Mudbox from other software, such as Autodesk Maya, is that when you create joints with Mudbox, it is more temporary and is mainly used for posing one piece at a time. In Maya, you would place all the bones of your object in locations that will allow proper deformation of your model. These bones would each have weights painted, giving every joint a certain percentage of influence over the vertices of your model. These bones can then be animated or posed to bring life to your model.

The next recipe will go over how to bring joints in from another program , such as Maya. That way you don't have to throw away all your hard work if you have already created what is called a *rig* for your character.

See also

- The *Creating a human rig by importing joints* recipe

Creating a human rig by importing joints

This recipe will show you how to import joints from another 3D package. Autodesk Maya will be used to create the rig for this character. A **rig** is a system of bones used to control animation or posing of models within a 3D package.

Getting ready

For this recipe, you may use the skeleton located in the code files of this book. The file is named `Joint Recipe Man.fbx`. This mesh was exported using Maya's FBX export option with default settings. Most 3D packages will have a `.fbx` exporter; it is a common file type. Next to a `.obj`, I would say, the `.fbx` is the next most widely used file type for bringing assets from one package to another.

How to do it...

The following steps will help you import joints from Autodesk Maya:

1. First off, be sure to export the `Joint Recipe Man` file from your 3D package as FBX so that you can bring the joints with your mesh. The `.obj` file type does not support joints, only the mesh. The `.fbx` file type is supported by Mudbox and will allow proper transfer of your skeleton.
2. Next step is to import your `.fbx`. If you do not have a 3D package to create and export your skeleton as a `.fbx`, then you can use the one in the code files of this book. As mentioned earlier, the filename is `Joint Recipe Man.fbx`. Now, click on **Import** under the **File** tab in Mudbox to import your FBX model. The following screenshot displays the menu in which you will find the **Import** option:

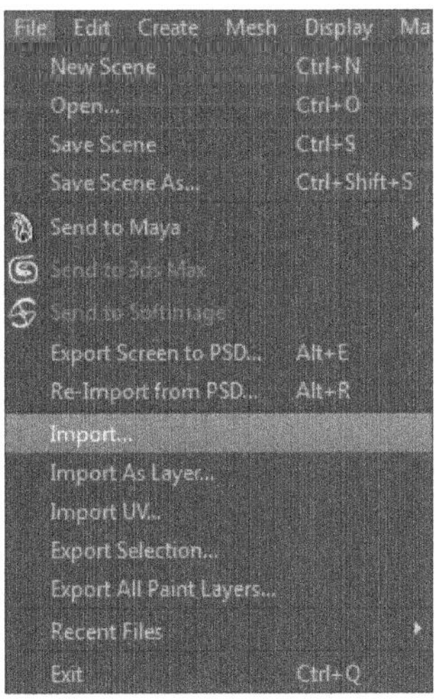

The following screenshot shows that the model is imported along with the joints and skinning from Maya. Custom controls and functions will not be imported with the skeleton:

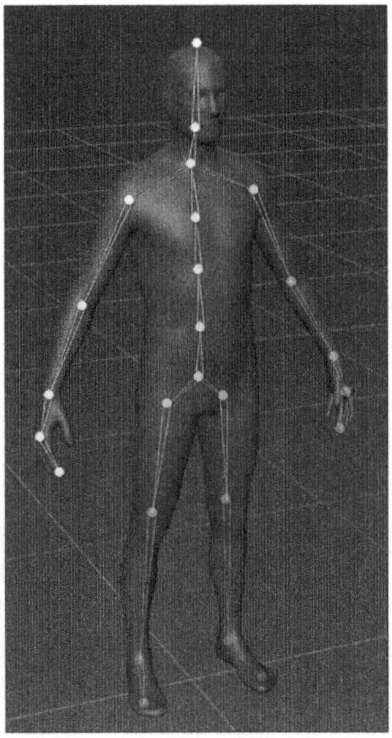

You can now transform these joints in Mudbox to pose your model. Just use the **Pose** tool from the **Pose Tools** toolbar in the bottom left-hand side of the Mudbox interface.

See also

- The *Posing a lamp cord by adding joints to your mesh* recipe
- The *Adjusting joint pivots and painting weights* recipe

10

Get Baked

In this chapter we will cover:

- Extracting sculpt information as a normal map
- Extracting an ambient occlusion map
- Add grunge inside crevices using the Dry Brush
- Adding and using a vector displacement map for sculpting

Introduction

This chapter will cover texture extraction practices within Mudbox 2013. You will learn how to extract texture maps that can be used to simulate higher polygon counts and therefore adding more detail without the performance hits. You will also learn how to extract maps that will add self-shadowing on your object, which will make it more believable. Ever wondered how you can make a tiling texture within Mudbox? This chapter will also cover a technique you can use to make tiling textures.

Extracting sculpt information as a normal map

This recipe will show you how to extract a normal map from your sculpted model. Normal maps are an excellent tool for adding more detail to your objects without all the polygons. This is an essential tool if you are creating assets for next generation games such as the *Call of Duty* series or *Mass Effect*. The texture will pick up light information in a way that suggests more detail than is actually modeled into the object.

Getting ready

For this recipe you will need a model with multiple subdivision levels so that you can bake information from the high resolution level down to the lower resolution level. If you have a sculpt that you have created in Mudbox and you'd like to follow along, then go ahead and load it up now. If you do not have a sculpt of your own or you would just like to follow the recipe more closely, then you can open up `Victorian Lioness Not UVed.mud`. When you open up the file you should see the following screenshot:

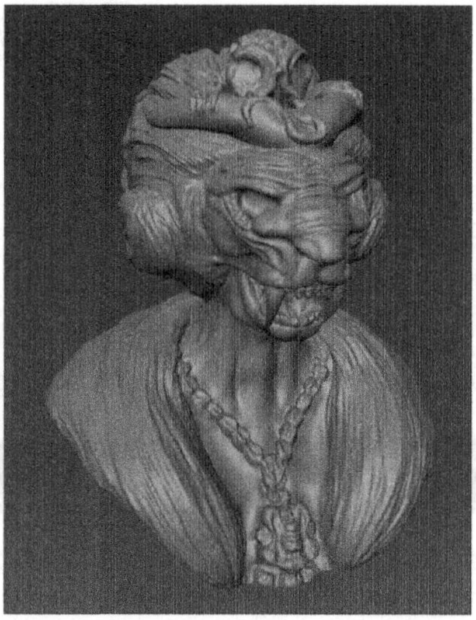

This sculpt was created by starting with the default bust mesh that comes with Mudbox, as shown in the following screenshot:

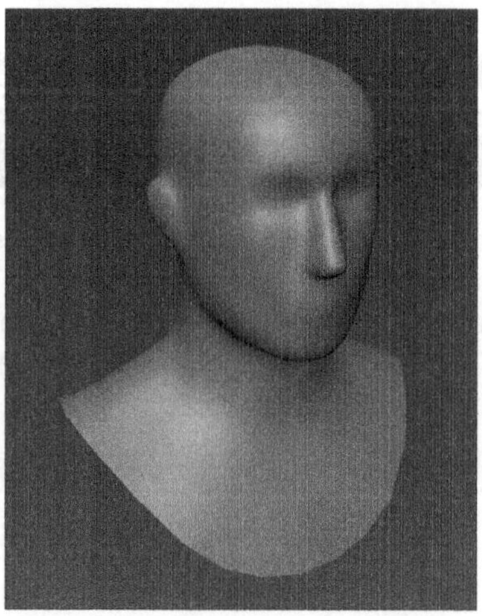

The UVs for this bust comes set up for you by default, but if your sculpt changes too much from the original shape of the bust, you will need to recreate the UVs of your low poly model. This step is needed to give room in your texture for detail information. I have listed the following steps you can take to export your low poly model, adjust the UVs, and import the UVs back into Mudbox:

1. First, we need to get the model out of Mudbox and into another 3D package. Whichever program you bring it into, just make sure it has the ability to manipulate UVs.

   To export the model we will be begin by clicking the *Page Down* key until you reach **Level 0** on your model. The following screenshot is of the Victorian Lioness low poly with the wireframe turned on:

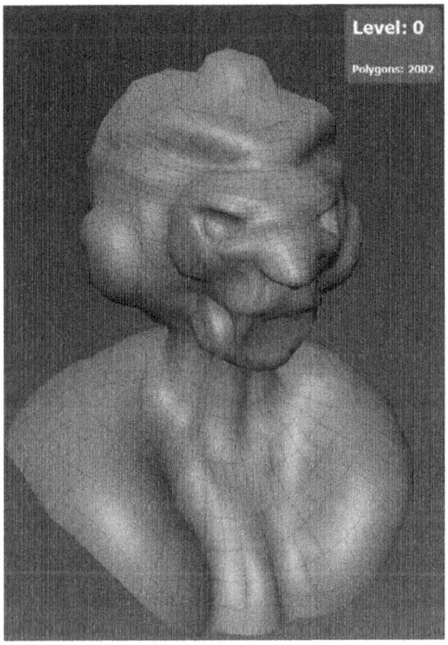

2. Now we are going to right-click on the model and choose **Select Model** from the menu that pops up, as shown in the following screenshot:

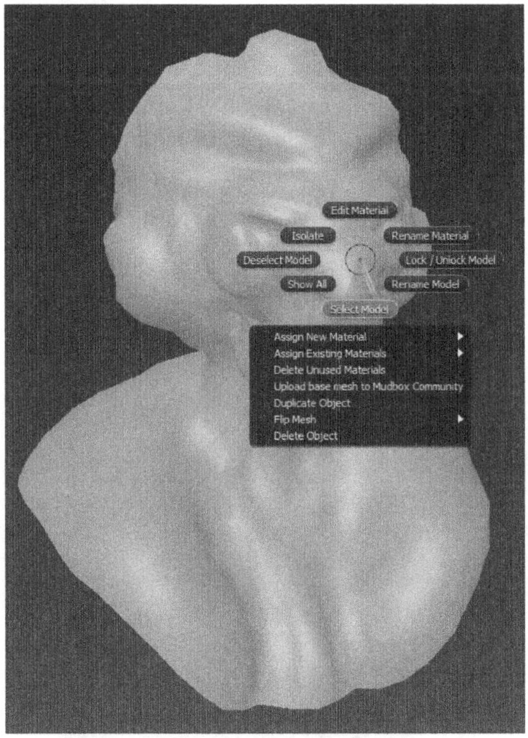

3. Next, choose **Export Selection** from the **File** menu in the upper left-hand side of the Mudbox interface. Now give it a name and click on **Save**.
4. Now, in the software of your choice you're going to adjust the UVs to how you want them. The code files of this book have a UV'ed and a non-UV'ed version of the low poly in case you don't have other software to use.

   With this particular model you can get away with just using a smooth UV tool in your desired software. UVing is beyond the scope of this book, but if you'd like to learn more about UVing there are plenty of resources available online.

   Once your UVs have been laid out you will need to export the model as a `.obj` file or a `.fbx` file to bring the UVs back into Mudbox.

5. Now that you have your UVs the way you want them, you will need to get those UVs onto the low poly version of your model inside Mudbox. To do this, you will need to go to **File** | **Import UV** in the Mudbox menu bar. Now choose the file called `Victorian Lioness Low Uved.obj` or the file that you created yourself, if you reworked your own UVs.

6. A window will pop up asking how you would like to match the UVs. Your choices will be **Vertex ID** and **Position**. You are going to choose **Vertex ID** for this model. The window that pops up should look as shown in the following screenshot:

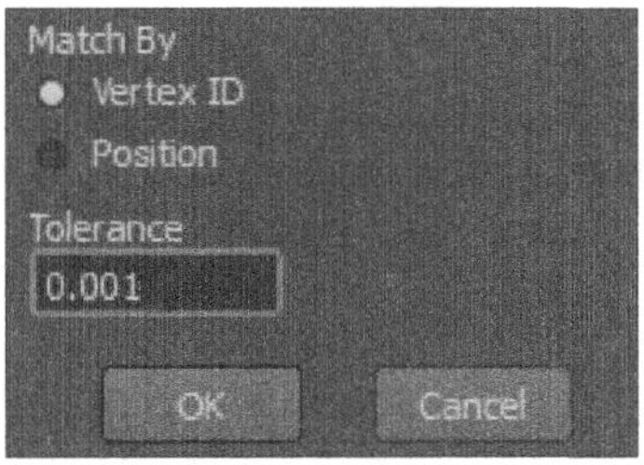

The reason **Vertex ID** is the best choice for this model is because we have not made any changes to the mesh, by adding or removing any vertices. Each vertex has a number and as long as these numbers stay intact Mudbox will be able to easily import the UVs of your object.

If you make any adjustments to your model, by adding or removing vertices, then you should go with **Position**. If you choose **Position**, then Mudbox will try to determine the UVs based on the world coordinates of your vertices.

7. That's it! Your UVs should be ready to go. The following screenshot is a comparison of the UVs. Mudbox's default UVs are on the left while the adjusted UVs are on the right.

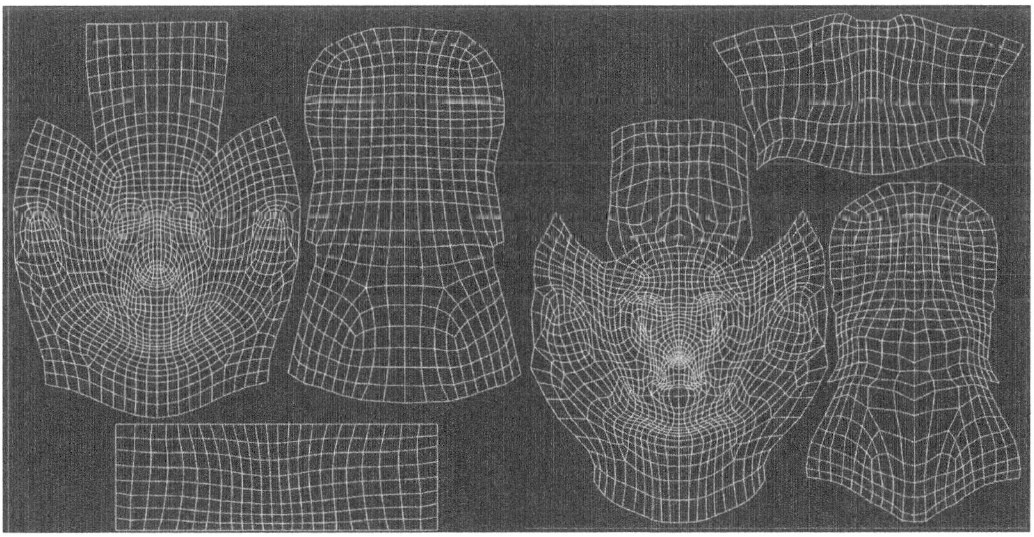

How to do it...

The following steps will help you to extract a normal map from your sculpted model:

1. Now that your UVs are all set up, click on the **Maps** tab at the top of your screen and select **New Operation...** under **Extract Texture Maps**. The following screenshot shows what the menu looks like:

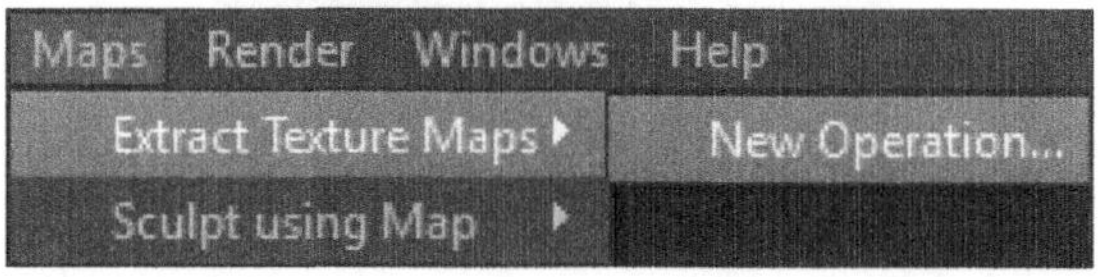

2. This will bring up a window to name the operation and select its type. Name the operation **Normal Map Extraction** and select **Normal Map** from the options under **Maps to Generate**.

   Naming the operation will allow you to easily utilize the same options and functions for re-baking your normal map or in baking other models without having to select the same inputs again.

   The following screenshot is what you should see at the top of the window, after selecting **Normal Map** and naming the extraction:

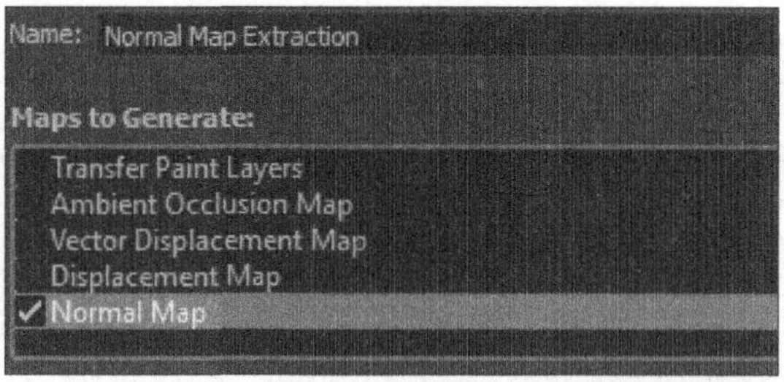

3. After clicking on **Normal Map** the new window that appears will reveal the settings that you can use to tweak your texture bakes. These settings allow you to customize the parameters of baking the normal map and you can choose where to save the normal map. The following screenshot is of the settings portion of the **Extract Texture Maps** window with the settings that will be used for this recipe:

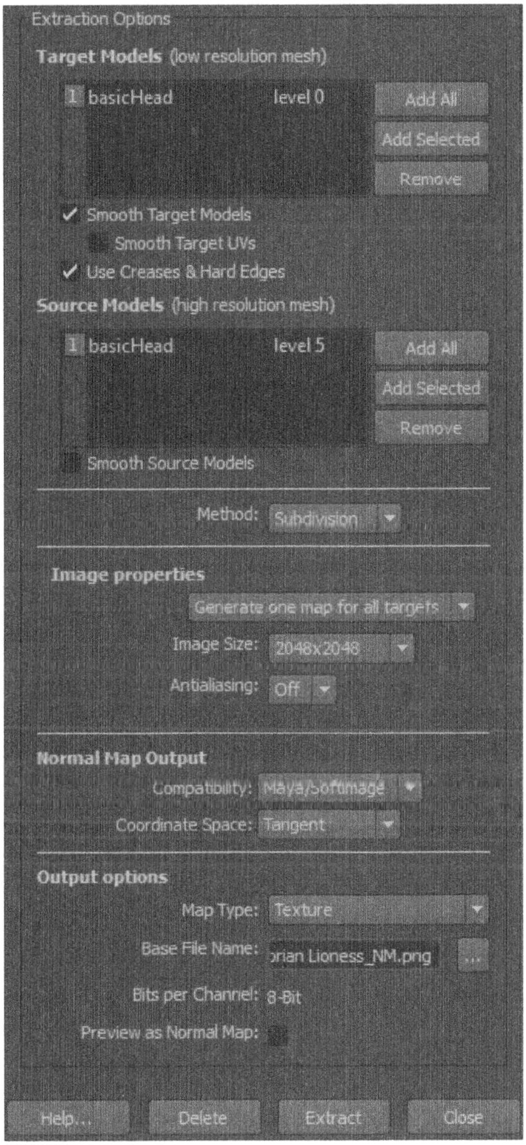

4. Now, we will go over some of the settings and figure out what they do. First off, make sure that the **target model** has the resolution of the model you wish to bake onto. The **source model** should be the resolution of the model you want to bake from, onto your target model.
5. The Method drop-down menu will give you two choices:
   - The first choice is **Subdivision**, which is the method that we will be using for this sculpt. This method uses the vertex position of the high subdivision level in relation to the low subdivision level of your sculpt. This method will produce fewer artifacts than **Ray Casting**, but **Ray Casting** will capture the height differences better than **Subdivision** method.
   - Next choice is **Ray Casting**. This method samples the distance of the source model and target model using sample rays cast along the normals of the target model.

   In the following screenshot, you will notice an artifact that is created by the **Ray Casting** method that is not present in the **Subdivision** bake:

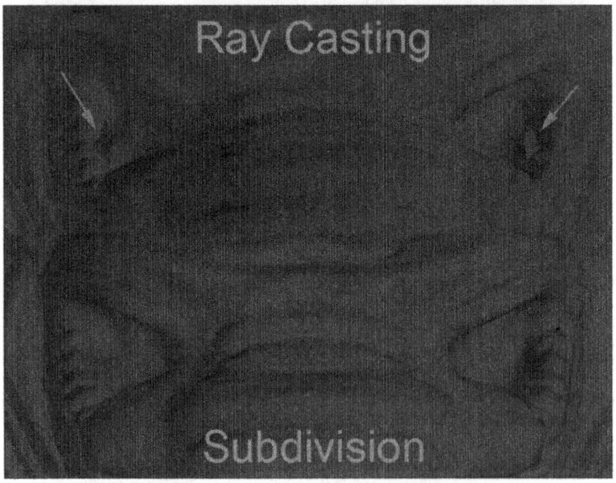

6. **Generate one map for all objects** can be used for baking a single normal map from multiple objects in your scene. This is useful when multiple objects have UVs on the same map file. Otherwise, you can select **Generate a map for each target** to create separate normal maps per object.

7. If you are creating a **Ray Casting** method bake, then these settings will become available. The following screenshot shows this menu:

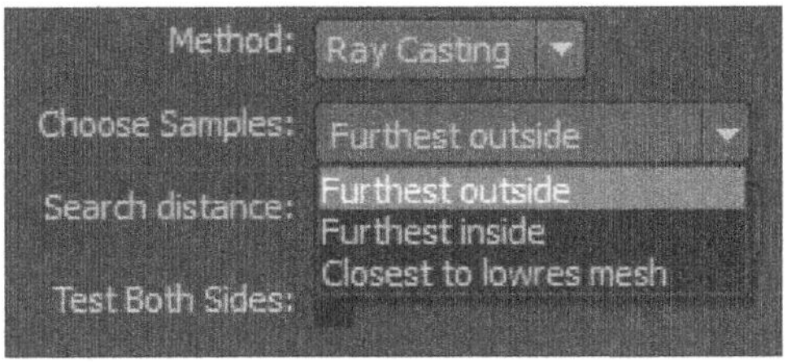

  - **Choose Samples** will determine which value to use when a particular sample intersects the source model more than once. Depending on the nature of your sculpture, one may yield better results than the other.
  - By default, **Furthest outside** is selected and usually does not need to be changed. This will take the furthest value from the source model while **Furthest inside** performs the opposite. **Closest to lowres mesh** will use the sample closest to the target model.

8. Select the **Image Size** based on what you need the normal map for. A higher resolution size will increase the number of pixels Mudbox will produce for the normal map.
9. **Antialiasing** will soften the result of baking high resolution down. Setting this to **2x** should offer enough softening if desired.
10. After you have determined all the values you want and established where to save the image, click on **Extract** to bake the normal map.
11. If you decide to check the box for **Preview as Normal Map**, then Mudbox will automatically update your model with the normal map by adding it to your **Paint Layers**. Lower your model's resolution to its base level 0 to see the effect of the normal map on your low poly model. The following screenshot shows the file at different stages:

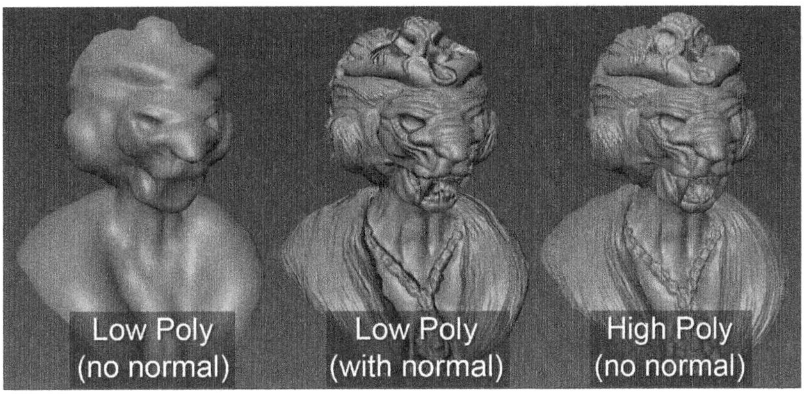

12. If you open up your normal map it should look something similar to the following screenshot:

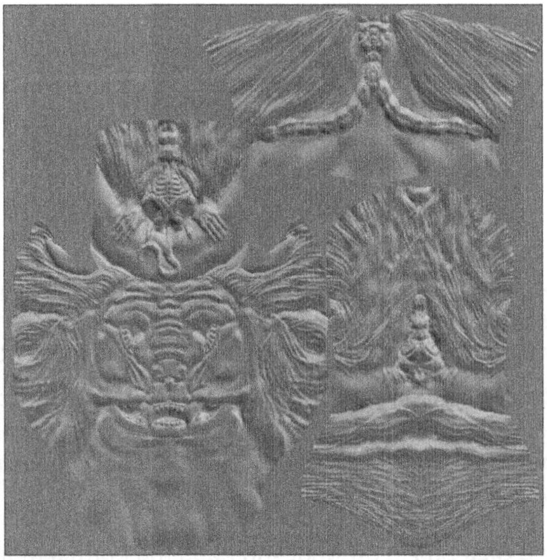

How it works...

When Mudbox extracts a normal map, it is recording the difference in placement of the surface from high poly to low poly, or from source model to target model. The resulting normal map is a variety of reds, greens, and blues which each represent a different direction in world/tangent space. When you look at a normal map image you just see the RGB values, but when you plug the map into the normal channel of a game engine or 3D software, then the software will interpret the colors as coordinates for the light to bounce off from.

There's more...

This sculpt's low poly was created by Mudbox, based on the details I added to the high poly version of the sculpt. Typically, the topology of the low poly model will not be exactly how you want it to be and will require some retopologizing. So, when you export your low poly to redo the UVs, you may also want to clean up some of the geometry as well. This may require exporting the high poly version, to be used as a guide. Just follow the same steps as you did for the low poly to achieve this.

Retopoligizing just means that you are going back and recreating the low poly model to match the shape of the high poly model so that your distribution of polygons are laid out more evenly and more efficiently, and with consideration of any areas that will be deformed during animation. The other important thing that retopologizing allows you to do is to create a better UV layout for the low poly model.

There are many tools out there that you can use for retopologizing your low poly models. The following are a few good ones:

- NEX Tools plugin for Maya, found at `draster.com`
- 3D Coat, found at `3d-coat.com`
- Topogun, found at `topogun.com`

See also

- The *Extracting an ambient occlusion map* recipe
- The *Extracting and using a vector displacement map for sculpting* recipe

Extracting an ambient occlusion map

This recipe will show you how to extract an ambient occlusion map from your sculpted model. By adding an ambient occlusion pass to your textures, you will notice a big improvement on how real your object will feel. The ambient occlusion map simulates the way light bounces off the surface of a real world object and leaves more shadows in the crevices and corners of the object. This is a standard addition to textures and renders within the movie, television, 3D visualization, and game industries.

Getting ready

For this recipe, you will need a model with multiple subdivision levels so that you can bake information from the high resolution level down to the lower resolution level. If you have a sculpt that you have created in Mudbox and you'd like to follow along with, then go ahead and load it up now. If you do not have a sculpt of your own or you would just like to follow the recipe more closely then you can open up `Victorian Lioness Not UVed.mud`.

You will also need to set up the UVs for your ambient occlusion map to bake to. Just follow the steps listed in the *Getting ready* section of the *Extracting sculpt information as a normal map* recipe.

For easier results in determining the outcome of your ambient occlusion map, set your model material's **Diffuse** color to white and reduce the **Specular** and **Gloss** to black. This will let you see how the ambient occlusion map is affecting the look of your model. To adjust these settings, you can right-click on the model in Mudbox and choose **Edit Material**. You should see a menu as shown in the following screenshot:

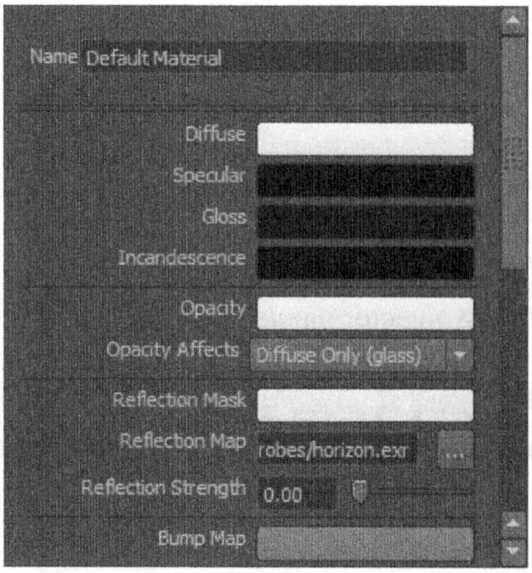

The model's material should look similar to the following screenshot:

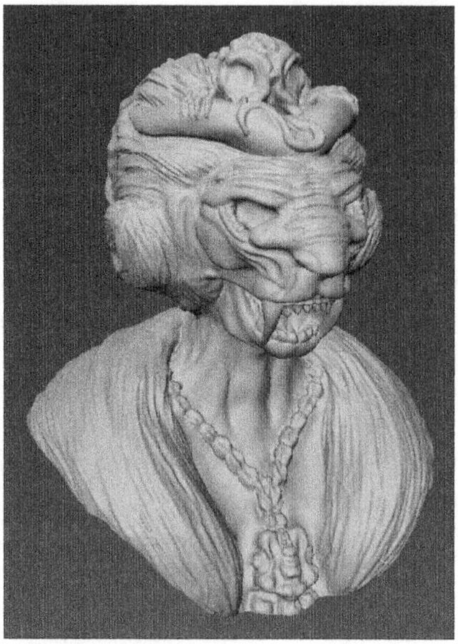

How to do it...

The following steps will help you to extract an ambient occlusion map:

1. Click on the **Maps** tab at the top of your screen and select **New Operation...** under **Extract Texture Maps**:

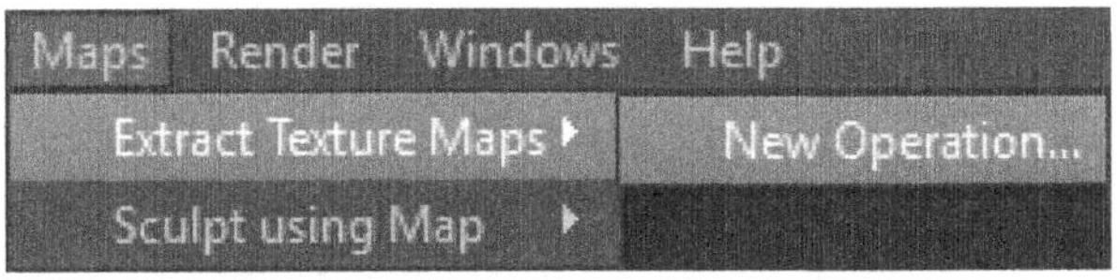

2. This will bring up a window to name the operation and select its type. Name the operation **Ambient Occlusion Extraction** and select **Ambient Occlusion Map** from the options under **Maps to Generate:**, as shown in the following screenshot:

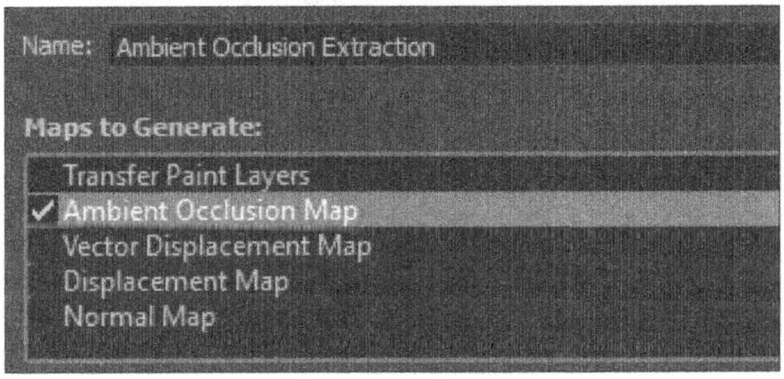

3. After clicking on **Ambient Occlusion Map**, the window will extend with more options. This allows you to customize the parameters of baking the ambient occlusion map and to decide where to save it. The following screenshot has the settings that we will be using for the Lioness bake:

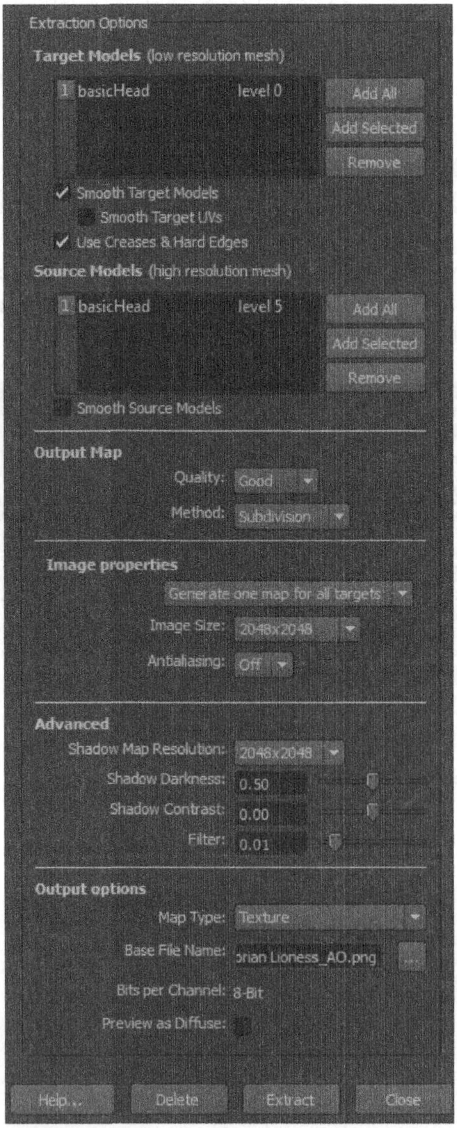

4. Make sure that the target model is the resolution of the model you wish to bake onto. Otherwise, the UVs and surface detail may not line up correctly with the intended low poly model.

5. The **Quality** setting will affect how fast your bake will render and the quality of the map. **Fastest** is good for doing tests with large ambient occlusion bakes while **Best** will give you a better final output.
6. Select the **Image Size** based on what you need the ambient occlusion map for. A higher resolution size will increase the number of pixels Mudbox will produce for the ambient occlusion map.
7. **Antialiasing** will soften the result of baking high resolution down. Setting this to **2x** should offer enough softening if desired.
8. **Shadow Darkness** will determine how intense the shadows will be. A lower value will result in a brighter map and a higher value will result in a darker map.
9. **Shadow Contrast** affects the contrast between areas with shadow and areas that have no shadow. Increasing the value increases the contrast and decreasing it decreases the contrast. The default value offers a great starting point.
10. Set the **Filter** to a lower value for sharp details. Higher filter values result in a softer output, which will help to hide any artifacts.
11. Before extracting your ambient occlusion map you may want to check the box labeled **Preview as Diffuse,** if you would like to see the map on your model once the bake is complete. Now, click on **Extract** to bake out the map.
12. Set the display to flat lighting, by right-clicking in the viewport and choosing **Flat lighting**, to see the effects of the ambient occlusion map without the default lighting getting in the way. The following screenshot displays the default lighting version on the left and the flat lighting version on the right:

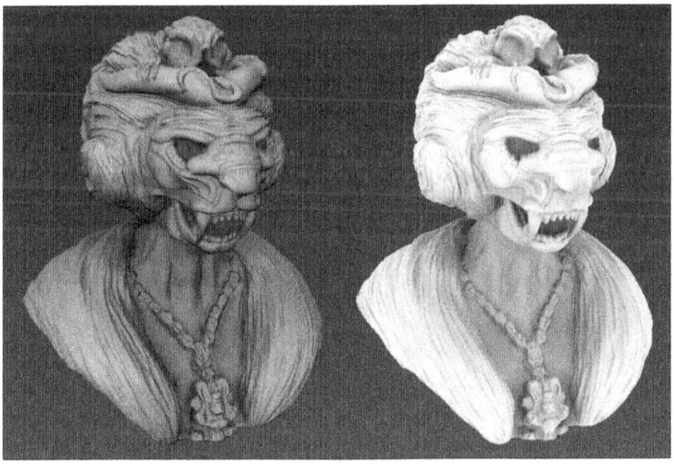

13. Now, this map can be used as a **Multiply** layer in your **Diffuse** layers. Make sure you place it above the rest of your diffuse texture by dragging the layer in the **Layers** tab.

14. Once your layers are in place, you may want to intensify your ambient occlusion map. To do this you can right-click on the ambient occlusion layer and choose **Adjust Color** from the right-click menu. In the window that pops up, you will be able to adjust **Hue**, **Saturation**, **Value**, and adjust the **Curves** of the layer. To intensify your ambient occlusion map, we are going to drag the curves around to get the contrast that we want.

Curves can be a little tricky to understand at first. Basically, the *X* axis represents the dark and light areas of your texture, while the *Y* axis determines how bright or dark those areas will become.

For example, if you drag the right-hand side of the curve upwards, then the highlights in your texture will get brighter; if you drag it downwards the highlight areas will get darker. Meanwhile, if you drag the left-hand side of the curve upward, then the shadow areas of your texture will get brighter, while dragging the left-hand side of the curve downward will make your shadow areas even darker.

The following screenshot shows one configuration you might use with a basic stone texture:

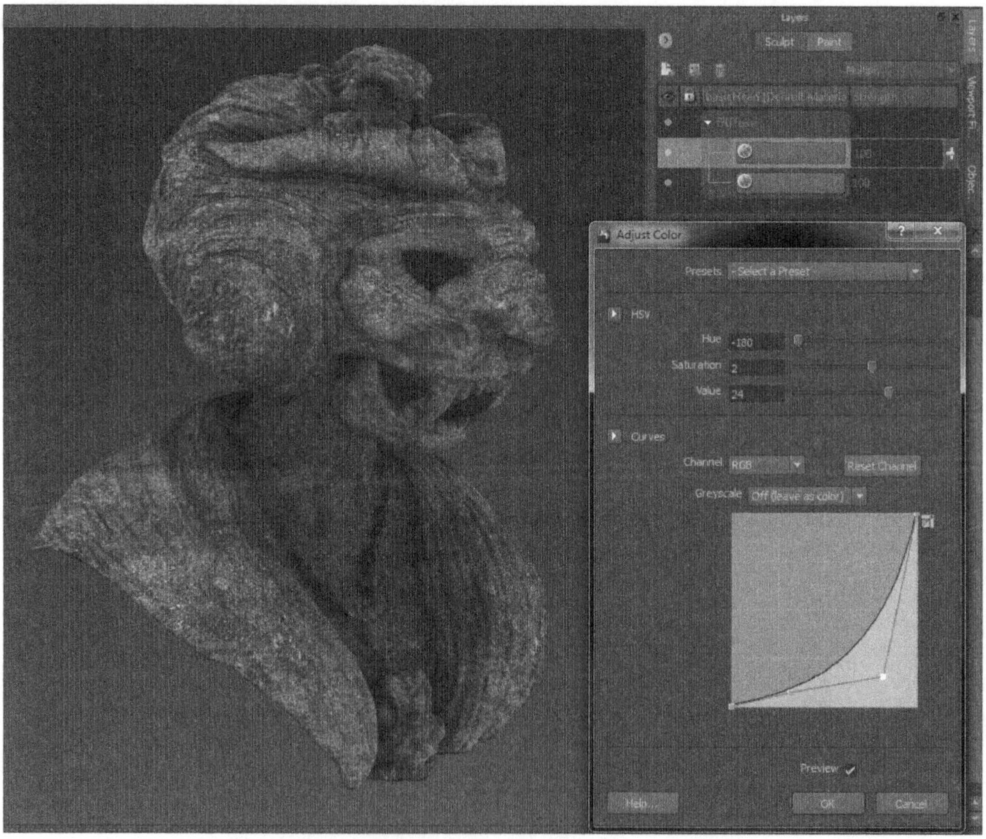

I recommend you keep playing around with these settings until you get a feel for what they do. **Curves** are a very powerful tool and you will find yourself wanting to use them for the control that they give you.

See also

- The *Extracting sculpt information as a normal map* recipe
- The *Extracting and using a vector displacement map for sculpting* recipe

Adding grunge inside crevices using the Dry Brush

This recipe will show you how to add grunge inside the crevices of your sculpts. We will be looking at the Victorian Lioness sculpt to show you how you can paint within the crevices or avoid crevices using the **Dry Brush**.

Getting ready

First, you will need to open the `Victorian Lioness Statue.mud` file. When you open the file, you will see the result of this recipe. If you would like to follow along, then you should hide the **Grunge** layer. Feel free to bring your own model in and apply this technique to your own work. The following screenshot shows the grungy, old statue that you should see when you open the `Victorian Lioness Statue.mud` file:

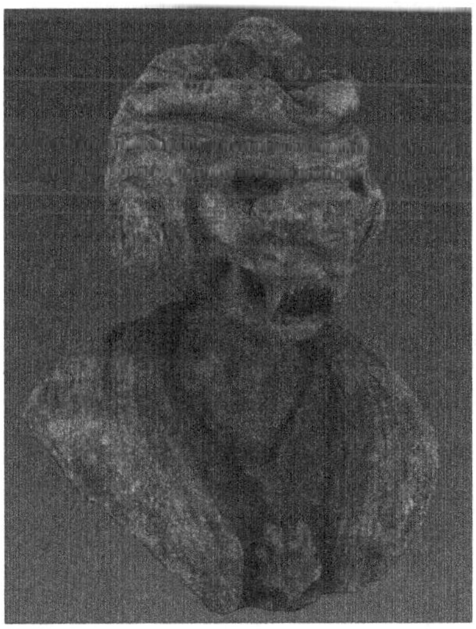

If you have done the *Extracting an ambient occlusion map* recipe you may notice a little difference in the color of the statue. This is a result of some more **Adjust Color** adjustments. If you have not read that recipe yet, I recommend that you do.

How to do it...

The following steps will help you to add grunge inside the crevices of your sculpts:

1. Now that you have the sculpt you would like to add details to, you will select the **Dry Brush** from the **Paint Tools** toolbar present in the lower-left corner of the interface, as shown in the following screenshot:

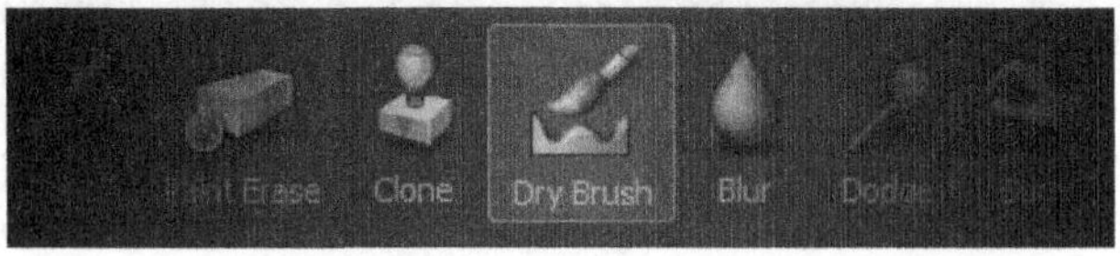

2. Now choose a color that you would like to paint into the crevices. You can also choose a stamp if you'd like to add some variation in the paint. The following screenshot shows the settings that I started out with:

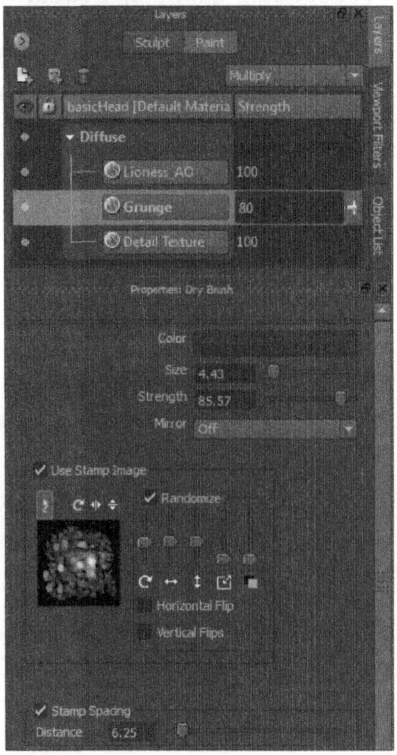

3. Begin painting in the grunge or other details where you would like them while holding the *Ctrl* key. This will make the brush have the opposite effect of its standard function. Normally, the **Dry Brush** will only affect the raised surfaces of your sculpt but because we are holding the *Ctrl* key it is only affecting the parts of the sculpt that lie within crevices. Just to illustrate what is happening, I have added some bright red paint to the crevices of this model using the **Dry Brush**, as shown in the following screenshot:

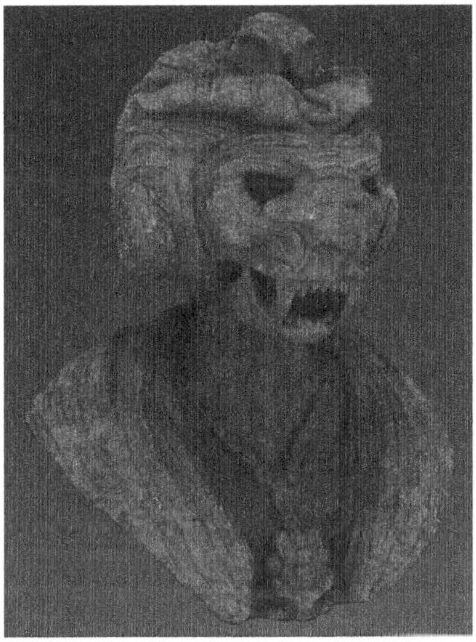

4. Now, add more details in the crevices and on the outsides of the crevices until you have built up your desired details. I recommend using a combination of **Dry Brush**, **Sponge** brush, **Burn** brush, and the **Dodge** brush to tweak your painting.

See also

- The *Enhancing your scene with viewport filters* recipe in *Chapter 8, Ready for My Closeup*
- The *Adding a stencil or stamp to your toolbox* recipe in *Chapter 4, Fine Tooth Comb*
- The *Extracting an ambient occlusion map* recipe
- The *Extracting sculpt information as a normal map* recipe

Extracting and using a vector displacement map for sculpting

This recipe will go over how to create a vector displacement map so that you can use it to sculpt with complex stamps. This feature is unique to Mudbox and takes the idea of a displacement map one step further by allowing crevices and overhangs to be captured by the extracted texture map. Vector displacement technology is a very recent development and presents some unique methods to add to your workflow as an artist.

Getting ready

The first thing you are going to need is a sculpt that you would like to turn into a vector displacement stamp, or stencil. If you do not have your own details sculpted you can use the `Vector Displacement Sculpt.mud` file to follow along with the recipe more closely. The following screenshot shows what this sculpt looks like:

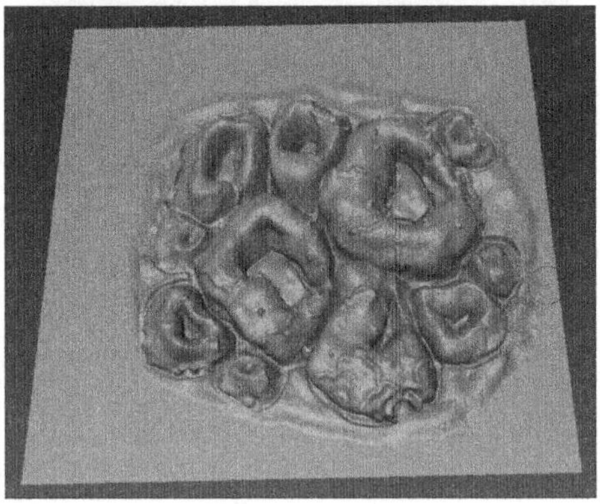

Keep in mind that if you create your own details, they should be done on a flat plane for this exercise.

How to do it...

Now that you have your sculpt ready to go, we can start the extraction process as mentioned in the following steps:

1. We are going to bake this vector displacement map down to a flat plane to allow for a better stamp, or stencil. If you reduce your sculpt's level down to 0 you will notice that the plane is not flat, as shown in the following screenshot:

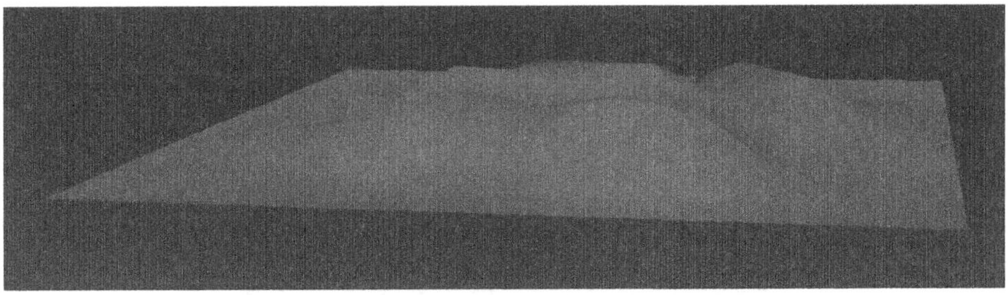

For this reason we are going to create a new plane to bake to, instead of baking down to level 0 of the high poly sculpt.

2. To create a new plane you will need to go to the menu, at the top of the Mudbox interface, and go to **Create** | **Mesh** | **Plane**. The following screenshot displays what the menu should look like inside Mudbox 2013:

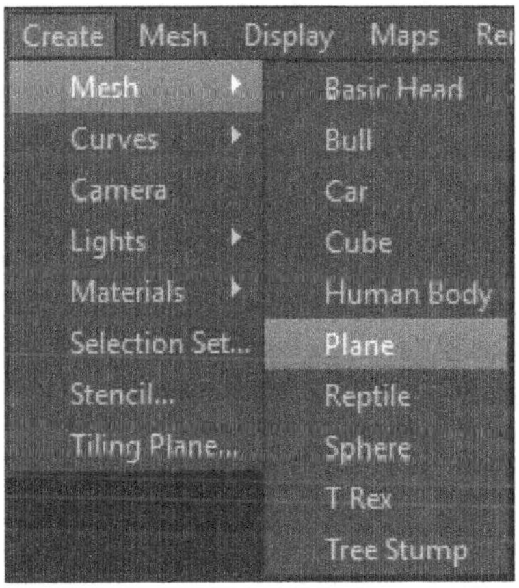

3. Now you should rename the new plane so it is easier to tell which plane is which. Select the new plane, if it isn't selected already, and go into its **Properties** on the right-hand side of the Mudbox interface. Find the **Name** textbox and change the name to **Target**. The following screenshot shows what the **Properties** window looks like:

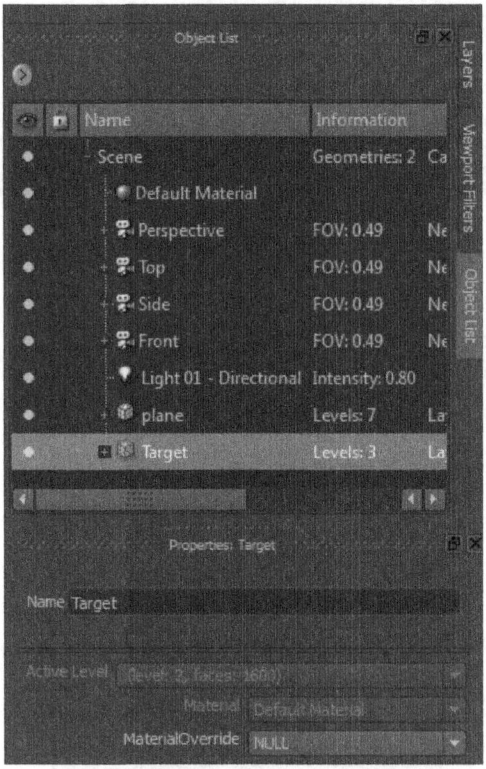

4. Now, go into the **Maps** menu item, at the top of the Mudbox interface, and create a **New Operation** by going into **Extract Texture Maps**.
5. In the **Extract Texture Maps** window that pops up, you will rename your extraction to **Vector Displacement Extraction** and choose **Vector Displacement**, as shown in the following screenshot:

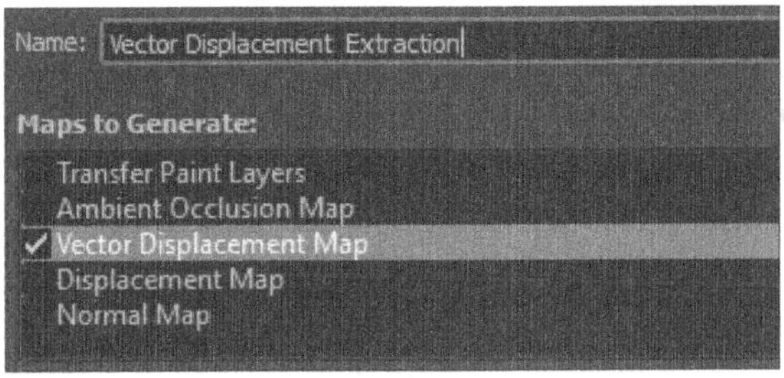

6. When the window extends, revealing the vector displacement options, you will need to enter in the settings shown in the following screenshot. We will go over these settings in the following steps:

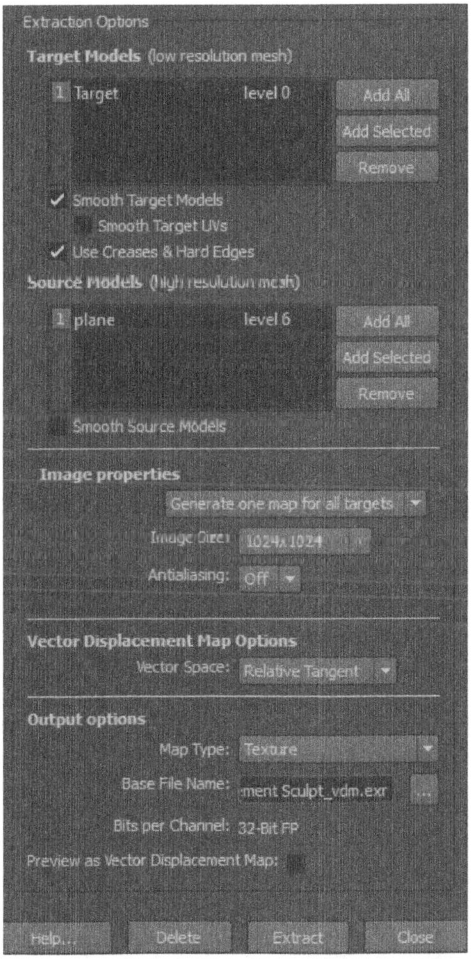

7. To set up the target model, that is the model with the UVs you are baking to, you will need to select the plane we had labeled **Target**. Now click on **Add Selected** next to the **Target Models** window. **Target** should show up in the box on the left.
8. Now, do the same thing for the **Source Models** section. The source model will be our high poly sculpt that has the details we would like to capture.
9. Next, designate the resolution you would like to use. In this case we will be using a **1024x1024** map. This should give us plenty of resolution for details given the size of the details that the sculpt is representing.
10. As long as you are using the vector displacement map inside Mudbox you can leave the **Vector Space** set to **Relative Tangent**.
11. Now, select a **Base File Name** and location that your bake/extraction will be rendered to. Note that you will need to add `_vdm` to the end of your filename if you are planning on using the map as a stamp or stencil, which we are.

    You can choose `.tif` or `.exr` extensions if you are only working on Mudbox. If you plan on working outside Mudbox, you will need to look at what your other software can read.

12. Now, click on **Extract** and voila! You have a vector displacement map.

There's more...

Now that we have the vector displacement map it's time to create a stamp with it!

1. To do so you will first need to browse to the vector displacement map using the **Image Browser** interface. You can add a stamp in other ways as well, which are covered in *Chapter 4, Fine Tooth Comb*.
2. Once you have navigated to the folder where the image is located, you should see an image that looks something as shown in the following screenshot:

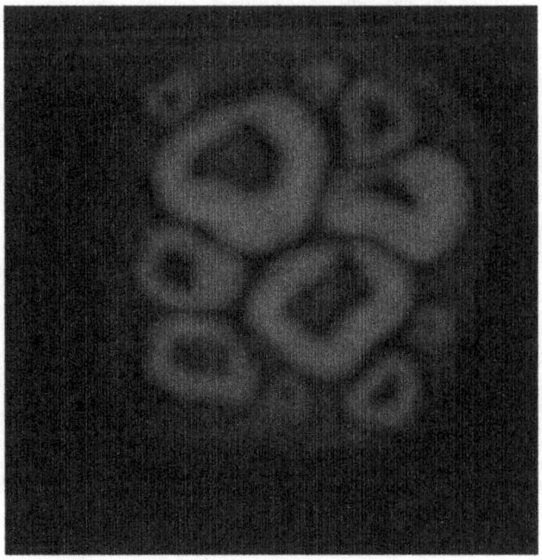

3. With the image selected, you can click on the **Set Stamp** icon at the top of the **Image Browser** interface. This will set the current image as a stamp on your current brush. In this case, make sure you are selecting the standard **Sculpt** brush. The following screenshot shows what the **Set Stamp** icon should look like:

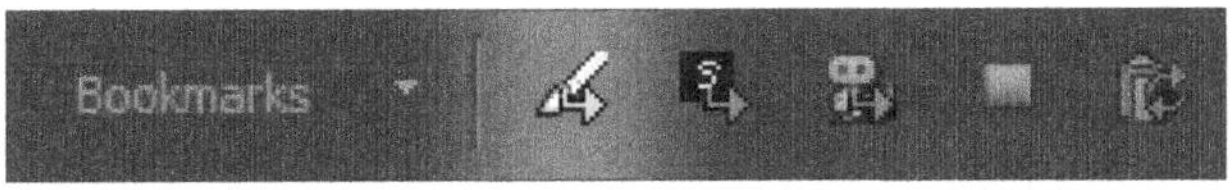

4. Now you will need to adjust your stamp settings by clicking on your **Sculpt** brush's **Properties**, to reveal the stamp settings. The following screenshot shows the settings that I used for this demonstration:

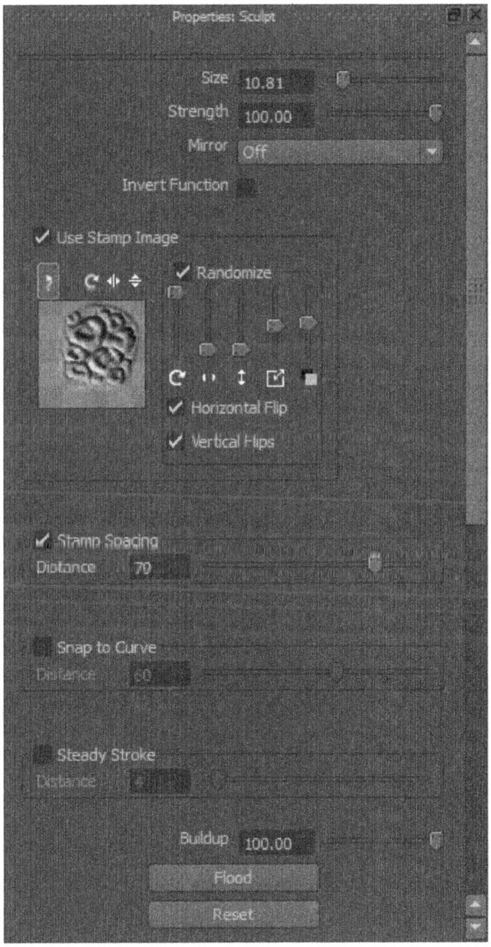

5. The important settings here are as follows:
    - **Strength**: This should be set to **100** to get the full details from the map when you paint
    - **Use Stamp Image**: This should be checked for obvious reasons
    - **Stamp Spacing**: This should be set high enough that you are not piling the details directly on top of each other on every brush stroke
    - Setting **Buildup** to **100** will help in a similar way as it did in the case of **Strength**
6. Now that our stamp is all set up let's give it a try! Go to **File** | **New Scene** and choose a **Starting Point**. I will be choosing the reptile for this demonstration. The following screenshot shows what the mesh should look like:

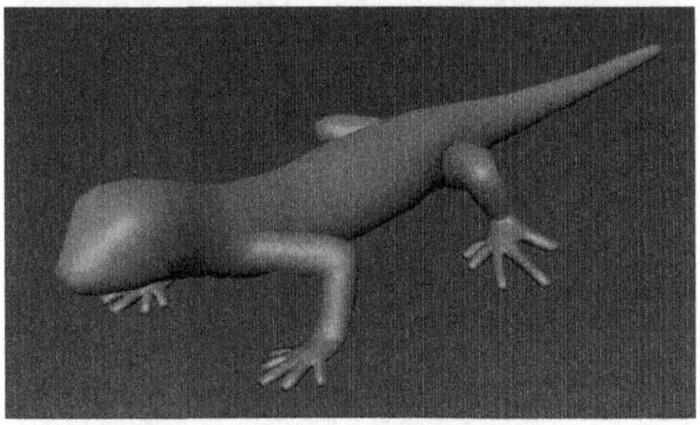

7. Press *Shift* + *D* several times, until you reach level 5 or so. This will give us enough resolution to sculpt on.
8. Notice that when you click on the **Sculpt** brush your stamp is still attached and the settings are intact. Mudbox will remember what you were using from one project to another. Now, use this brush to add some of our new vector displacement map details! The following screenshot shows a segment of the reptile with the stamp's details applied:

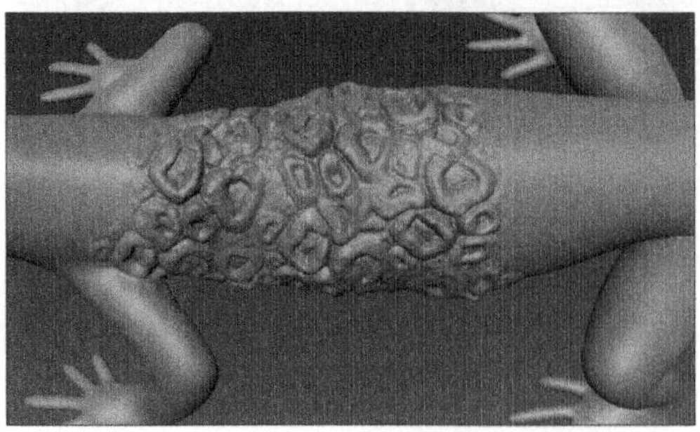

See also

- The *Adding a stencil or stamp to your toolbox* recipe in *Chapter 4, Fine Tooth Comb*
- The *Extracting an ambient occlusion map* recipe
- The *Extracting sculpt information as a normal map* recipe

Index

Symbols

A

B

C

H

I

J

K

L

M

N

O

P

Q

R

[PACKT] PUBLISHING

Thank you for buying

Mudbox 2013 Cookbook

About Packt Publishing

Packt, pronounced 'packed', published its first book "*Mastering phpMyAdmin for Effective MySQL Management*" in April 2004 and subsequently continued to specialize in publishing highly focused books on specific technologies and solutions.

Our books and publications share the experiences of your fellow IT professionals in adapting and customizing today's systems, applications, and frameworks. Our solution based books give you the knowledge and power to customize the software and technologies you're using to get the job done. Packt books are more specific and less general than the IT books you have seen in the past. Our unique business model allows us to bring you more focused information, giving you more of what you need to know, and less of what you don't.

Packt is a modern, yet unique publishing company, which focuses on producing quality, cutting-edge books for communities of developers, administrators, and newbies alike. For more information, please visit our website: `www.packtpub.com`.

Writing for Packt

We welcome all inquiries from people who are interested in authoring. Book proposals should be sent to `author@packtpub.com`. If your book idea is still at an early stage and you would like to discuss it first before writing a formal book proposal, contact us; one of our commissioning editors will get in touch with you.

We're not just looking for published authors; if you have strong technical skills but no writing experience, our experienced editors can help you develop a writing career, or simply get some additional reward for your expertise.

[PACKT] PUBLISHING

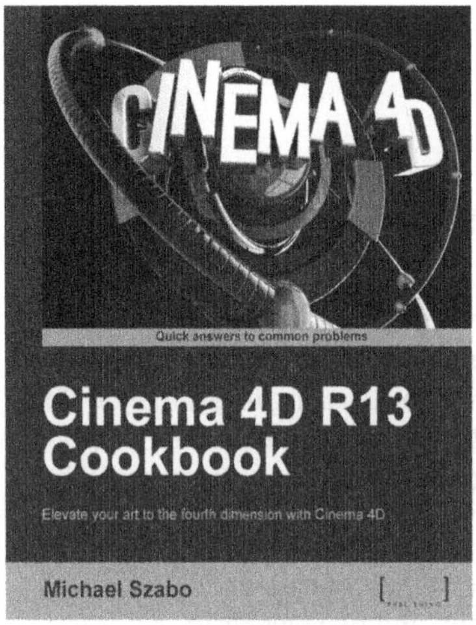

Cinema 4D R13 Cookbook

ISBN: 978-1-84969-186-4 Paperback: 514 pages

Elevate your art to the fourth dimension with Cinema 4D

1. Master all the important aspects of Cinema 4D
2. Learn how real-world knowledge of cameras and lighting translates onto a 3D canvas
3. Learn Advanced features like Mograph, Xpresso, and Dynamics
4. Become an advanced Cinema 4D user with concise and effective recipes

---

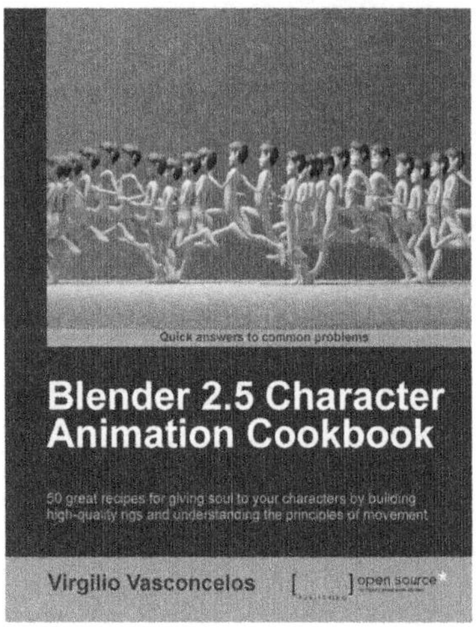

Blender 2.5 Character Animation Cookbook

ISBN: 978-1-84951-320-3 Paperback: 308 pages

50 great recipes for giving soul to your characters by building high-quality rigs and understanding the principles of movement

1. Learn how to create efficient and easy to use character rigs
2. Understand and make your characters , so that your audience believes they're alive
3. See common approaches when animating your characters in real world situations
4. Learn the techniques needed to achieve various setups, from IK-FK blending to corrective shape keys and eyes controllers

Please check **www.PacktPub.com** for information on our titles

[PACKT] PUBLISHING

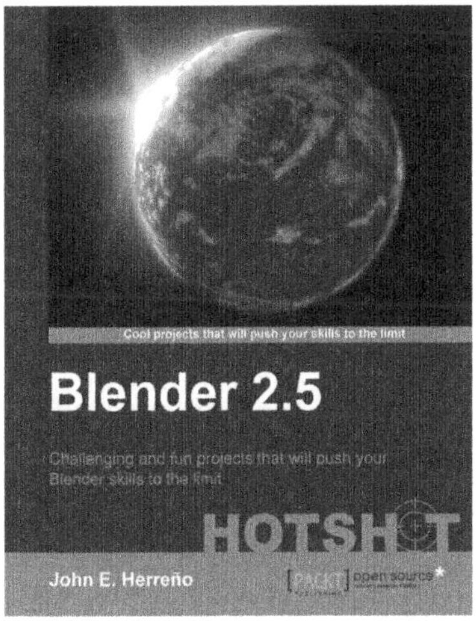

Blender 2.5 HOTSHOT

ISBN: 978-1-84951-310-4 Paperback: 332 pages

Challenging and fun projects that will push your Blender skills to the limit

1. Exciting projects covering many areas: modeling, shading, lighting, compositing, animation, and the game engine
2. Strong emphasis on techniques and methodology for the best approach to each project
3. Utilization of many of the tools available in Blender 3D for developing moderately complex projects
4. Clear and concise explanations of working in 3D, along with insights into some important technical features of Blender 3D

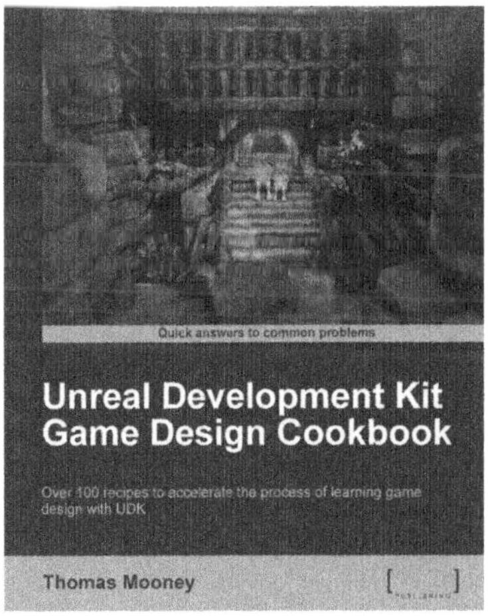

Unreal Development Kit Game Design Cookbook

ISBN: 978-1-84969-180-2 Paperback: 544 pages

Over 100 recipes to accelerate the process of learning game design with UDK

1. An intermediate, fast-paced UDK guide for game artists
2. The quickest way to face the challenges of game design with UDK
3. All the necessary steps to get your artwork up and running in game

Lightning Source UK Ltd.
Milton Keynes UK
UKOW07f2142150415

249719UK00006B/244/P

9 781849 691567